THE INTRINSIC AND EXTRINSIC CITY

DS11 2008-2017
EDITED BY ANDREW PECKHAM AND
DUSAN DECERMIC
WITH SAM GILES AND TOBY PLUNKETT
SEVEN CITIES EIGHT PROGRAMMES

'Studio as Book' is a new series of yearly publications that tender the extraordinary creative work undertaken in the Department of Architecture's design studio - in detail. The series includes undergraduate and graduate level work, and is intended to sit alongside the Open Exhibition and catalogue. Each book in the series covers the work of a single design studio over the course of at least two years. Its objectives are:

- To record, archive, and present the pedagogical programme and creative student outputs of a design studio.
- To position the work of a design studio within a broader intellectual, scientific or aesthetic field.
- To advance the design driven research being undertaken in the Department's design studios.
- To provide a reference for future iterations and variations of a design studio.

Reducing the creative output of a multi-year design studio to a single volume, using a pre-designed work template is no easy undertaking, and it is necessarily selective. At the same time, it provides a consistent, sure platform for the wide range of approaches to the discipline of teaching architectural design which characterise the department.

Each 'Studio as Book' has been peer-reviewed on the basis of a proposal submitted by the studio's tutors to an editorial committee. In addition to studio briefs and student work, each book includes content that draws out the studio's research and pedagogical agenda. The format that this takes varies from book to book — reflective essays by tutors or past students, interviews, theoretical essays from parallel fields, and so forth. The 'Studio as Book' Series will later be accompanied by a Studio Pamphlet Series for design studios of a shorter duration.

Harry Charrington

Head of Department of Architecture
University of Westminster

I wish to acknowledge the contribution of the following in bringing this project to fruition: Lindsay Bremner, Director of Architectural Research, who was the driving force behind the series, Mark Boyce author of 'Sizes May Vary, A workbook for graphic design (Lawrence King, 2008) - and the designer of 'Studio as Book', and Filip Visnjic, designer of the series' web site, http://www.studioasbook.org.

THE INTRINSIC AND EXTRINSIC CITY

DS11 2008-2017
EDITED BY ANDREW PECKHAM AND DUSAN DECERMIC

WITH SAM GILES AND TOBY PLUNKETT
SEVEN CITIES EIGHT PROGRAMMES

STUDIO AS BOOK
NO. 03

DEPARTMENT OF ARCHITECTURE
UNIVERSITY OF WESTMINSTER

FOREWORD
LUCIANO LAZZARI

8 - 13

PREFACE
ANDREW PECKHAM

14 - 15

SHORT CUTS
WILLIAM FIREBRACE

16 - 27

7 Cities///8 Programs

28 - 221

CITIES

30 - 31

172 - 199   2008/2009

WROCŁAW:
SOUTH WEST POLAND

WRO:
RECOVERING WROCLAW/
CITY AS PALIMPSEST/SILESIAN FIELDS

102 - 123   2009/2010

TRIESTE:
NORTH EAST ITALY

TRIESTINITÀ:
COSMOPOLITAN 'REGIONS'/
GLOBAL LOCALE

56 - 81   2010/2011

ANTWERP/GHENT:
LONDON TO FLANDERS

ANTWERPEN/GENT:
RECOMBINANT ARCHITECTURE

200 - 221   2011/2012

KRAWKÓW/KATOWICE:
MINING THE SEAM

SILESIAN TERRITORIES:
DUAL IDENTITIES

32 - 55

2012/2013

COPENHAGEN/MALMO:
CENTRAL DENMARK, FOURTH ISLAND

KØBENHAVN:
NORDIC NOIR

	ARCHIVE	CATALOGUE
	222 - 235	246 - 261

2013/2014 124 - 149	BIBLIOGRAPHY	AFTERWORDS
TRIESTE/REVISITED: NORTH EAST ITALY	236 - 241	262 - 283
TRIESTINITÀ: CITY AS MEDIUM		
2015/16 82 - 101	QUOTES	DIFFERENT REALMS OF PRACTICE LUCY BROOKE
GENOA: NORTH WEST ITALY	242 - 245	264 - 269
GENOVA: MODES OF EXCHANGE		
2016/17 150 - 171		INTRINSIC AND EXTRINSIC CITY ANDREW PECKHAM DUSAN DECERMIC
BUDAPEST: NORTHERN HUNGARY		270 - 279
BUDAPESTI: ARCHITECTURES OF STASIS AND FLUX		
		NOTES FROM THE HEART DUSAN DECERMIC
		280 - 283

AT THE FRONTIER - SIMHIKA RAO 50-55 THOUGHTS ON PRACTICALITY AND COLLABORATION LOUISE SCANNELL 74-81 STUDIO CULTURE TOBIAS PLUNKET 96-101 GLOBAL COUNTERPOINTS JULIANNE CASSIDY 118-123 EXPERIENCES IN THE STUDIO HANNAH GAZE 138-143 STUDIO: MYTHS OF A RECURRENT PRESENT MATTHEW STEWART 144-149 PLUS ÇA CHANGE SAM GILES 166-171 THE AGENCY OF ARCHITECTURE HELEN MISSELBROOK 194-199 THE VALUE OF STUDIO CULTURE CATRIONA HUNTER 216-221

ACKNOWLEDGMENTS

284 - 285

FOREWORD

F.

LUCIANO LAZZARI

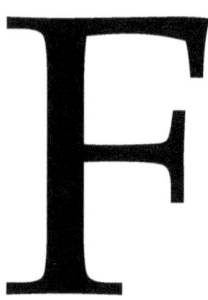ast forward to 2017. In the last few years, through Andrew and Dusan's visits to Trieste to undertake studio projects, I reconnected to Westminster, giving guidance and background support to their visiting students in and being invited to participate in studio 'crits' for their final design thesis proposals. What had changed? The vision and the freedom that can only come from a wider and deeper range of

My connection to the University of Westminster goes way back to the 1970s, when I graduated there at what was then the Polytechnic of Central London (PCL). The entry 'portico' was just an open colonnade without security barriers or any controls, leading onto a windswept, open space where ideas, people and weather interacted freely. It was a time of 'movements' and 'masters'. At the school Archigram was an important presence and David Greene my tutor; as our lecturers, we had the likes of Kenneth Frampton, Alan Colquhoun, Peter Cook and even a young assistant Daniel Libeskind. The atmosphere at the school was intense, involved, reasoned and thoughtful but ultimately, in retrospect perhaps, rather circumscribed. Studio work was channeled into defined currents of thought.

experience; the difference that one could say lies between climbing a mountain and instead now being able to fly, higher, faster, further and with greater vision. This is part of the appeal and the challenge of architectural education today.

The attraction and inherent difficulty is that of having such a large range of stimuli and such a vast reservoir of information and knowledge; of theories and of subjects to explore; access is now just a click away. The global connection is almost inexhaustible and the statistics staggering. There are 600,000 architects in Europe today and global architects number between three and four million. Europe has an average of one architect to 1000 of population although Italy has 2.6, resulting in the city of Rome alone having 22,000 registered architects, which is twice the number of architects in Holland (11,000). But how many students of architecture do we have now? A quick count identified 107 schools of architecture in India alone, Europe probably has around three times that number.

Consequently, on a purely numerical and quantitative level, the potential for sharing overwhelming quantities of data and information is enormous — making, such a diversity of cultures and social and climatic conditions, an avalanche that threatens cognitive discernment.

There is then the visual carousel — innumerable images constantly mirrored from the screen to our retinae, creating an inexhaustible kaleidoscope of archi-jumble. Cheap travel is available to all, so we have a Ryanair culture of easy consumption supplemented by the infinite inducement of 'copy and paste' mechanisms; suddenly everyone is empowered to be an expert inspired by the 'glossies' and Google.

Here, lies a less obvious problem, and of course a challenge. So, I would argue that this wealth of information and of experience, real or virtual, is the first issue to be addressed and exploited. This makes it an exciting time to be an architectural tutor. Teaching is no longer simply the transfer of a preset body of knowledge but in the true sense of the concept involves guidance and discrimination. Without predefined routes; without dogma, and without the imposition of a set of instructions, discursive freedom properly managed can make the journey through an architectural education memorable.

This journey towards becoming an architect begins the day one decides that is what one wants to be and ends the last day one draws breath. Architectural education is no longer a staged process that develops from university to internship, to practice, or to research or teaching. The traditional format of schools is becoming blurred, with experimentation taking place between work and study. Offices are now often involved in research, with research based design being the successful result. Naturally, all design is research based, or should be, but I view research being a driving force in the development of design within an architectural office, drawing from external as well as internal expertise and data.

Erasmus was the first major project for the internationalisation of student experience and this process is now being brought to fruition in architectural offices everywhere. Technological progress has also broken the barriers of work allocation in the office environment. A graduate can have skills that the senior partner lacks and so immediately the hierarchy has changed. One does not any longer have to experience months of mind-numbing drainage details as 'training' in the workplace, but is immediately catapulted into a more inclusive and effective participation in the design team. Conversely, the older generation is brought into contact with new ideas and exposed to wider possibilities of representation, presentation and understanding.

In this regard, there is a strong movement in Europe to bring down the barriers between the schools and the profession, between traditional ivory towers and the acumen of the financially driven practitioner. The value of this desirable and increasingly sought after collaboration has come about through the new-found processes of access and exchange, aided by legislation such as the Professional Qualifications Directive, which allowed automatic recognition of qualifications throughout the EU, but also through mechanisms such as 'continued professional development', which helps to reawaken the thirst for learning in a conscious awareness of the need to hone and maintain one's skills.

A wealth of knowledge, interaction, freedom of movement and of thought, blurring of boundaries, a continuum of development going in both directions – this is what we now have on offer. But in the absence of a predefined route, what is our compass? In the absence of a set curriculum of study, what skills should we acquire? The answer to the first question is straightforward and expressed in one multi-faceted word: responsibility. We need a reaffirmation of our commitment to a responsible attitude in the practise of our profession. The concept of a 'responsible architecture' includes the spirit of sustainability, but beyond that and returning to the original meaning of the term we need to pursue responsible design that takes into account at all scales the need for energy efficiency, flexible spaces, life-cycle costing of buildings, serious maintenance plans, and smart and inclusive re-use.

Climate change is probably our single biggest threat, one that can jeopardise our very future and change the face of the world. Our ancestors always took a sustainable path. Unfortunately, during years of unbridled development we lost this sensitivity. Now, having realised that growth cannot be infinite and the world and its resources are not unlimited, we must rediscover the pragmatism of acting in ways that are compatible with dwindling resources, and environmental and social fragility. Forty years ago, these attitudes were present, but they were essentially political choices. Now they should be considered fundamental necessities. Architects' practices impact on the way millions of people work, study and live. Our works can last a thousand years, but our mistakes even longer—we cannot and must not act alone in the process of creating the built environment, but as architects we have a unique holistic knowledge and potential vision that others may not necessarily have.

This brings us to the question, of skills. The 'generalist' versus the 'specialist' debate is a longstanding topic in the schools of architecture. It used to be phrased as 'are we in the business of teaching architecture or creating architects', and now it concerns the aspiration to specialise in all the various facets of the profession to become a person with a knowledge of everything, but as a specialist of nothing. Comparison is often made with the medical profession, which is split between the GP or the specialist consultant. But the analogy is questionable—no GP has a training that leads naturally to the ability to coordinate the complexities of a design team, one that requires the architect to be psychologist, sociologist, economist, technician, visionary and priest, and poet and artist. I have heard that architects make excellent restaurateurs, and can imagine they might also make great film directors or writers, travel guides or musicians (let us not forget that Pink Floyd's Gilmour, Waters and Mason, began their careers as students of architecture at Regent Street Polytechnic!).

Let us form graduates with conscience

With the ability to have a longer-term vision

With curiosity and open mindedness

Innovative and prepared for change

And we shall be creating Architects

June 2017 Luciano Lazzari RIBA hon. AIA hon. CCA President Architects' Council of Europe (RIBA President's Medal July 2017)

PREFACE

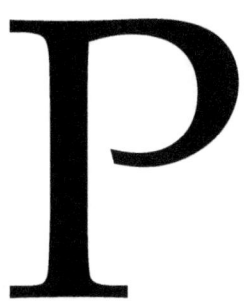

From the outset, this studio book was not predicated on a fixed research agenda identified with a design studio where tutors, like-minded critics and students validate a performative practice of teaching, design and research or a theory of architecture. Instead, Design Studio 11 (MArch part II) has been conceived as a supportive self-reflexive, but critical, framework. This publication presents the work of the studio while questioning the definition and efficacy of 'design research'. At its core is the development of a series of urban programmes identified with individual cities, over an eight-year period of our studio collaboration.

Luciano Lazzari and William Firebrace, both with a longstanding experience of architectural education and practice in Europe, provide introductions examining current architectural imperatives and the vagaries of 'studio' culture. Our central preoccupation was to consider the 'after-life' of the design studio: whether as a conceptual proposition; as work in practice, or as acted out in subsequent research or teaching—subjects explored in our now ex-students' reflections on the relationship between their studio-based education and their subsequent experience of practice.

It was also our somewhat indulgent polemical intention to engender a critical review of the cult of the design 'studio' in schools of architecture, whether viewed as an obsolete shibboleth or a practice in a state of contemporary flux. Resisting the view of design work produced as a model practice; reflected in distinctions, prizes and attendant exhibition spectacle; it was the longer-term effect of a studio education and its embodied research, that we sought to address.

The book is structured as a series of introductions to studio programmes from 2008–2017 (with a break in 2015) focused on particular European cities: from Wroclaw to Trieste; from Antwerp and Ghent to Kraków; from Copenhagen and Malmo back to Trieste, and from Genoa to Budapest. Outlining the titles of the series of short projects and studies that initiated each year, these typically present one in detail and sample student project work each year in the format of a graphic landscape. Retrospective 'reflections' by individual ex-students are interspersed in this structure—

bookended by full-page images of their work in the studio and subsequently in 'practice'. Our teaching evolved to include the design of a catalogue which acted as a springboard towards the formulation of each student's individual architectural (or design thesis) project that followed—and sampling these catalogues concludes the book.

The project notes published here (they were never intended for publication), essentially set out the preparatory work done 'at a distance' before embarking on a mid-year city visit. A city survey each year focused on what we have defined as intrinsic and extrinsic aspects of urbanity. This was conducted while students also researched their own projects and choice of sites. The overall preparatory work tested our students' abilities to conduct pre-emptive research (working individually and in small groups) research characterized in the form of short projects related to each city. Capitalizing on the availability of digital culture and information, these weekly studies aimed to acquire formal, social and historical knowledge, incorporating assumptions to be subsequently tested 'on location'.

We deliberately sought to avoid any valedictory connotation to the conclusion of this sequence of projects, setting out the briefs in an arbitrary rather than a chronological fashion. The final focus on Budapest (2016–2017) is however differentiated from the earlier years in presenting the thesis project of a single student, largely for its explicit formal derivation from the introductory work. Without sufficient time for realistic comment on post-MArch studio experience in so recent a past, there is instead a record of interviews for different courses and one practice, which suggest (unflatteringly) that in their conduct the terms and expectations of education and practice are not dissimilar: that is in terms not of specific skills and abilities, but in their conduct and in the judgements made by the interviewers. A salutary tale.

More positively we hope this book offers insight into the range of issues engaged in the studio as a collective enterprise in architectural design, one which recognizes the transnational cultures, conflicted histories, multicultural social life and municipal institutions that continue to inhabit, or have inhabited, these cities in the dissolute era of Brexit.

Andrew Peckham
& Dusan Decermic

SHORT CUTS

STUDIO CULTURE

WILLIAM FIREBRACE

ACT I
WESTMINSTER

* * * * *

Sc

University of Westminster, Department of Architecture, autumn 2016. 1970's brutalist building. On the fourth floor, large open plan studio spaces and minuscule offices for the staff. Various drifting sounds of conversations from the studios, quiet in the small office above.

Andrew Peckham: The myth of the design studio?
Pause.
Peckham: What might these myths be?
Dusan Decermic: First we need to be clear about our own position.
Decermic spends several minutes operating expresso machine.
Peckham: We are urbanists but doubt urbanism.
Decermic: But we enjoy a touch of landscape.
Peckham: We can tolerate a suggestion of irony.
Decermic: We like a certain mood.
Pause.
Peckham: We have a fondness for Mitteleuropa: Wroclaw, Trieste, Krakow, Budapest.
Decermic: Belgrade, don't forget Belgrade.
Peckham: We love the atmosphere of those vast semi-forgotten cities, the remains of various empires.
Decermic: Well you do, certainly. I am not entirely opposed to cities with a bit of sunshine. Possibly even by the sea. Anyway, we are different from other studios.
Peckham: We certainly wish to be different from them. But how do we explain how we are different?
Pause.
Peckham: So, if we are now going to explain the attitude of our studio and its relationship to other teaching methods, for comparison we need an outside view from someone who knows how other schools operate, who has experience of the academic world in other lands. Someone who knows about myths.
Decermic: Even if he or she might not be an Arsenal supporter.
Pause.
Peckham and Decermic together: Then we should ask....
An etiolated figure appears at the doorway. Enter Firebrace, shiftily.
Peckham: Ah, there you are William. We have something to ask you. We know you have been around a bit and seen a few architecture schools. You are rumoured to have international experience. Even if for some reason you have ended up here.
Decermic: We would like you to write something for us about the studio systems in other schools, and how it compares with what we do here. Something about teaching design. What do you think?
Short but healthy silence. Exit all in fine spirits towards the Angel public house.

ACT II
MOSCOW

* * * * *

Moscow University, Department of Architecture, 2010. Nineteenth century building in the neo-classical style, grand staircases, high rooms with ample windows. Office of the director, grand space with views of a garden, contemporary furniture, sculptures, models. The director, heavily bearded and with blue-framed spectacles, wears a fashionable suit. He speaks through an interpreter, but possibly understands more English than he wishes to reveal. He sits in a Breuer chair, on a raised dais, slightly above the level of the visitors.

Director: Have you come to Moscow to learn from us? Or do you wish simply to show us what you do.
English visitor, also via translator: Of course we wish to hear what you do.
Director: So this is how our course runs. All students in any year do much the same projects. Year one: exercises in pencil drawings of statues in Academy of Fine Arts. You see here on wall behind me, such beautiful images of busts of roman emperors, classical columns, goddesses.
Visitor: And then?
Director: Year two. Design of BMW showroom in central Moscow. Look here on the screen at these 3-D models and animations. Very talented students.
Visitor: Yes, there seem to be plenty of expensive motor vehicles, and the women in the images all have short dresses.
Director: Modern Russian world. Modern Russian people. Year three. Strategic planning for new city with population of 10,000, near Novosibirsk. Housing, factories, highways, cultural buildings,

ACT III
STUTTGART

* * * * *

Stuttgart Academy of Fine Art, Fachbereich Architektur und Design, 1997. A 1980's brutalist building, on a site above the city. Wide corridors and many small rooms.

A taxi pulls up at the entrance. The guest professor has arrived from the airport. A well-known English architect, he wears a baggy corduroy suit. His assistant greets him and carries his coat and bag upstairs. The students already have their work lined up in the corridor. A series of large cardboard models show proposals for an art gallery in a Stuttgart inner city street.

Guest-professor: I am here.
Pause
Guest-professor: I see you have all been working hard. I will start the critique.

The assistant comes with a tray for the coffee and biscuits for the guest professor. He carries a small notebook and writes down all the professor's comments. The guest professor walks slowly down the corridor and gives out a few comments on each of the projects. The students wait patiently for the assessment of the projects.

Student: Have we done what you required?
Professor: I see you have all understood the brief. I have said the aim is to learn to design in an appropriate style, not too individual but also not too conformist. I seek a balance between individuality and anonymity, is a delicate one.
Student: Do you wish us to produce an architecture which is like your own.
Professor: Hmm, well. Yes… no. No of course not, I want you to be individuals. But to be inspired by my work, to see it as a kind of example to follow. I would certainly find this praiseworthy.

The assistant hands out the comment sheets and the brief for the new project.
Professor: Excellent. I really must be going. My plane for Tokyo departs in an hour. I am going to design an art gallery for them. I say…work hard, and I will be back next month.

airport, stadium, rail station, motorways. See here on other wall, large scale plans and models.
Visitor: Very impressive. Which of these design projects from the three years seems to you realistic and appropriate to Russian society today?
Director: All realistic. We are realists here. And also of course idealists. This is Russian tradition, realistic and idealistic. With pencil drawings, students learn to see and to care about tones and lines of drawing, they understand tradition. With car show-room they learn how to deal with a realistic project for people with enough money to afford architects.
Visitor: And the new town project?
Director: With design of new town they learn to plan for social world.
Visitor: Does this social world of mass planning still exist.
Pause.
Director: Not much, but it is part of our heritage. We are interested in a partnership with the West but we work within great Russian social and political tradition. Do you have any other questions?

ACT IV
ARCHITECTURAL ASSOCIATION

* * * * *

The Architectural Association, 1984. The chairman's office, a fine room on the second floor, decorated with drawings and models of student work. A desk in the corner, a settee and several comfortable chairs.

Alvin Boyarsky, chairman: William, please come in. Just the right moment, here is a parcel which has arrived today from New York. Please help me open it. Ah yes, what is this? It's the book from the Cooper Union, the catalogue of their student projects for the last few years. Edited by John Hejduk. What a surprise.

Firebrace: It looks interesting.

Boyarsky: Interesting? Maybe.

Firebrace: But they have the same unit system as us.

Boyarsky: Hmmm...

Firebrace: They are also innovative and keen to try new things...

Boyarsky: No......no....no, oh no...what a disappointment. They are trying hard, but really this is all quite weak. Poor John, all this work and it's just going nowhere.

Firebrace: But I quite like some of this...

Boyarsky: No, William, no, you really must learn to understand that what we have here is special. No one else can do what we do. We – or rather I – thought of it first. The AA invented the unit system of small individual groups, working together with a group of inspirational teachers with a specific design method. Units with very different programmes, with different attitudes, but all in one school. And working to the highest standard. No one else has the internationally renowned teachers we have. The others are merely imitations, feeble, provincial, imitations.

Firebrace: Alvin, could I ask you something.

Boyarsky: Yes, of course.

Firebrace: I have a second year student who is a bit of a problem.

Boyarsky: A problem? Well we don't like problems. Just remember William that you were once a very poor second year student, in fact one of the worst, you could hardly draw.

Firebrace: ...yes... but that was a long time ago...

Boyarsky: And in the end you pulled yourself together and now you even teach here. So please don't think of students as problems, just as people who need a particular kind of attention.

Firebrace: I am glad you reminded me of all this.

Boyarsky begins to carefully repack the book for the next visitor.

ACT V
DELFT

* * * * *

Delft University, Department of Architecture, 1985. 1970's building with wide open spaces. A big room with tables, on which are placed a very large number of timber models of the Rietveld Schröder House in Utrecht. Somewhere in the distance a brass band plays traditional music.

Young teaching assistant: The aim of this exercise is to examine a classic piece of Dutch architecture, to understand how it works in three dimensions, to understand the basis of 1920's colour theory and to learn how to make an exact model of a building using timber. Here in our workshops we have excellent facilities for working with all kinds of materials, we consider the development of architecture as a craft an important part of education.

Second assistant: how do you feel about the way all the models are so similar? What do the students learn about their own creativity?

First student: We are an architectural department in an art academy, not a technical university or a polytechnic. There is a kind of masterclass system here, but really there is little difference between the teaching of the professors. They are all pragmatists.
Second student: We students believe we should have the freedom to explore architecture as we wish, not just follow the wishes of our professors. For this reason we have invited you to be our guest professor.
Firebrace: Why me?
Third student: Because you are not very technical. And not very pragmatic. You have a reputation for being experimental.
Firebrace: This is most flattering. And the nightlife here in Berlin is delightful. We are going to start by making films.
Fourth student: Films? We don't know anything about films. We don't even have movie cameras.
Firebrace: I would like each of you to make a short film of the city.
Fifth student: Can we make whatever kind of film we like?
Firebrace: Yes. Kind of. It must be short. With no boring bits.
Sixth student: Can we do drawings?
Seventh student: Can we do models?
Eighth student: Can you suggest some theory books?
Firebrace: I will be back in two weeks and the films must be finished. You wish to be experimental, now is the chance.
Ninth student: Experimental - I might read some Deleuze Guattari.
Firebrace: Nein. No reading permitted.

ACT VIII
ANGEL

* * * * *

The Angel in the Fields pub, London, April 2017. Downstairs room, usual mix of tourists, idlers, businessmen, academic apparatchiks. Peckham, Decermic and Firebrace sit at a table.
Peckham: Success is not to be sneered at.
Decermic: But how do we decide what is a successful student project. An interesting form? Good graphics? Social issues? The world of academia is different from the world outside.
Peckham: The world outside mostly expects a degree of pragmatism from architects, together with a certain style. A hint of experiment, but not too much. The world has surely a right to expect a level basic competence after seven years of architectural education?
Decermic: But if all we are teaching is office competence then our ambition is hardly high.
Peckham: So we should look for individuality, but how many individuals are actually so very individual?
Firebrace scratches his head and is about to speak.

ACT VII
CORK

* * * * *

Cork University, Department of Architecture, 2014. 1960's commercial office building, converted to studio spaces. Temporary screens covered in drawings.
Year leader: The students here almost all come from the area around the city. We feel Cork is special, and the work should also be special. We are very different from Dublin, we have a different approach to the world. All the students in the year are working on the same project, in Prague. They will show you their work.
Student: My project is concerned with parks. And routes. And the poetry of James Joyce. And Kafka, but not so much Kafka. And dance moves. And methods of recording sounds.
First critic: That's quite a lot of themes.
Student: Yes, sometimes I am a tad confused, but I think I am getting there. Here is the plan, it's a concert hall.
Second critic: It's all rather beautiful. I like those curved walls and the colours. Is there a section?
Student: Not yet, I am still wondering how to fit the James Joyce bits in. And the Kafka.
First critic, waving his arms encouragingly: Remember Samuel Beckett. Fail, fail again, fail better.
Pause.
Bob Dylan, softly in the background: My love she speaks softly. She knows there's no success like failure. And that failure's no success at all.
Student: But I would like to succeed.

Decermic: Studios seem to be the standard system of teaching architecture design in this country. They have the advantage of organising smallish groups of students around one or two tutors.
Peckham: But the system only makes sense if the studio has an identity, and an aim.
Decermic: But if has too narrow an identity all the work looks the same – just visit the Bartlett.
Peckham: Is that what students want, just to follow the studio line?
Firebrace blows his nose.
Decermic: Maybe. Those that don't particularly wish to follow a line of their own.
Peckham: What anyway might be the alternative? To teach a pragmatic architecture, like we see in some schools. This would be dull for all concerned.
Decermic: Anyway, things have changed so much recently, it is difficult to know quite where architecture departments are going.
Peckham: Where once we had an idea of education being a part of society, for the benefit of all, now we have the notion of students as customers. From the myth of the studio - to a production line?
Firebrace raises one hand.
Peckham: Anyway William, you were course leader here for two years. You have some responsibility for how things have worked out. And what about the studio you ran here, in the department? Did you have a design attitude, which all the students had to follow? Your students made films, but was this just another technique or a new time-based representation of the project? We liked watching the films, it made a change from just looking at drawings
Firebrace looks sheepish.
Decermic: William, are you going to say something? About that text.
Firebrace: Indeed, indeed.
Pause
Firebrace: Doesn't the writing will speak for itself? And surely, I have already said enough...
Peckham: Well anyway you will need to write some more. But don't make us sound like characters, speaking lines written by you. Not a pair of talking heads. We are our own people, allow us personalities...
Decermic: And remember we have a deadline.
Peckham: This is 'design research'. Everyone does design research nowadays, it goes with the territory. A policy initiative, and we need to pay close attention to education initiatives. Design research brings in status and funding—if rather little else. So, don't be too literary or too clever, or too imaginative, think research.
Exit Firebrace, slyly.
Peckham: Did he buy his round?
Decermic: And we never nailed him down on who might be the new Arsenal manager.

ACT IX
TOKYO

* * * * *

Tokyo University of the Arts, Department of Architecture, 2001. 1980's building with small spaces. A corridor with several automats dispensing tins of hot coffee. Metal chairs scattered around low tables.

First lecturer: The teaching system here in the department is not really a studio system. In the part of the school in which I teach it's more like a year system. All the students from each year do much the same project, but with different tutors.
Second lecturer: And now of course with the internet and all schools having their own sites, everyone knows very quickly what is happening elsewhere. As soon as an approach to design which seems new is produced, it spreads very quickly. So what is the point of all student projects trying to be different when they all end up looking much the same.
First lecturer: We really would like though to do social projects, towns, hospitals, housing. Making the world somehow better. Surely this must be the aim, rather than just being stylish.
Second lecturer: But of course, and with a good colour scheme.
Visitor: And when you were a student?
Second lecturer: Ah, long time ago. Then I worked on my project alone in my room. I worked every night and slept in the day, but I never slept much. I hardly spoke to anyone and never to my tutors. I hardly even went outside. The project was so complicated, like a game with very exact rules. The design became almost indistinguishable from my psychological state. Every time I thought I got near the end, I realised that I had hardly started. I thought it could never be finished. It might take me years, perhaps my entire life to finish. My parents kept on asking me when I would get my diploma. But I had to finish. So one day I handed it in, even if it wasn't really finished. I felt so pleased it was done, but also lost because I now I had nothing to work on.
Visitor: And how do you feel today about the project?
Second lecturer: I am happy. But I never look at that project. It is in a box, at the back of the cupboard. Perhaps the mice have devoured the drawings. I do other things now, I work for a company specialising in supermarkets signs, we produce them very quickly and are very successful.

ACT X
VIENNA

* * * * *

Vienna Universität der Angewandete Kunst, 1992. Another fine nineteenth century building. A room in the basement, with tattered red armchairs, wooden tables, several bottles of vodka rapidly emptying.

Student: We have here the Meisterklasse system. There are three studios, each led by a distinguished architect, who has a professorial position for life. Students are accepted into a particular studio when they arrive, and remain there for their whole student career – three years, five years, maybe even longer. Each studio follows the work of the professor.
Firebrace: And does the system work?
Second student: Yes, very well, we have the highest level of student work in Austria.
Firebrace: Do the three professors get on?
Third student. Not really. In fact they hardly talk to each other. For one everything must be designed in the traditional way. For the second everything must be evolved by instinct and inspiration and always have plenty of angles. And the third is post-modern, he likes a kind of pop-art approach.
Firebrace: Can you cross over from one to another?
Fourth student: No, that would be pointless, there cannot be links between the three paths.
Firebrace: At least you can drink vodka together.
Fifth student: This is the deconstructivist vodka, the traditionalists and the post-modernists drink other brands.

ACT XI
COPENHAGEN

* * * * *

Royal Danish School of Architecture, Copenhagen, 2001. A series of long buildings, originally built for the navy. Sequence of auditoriums. Room with tables and chairs, looking out over water. Light snow. Students making soup with homemade dumplings.

Student, standing beside window and smoking: I have been in this university for eleven years. Yes, I still have some more modules to do. But I am in no hurry, I like it here and the people are very pleasant. There is more to student life than just learning, just moving on to professional life. The students are a community, with our own lifestyle. We provide an alternative economy to parts of the town, keep alive areas which might otherwise sink. Last year I got a grant, I went to Romania, out into the countryside, to study the barns and agricultural buildings. And now I have my partner, and our daughter, they are important to me. I work part-time in the university café, doing the baking. After all this time training to be a professional and I work in the café, but I contribute to the community by the work I do.

Visitor: Maybe you should become a baker.

Student: Maybe. But I always wished to become an architect. Or at least an architect-baker.

Visiting teacher: What is the system here? How do you work with the professors?

Student: Mostly we choose our own project and also how long it takes us to finish. We sign up with a professor who agrees to do the supervision, but we don't see them much. We respect the professors, they have their own interests, but we don't want them to interfere too much in what we do.

Visiting teacher: And have you done any work yet on my project?

Student: Oh yes, of course. I have thinking about it hard. And discussing it with others. We have long discussions, late into the night. And we have been reading detective stories, like you suggested. We have been finding clues. It's all becoming clearer. It's going to be very good.

Visiting teacher: Do you wish to show me now?

Student: Not quite yet. I want it to be a surprise for you. And now I have to pick up my child from kindergarten.

Visiting teacher: The final 'crit' is tomorrow.

ACT XII
MARSEILLE

* * * * *

Ecole National Superior architecture de Marseille, 2007. Elegant white and grey buildings some distance outside town, not far from the sea. Early afternoon, the sun shines down. A group of students sit outside, at a metal table, in the shadow of the pine trees. Paper coffee cups and tins of soft drinks. Several students work on laptops, one is turning the pages of a copy of Jean Baudrillard's *Simulacres et Simulation*, two others are drawing in small notebooks.

Visitor: I wonder please if you could tell me...

No reply. No one stirs. Sky pure blue. Rocks of mountains glimmer in heat. Lizards run. Faint sound of motor scooter approaching.

ACT XIII
EDINBURGH

* * * * *

Edinburgh University, Department of Architecture and Landscape Architecture, 2016. Centrally located nineteenth century building with studio spaces on the upper floors. Scattered around the rooms are large scale models of considerable complexity.

Senior tutor: We are keen to be difficult from the English schools and from the whole English system, which has just been copied everywhere. So the students join one of six studios and they stay in the same studio for two years. They work on one site, usually somewhere abroad, for that whole period. The aim is that for once in their lives they would have the time to work on one theme for a long period. My students are working a town in Greece.

Visitor: Two years - that is a long period to work on one project. Don't they need new inspiration?

Tutor: During the two years they have the opportunity to explore their theme in depth, and then to produce a really good presentation of their work, with drawings and models on which they work for weeks.

Visitor: Are the studios very different from one another?

Tutor: We would like to think so, but probably we are all rather similar.

Visitor: Do they never work on a 'Scots' project?

Tutor: Rarely. The whole idea of being 'Scots' is being outward looking, being international. Anyway the weather here is often dreich, which is depressing.

Visitor: Do the studios depend on the personality of the teachers?

Tutor: There are different personalities. And of course there are long standing rivalries. That's what happens in schools, the personalities are more at odds than the working methods. But because we are all working in one building we grow to be a bit like one another.

Visitor: And what is your personality?

Pause.

ACT XIV
BERLIN

* * * * *

Berlin, Weissensee University, Fachbereich Architektur, 1991. Socialist era building, walls decorated with paintings and fabrics. Lecture hall with students sitting at front, group of professors at rear.

Firebrace: Could you tell me how the school is organised?

Silence.

Professor: We are organised in the way we have always been organised.

Firebrace: But now that there is political change, will the school change? Do you wish to be more like schools in the West?

Professor: We are not sure what changes will be made. Everything is new.

Firebrace: And the way you teach?

Professor: We are pragmatic. We are not involved with political questions. We teach the students to solve the architectural issues they will encounter later in professional life. This year the older students are all working on the design of a hospital. They work with plans, sections and models. And technical details, they all draw technical sections through their buildings.

Firebrace: And what would you like me to teach...

Professor: We think you could teach the students about light and shadow. You seem to know about darkness. And maybe about light, the students need to learn about light.

Firebrace: Aha.

Professors and students clap with genuine enthusiasm.

EPILOGUE
WESTMINSTER

* * * * *

University of Westminster Department of Architecture, 2017. Back in the small room on the fifth floor.
Peckham: Darkness and light? What's he on about?
Decermic: That's myths for you: darkness and light.
Pause
Decermic: But definitely more light...always more light.
Peckham: Shades of grey?
They leave the room, and look down into the open plan studio space. A few students are diligently working. Some check their smartphones. Others snooze gently. Peckham and Decermic take the lift down to the ground floor, and move off together into the bright sunlight outside.

William Firebrace is former Professor of Architecture at the Stuttgart Academy for Fine Arts. He has taught in many European architectural departments, including a studio at the University of Westminster where he also ran the MArch Part II course. He is author of Marseille Mix, Memo for Nemo and Star Theatre, and is now working on a book on the German peripheral.

* * * CURTAIN * * *

7 CITIES /// 8 PROGRAMS

London
United Kingdom
2008-17

Copenhagen
Denmark
2012-13

Antwerp
Belgium
2010-11

Genova
Italy
2015-16

Trieste
Italy
2009-10/13-14

Budapest
Hungary
2016-17

Wroclaw
Poland
2008-09

Kraków
Poland
2011-12

12/13
COPENHAGEN

C

NORDIC NOIR

Todd Courtey

Sophie Determann

Timothy Bedingfield

James Williamson

Simhika Rao

Catriona Hunter

Vicky Tippell

Dominik Sedziki

Marta Ferriera

Samuel Gardner

Paul Motley

David Cloux

Owen Dore

Laura Gazey

Sofronis Marcou

Kristine Sutca

Adrian Manea

Gavin Kelly

Artjoms Kuzmics

Diana Lyubych

Lee Fox

Elena Neophytou

2012/2013

COPENHAGEN/MALMO:
CENTRAL DENMARK/SWEDEN

KØBENHAVN:
NORDIC NOIR

Landmarks:

AMALIENBORG/CHRISTIANSBORG/
FREDERIKSBERG/ROSENBORG/
FREDERIKSBERG HAVE/ FÆLLEDPARKEN/
AMALIEHAVE/ ØRSTEDSPARKEN/VALBY
PARK/KONGENS HAVE/THE BOTANICAL
GARDEN/LANDBOHØJSKOLENS
HAVE/BIBLOTEKSHAVEN/
KASTELLET/KØPENHAVNS RÅDHUS/
GEFIONSPRINGVANDET/DRAGØR/
RÅDHUSPLADSEN/KONGENS NYTORV/
GAMMELTORV/GRÅBRØDETORV/
VOR FRELSERES KIRKE/FREDERIKS
KIRKE/VOR FRUE KIRKE/HAVNEBAD/
HELGOLAND/BELLEVUE/AMAGER
SKUESPILHUSET/DYREHAVSBAKKEN/
ORDRUPGAARD/ZOOLOGISK MUSEUM/
SUPERKILEN/LANGELINIE/DEN LILLE
HAVFRUE/KUNSTINDUSTRIMUSEET/
MARMORKIRKEN/ARBEJDERMUSEET/
SØERNE/BOTANISK HAVE/DAVIDS
SAMLING/STRØGET/RUNDETÅRN/
KØBENHAVNS BYMUSEUM/TIVOLI/
NY CARLSBERG GLYPTOTEK/
KØBENHAVNS RÅDHUS/PRINSENS
PALÆ/THORVALDSEN/CHRISTIANSBORG
SLOT/SLOTSHOLMEN/TØJHUSMUSEET/
HOLMENS KIRKE/BØRSBYGNINGEN/
DANSK JØDISK MUSEUM/DET
KONGELIGE BIBLIOTEK/VOR FRELSERS
KIRKE/OPERAEN/SØNDERMARKEN/
ORLOGSMUSEET

Coordinates:

55°40′34N 12°34′06E

Region:

Capital (Hovedstaden)

Area:

86.39 km2

Elevation:

91 m

Population:

1921	3,267,831	—
1930	3,550,656	+8.7%
1940	3,844,312	+8.3%
1950	4,281,275	+11.4%
1960	4,585,256	+7.1%
1970	4,937,579	+7.7%
1980	5,122,065	+3.7%
1990	5,135,409	+0.3%
2000	5,330,020	+3.8%
2011	5,560,628	+4.3%
2017	5,748,769	+3.4%

Demonym(s):

Copenhagener

Patron Saint:

Sankt Knud

Copenhagen in Denmark and Malmo in Sweden (whose post-industrial economy has been boosted by the major infrastructure project of the Oresund Bridge), are two adjacent cities, physically linked at one point (but without a contiguous 'border') yet nonetheless increasingly identified with a trans-national region. The dichotomy between the two cities and cultures has been explored socially and psychologically in 'The Bridge', and identified with novels and films associated with Nordic Noir as a genre. An inversion perhaps of the Scandinavian ideal that permeated post-war architecture in Britain, one associated with enlightened social democracy. If those illusions succumbed to later socio-economic and political scrutiny, the legacy of Nordic Light lives on in the 'impression' of continuity within a modernist tradition; its ideals and aesthetic preferences; despite an antidote that is noir or gothic in projecting dark space and dystopian architecture.

Anti-Ikea

Bridging or assimilating cultures remains part of the experience of architects working abroad (regardless of global homogeneity). How to remake, refashion or reformulate another culture as your own, or conversely become implicated or accommodated within its particular history and contemporary everyday life? The experience of immigrant cultures in Scandinavia may be positive or traumatic, and that of the architectural tourist something else: an architectural migration, the anti-Ikea.

Transpositions

Is the relation between opposites: transparent or opaque; light or dark; digital or analog; theory and practice or optical and tactile, something 'given' or are they equally mental 'constructs'?

Dualities tend to be mutually reinforcing, so we are interested not in erasing differences or reconciling them, but exploring the interface between qualities (epitomised in the coding and naming of colours or perfumes for example). How to extend the range of a one-dimensional architecture, or to sharpen its particular and ordinary characteristics?

Genre in architecture

The attributes of Nordic Noir, acted out in stories, films or sagas, raise questions of genre and narrative. Rather than indulging in the myth of the architect as film director (or scenographer); assuming too literal connections between different practices; what are the implications of genre and multiple narratives in their application to architecture? An oblique take perhaps on traditional questions of style and typology.

Working knowledge

A linear chronological development is typically followed in design projects (however contrary their intentions may be): the gradual move from concept or image to strategy, building, detail and materialization, is engrained in architectural culture, together with remnants of a concurrent myth of (modernist) integration. Conditions of practice: perhaps....predictable remedies include discursive studies (implications often undeveloped), or occasional and extreme disruptive juxtapositions in scale. Our interest instead is in 'the project within the project': individual and group work, parallel, different in character, scale, atmosphere and intent, but not merely piecemeal details or cursory fragments.

COPENHAGEN/MALMO VISIT

Narrative Re-visit: Real/Fictional Three Conditions/Five Characters/Year One: Culture/Environment/Production of Culture/Year Two: Strategic/Local Knowledge Thesis/Report/Four Themes: 001 Walled-in: Experiential/Constituting Enclosure/Interface-Between Walls/002: Aperture: Opening Up/Viewing/Framing/003 Order and Contingency: Order/Hierarchy/Composition-Arrangement/004 Flow and Promenade

04 YEAR ONE: MEDIATEQUE PRINT PUBLICATION STUDIO

01 1000 SHADES OF GREY
001   manifest
002   representative project

02 GENRE AND NARRATIVE
001   theory
002   (recycled) city

03 RECIPROCAL
001   two regions
002   site/culture/identity

05 YEAR TWO: CATALOGUE RAISONNÉ

03 1000 SHADES OF GREY
001   dark, transparent and grey space
002   representative project

INTRODUCTION

Our intention was to confront directly at the outset, Noir as it may be understood in architecture. Background research is viewed as an opportunity to build up a contextual archive of material about Copenhagen and Malmo. The art of these short projects is to develop your own agenda within the parameters we set out, and to exceed these in making them your own. The expectation is of a high level of commitment and 'finish' to this initial work and you will need to demonstrate the confidence to act decisively without prevarication. There is no correct, preferred or 'right' way to pursue these projects, how you interpret them is down to your own judgement.

INDIVIDUAL PROJECT

Working individually draw up a 'manifest' of a particular architectural condition. In doing so consider the following two extremes of illumination (or its absence) and their median (or is the concept of grey space something quite different?):

dark space (black-out / tactile)

transparent space (light / optical)

grey space (fog / intangible)

There are many different terms, associations and implications linked to these categories, whether architectural, spatial, temporal, formal, aesthetic or philosophical. Work directly with these three categories of space, or refer to them as a model for a parallel triad (environmental, sculptural, formal or programmatic). What lies between the two extremes involved.

'1000 Shades of Grey' has both implicit and explicit connotations, in particular the nature of subtle variations and their naming or coding. There's the question of gradation and the absence of colour. Grey may be associated with ordinariness (among other things) but also aesthetic delicacy in its muted and multi-hued tones.

According to the dictionary a 'manifest' is a record (or list) of cargo, freight or baggage which requires the naming of items, while to make 'manifest' concerns visual or mental clarification. Your manifest should not only clarify the 'third' condition involved, but also identify what 'baggage' you bring to the project.

The presentation of your manifest should be a verbal, visual and architectural record of variations related to the condition you are examining, where change over time becomes an issue. The agenda that you bring to your manifest should be of architectural consequence.

FABLER FABRINA FADO FAMNIG FANSTA FANTAST FANTASTISKFÃ RGGLAD FARTYG FARUM FASTBO FATTBAR FAVORIT FEJKA FELICIA FENOMEN FIBBEFICUS FIGGJO FILLSTA FINLIR FINNGRUND FISKEVIK FIXA FLATEN FLIT FLOKATI FLORERA FLORÃ FLUKTAFLYGEL FLYN FLYT FLYTTA FNISS FOLKVIK FORMAT FORSÃ FRAKTA FRAMSTÃ

GROUP-WORK

Select the most consequential individual manifest, and design a 'representative' project located in Copenhagen or Malmo that exemplifies the qualitative variations recorded.

Identify a set of architectural elements, constituting a project, each re-formed individually, in multiples or in series, engaging the variations recorded in the manifest.

The choice of scale, construction type and site is entirely open, and you have to confront the problem of how to quickly produce a rhetorical design. This may be 'procedural' in following a particular logic, or be 'media' based in short- circuiting the design process. The project, should appear embedded in its context. Decide what to emphasise and consider both the residual and the generic? Suspend your usual way of working, take on board a shared group

perspective and don't agonize about individual design decisions and outcomes. You may appropriate 'ready-mades' and available documentation in utilising digital manipulation.

FINAL PRESENTATION
01 strategic explanation
02 contextualization 'on-site' / generic outline,
03 sectional articulation
04 the confines of the interior.

03 RECIPROCAL
001 two regions
002 site/culture/identity

INTRODUCTION:
RECIPROCAL: THE
PROJECT WITHIN
THE PROJECT
ORESUND

The third and final two-week project may be worked on individually, collaboratively. Our conception of this project is concerned with several key issues: your design methodology, the relationship between Copenhagen and Malmo, and the identity of the trans-national Oresund region.

WORKING
KNOWLEDGE

You are expected to question the normative way of working on a single project over time in a chronological sequence, gradually moving up the architectural-scale. The move from concept or image, to strategy, building, detail, materialization, and progressive 'integration' towards a complete description, is engrained in architectural culture. 'Conditions of practice' perhaps, but is not the design process often fragmented in fact, as are the current procedures of 'design and build', and of production and construction? Our interest is in what we have called 'the project within the project'. You have experienced reciprocal individual and group work, working in parallel on different architectural characteristics and at different scales. How, particularly with the final year thesis in mind, do you 'frame' a project to constitute a strategic and contrasting material intent from the start, where both aspects are worked up in parallel? A formal design strategy is progressively refined, just as is its material development. The intention is to avoid expedient or inconclusive strategic 'ideas', and conversely, prevarication that defers detailed design development held back in undeveloped form.

TWIN CITIES

Copenhagen and Malmo are twinned by their adjacency, connected by the Oresund bridge and tunnel. While they reflect their national cultures, like most cities on national borders one merges with the other, as do their communities. What interests us is the difference between their respective identities: one a capital and the other a provincial post-industrial city. What one embodies the other may require. The decline of their (marine) industries has followed a typical pattern, whereas the rise of administrative, media based corporate business and cultural tourism in Copenhagen, has followed a *different trajectory to the high-tech IT, digital and education 'industries' courted by Malmo (which retains a container port and the presence of Skanska). A service economy on one hand, and a revived, reconfigured or reinvented industrial economy on the other? Consequently, how might strategic architectural intervention map one city onto the other, or offer contrasting initiatives to reinvent their current identities? What distinctions prevail in their everyday multicultural life? And does Nordic Noir enliven, or in fact simply accept, the realities of both cities?*

TRANS-NATIONAL

The Oresund Region represents a trans-national identity increasingly favored within the EU. Or is it merely a strategic concept induced by the development of a new infrastructure and changed economic conditions? With what architecture(s) is it to be 'represented', and with what institutions? How might its infrastructure be turned to advantage? Or is it to be characterized by a 'lighter' networked economy predicated on communications, transport and the free market, invisible institutions, a transient culture, disparate places and diverse events? Could both cities be served by an alternative culture, a new economy and a revived social agenda (one distinct from the overworked conception of urban 'regeneration')?

THE PRODUCTION OF CULTURE

At this stage, we are introducing a general theme of the 'production' of culture'. Copenhagen in common with many European cities has a surplus of cultural institutions (museums, art galleries, theatres, concert halls etc) where the consumption of culture as a commodity or a spectacle has perhaps displaced an everyday focus on culture as a social and aesthetic activity. What of the 'production' of culture? In what wider range of places and institutions is culture 'produced'? In studios (of painting / design / film / digital media / graphics); workshops (making sculpture / scenery / printing / narrating), and factories, software production companies, archives, libraries or indeed domestic 'rooms'? Should a 'craft' or a 'industrial' connotation be celebrated or denied?

03 RECIPROCAL
001   two regions
002   site/culture/identity

Consider design ambition at two scales: a large geographical scale, and a detailed small scale. Define the boundaries of (internal and external) of two 'regions', within the remit of the larger Oresund Region. One should be associated with a strategic urban or territorial (XXL) scale (complex, island, city, district, zone, conurbation, hinterland or geographic area). The other (part or component of a typical, real or fictional building, urban space or landscape) with the small (S) intimate scale of the individual (lift, stair, ramp, threshold, lobby, foyer, hall, niche, waiting room, kiosk, booth, carrel, courtyard, bar, reception or information display). These lists are purely indicative. Represent the two 'regions' in a reciprocal relationship: either within each city (Copenhagen and Malmo), or as one region within the other. The resulting proposition may therefore be contextual (in urban terms) or more abstract and singular in nature. Similarly make an imaginative leap or connection (in physical or metaphorical terms) between the two regions. While a generic description, the graphic quality of their representation should carry material conviction. So, your initial task is to identify the parameters that define each region, setting out their relationship—whether through juxtaposition, association or formal configuration.

INITIAL
PRESENTATION
01: Draw up a 'map' (or a mapping) that outlines each of the two 'regions' and registers its scale, boundaries, thresholds and typical aspect. These maps may be two, or three, dimensional, and incorporate contextual material (projections, images, text or icons) related to the identity of each 'region'. Generic and schematic in nature they should be representative as much as descriptive. The two maps should be presented in reciprocal relation to one another.
02: Consider an architectural detail at either scale, which serves to describe an intervention in each 'region' (as you conceive them). The detail may be designed, invented, or 'found'. Each should be juxtaposed with their respective maps.

03 RECIPROCAL
001 two regions
002 site/culture/identity

WEEK 2: RECIPROCAL: SITE/CULTURE/IDENTITY

If you are working individually, develop a proposition for a site in one of the generic regions proposed earlier, while if working as a group you are expected to develop two sites in related regions. The design of the project for each site should be informed by the previous work. Develop an architectural proposition, whether that is framed within the context of the greater region or is consolidated locally in relation to the micro-region. In either case demonstrate how in working 'up', or 'down', in scale, each proposal develops as a building or a range of buildings. Their programme should be representative of the Oresund Region or be associated with the production of its culture. Location may be within the wider region, or within the districts immediately beyond the city centre of Malmo or Copenhagen (or on their urban periphery). You may submit the large-scale region to downsizing, and the micro region to multiplication or repetition as you develop these related propositions.

FINAL PRESENTATION

Consider the relationship between drawing, diagram and model. Each representation of the project should be composite in character.

01 Composite Drawing
02 Composite Diagrams
03 Composite Model

Each should in principle encompass different scales of object, boundary or region. The drawing should include a least three different projections. The diagrams should conceptualize or explain different aspects of each project. The model should be constructed of two elements of differing scale.

01_CN_S_001_002_002_P46_EP

01_CN_S_001_003_003_P46_HP

01_CN_S_001_012_012_P47_C

01_CN_S_002_013_013_P47_P

01_CN_S_002_004_004_P46_EP

01_CN_S_001_005_005_P46_SP

01_CN_S_003_006_006_P47_EP

01_CN_S_002_007_007_P47_HP

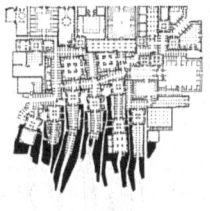 

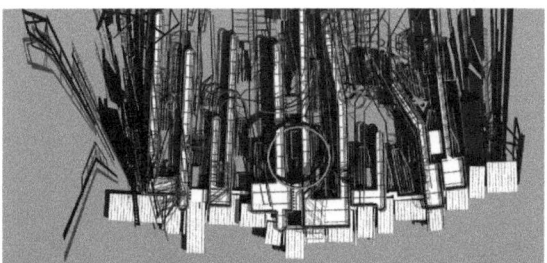
01_CN_S_001_008_008_P47_P

01_CN_S_001_009_009_P47_M

01_CN_S_004_010_010_P47_EP

01_CN_S_001_011_011_P47_IP

(L. Hilberseimer, *Größstadatarchiktur*)

THE HAZE HOVERING OVER THE CITY DULLS THE BRILLIANCE OF COLOUR. THAT IS WHY THE PRIMARY COLOUR OF ALL CITIES IS AN UNDEFINED GREY, THE [MUTE] COLOUR OF THIS ATMOSPHERE. (1)

01_CN_S_005_020_020_P49_M

01_CN_S_003_021_021_P49_IP

01_CN_S_006_022_022_P49_M

01_CN_S_001_023_023_P49_A

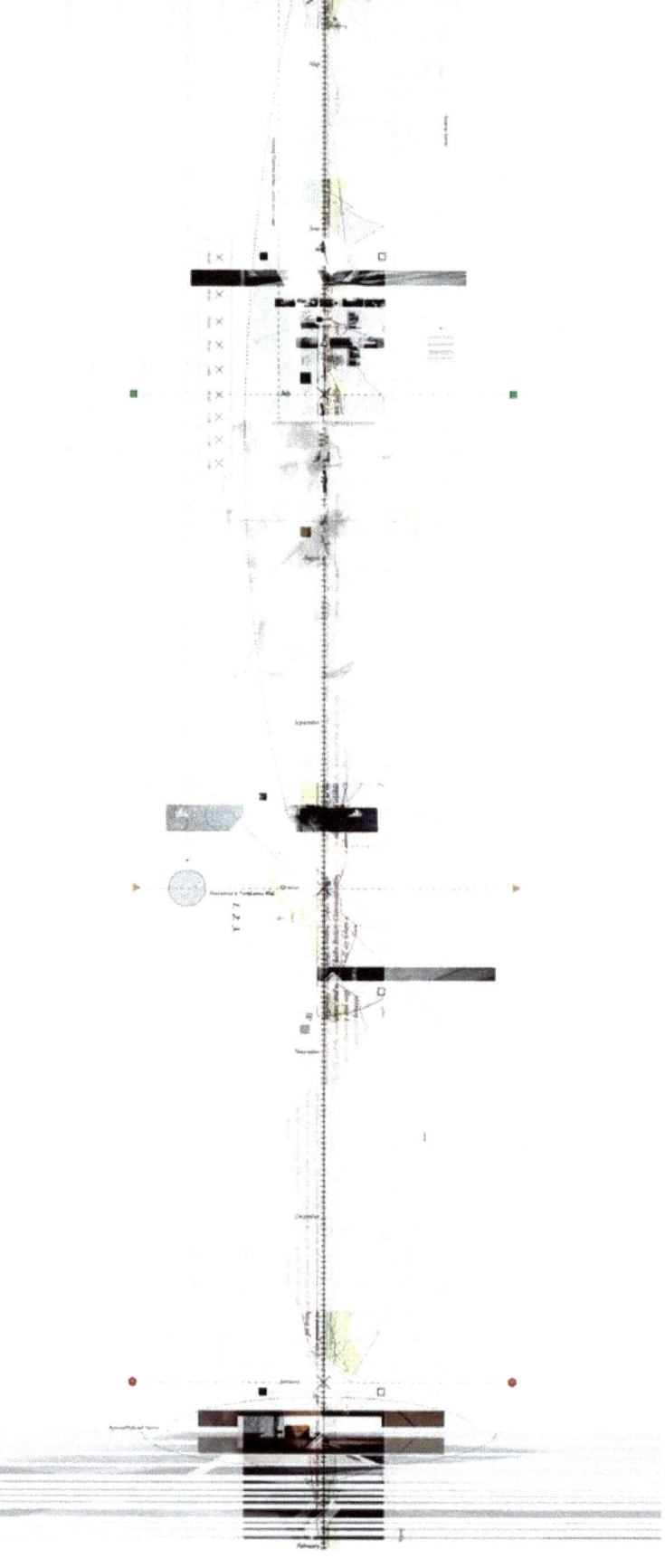

SIMHIKA RAO

AT THE FRONTIER

In my experience, design research is inherently about the process of retraining and rethinking design methodologies: that is with a view to being innovative and formulating progressive ideas that directly engage with the current issues facing the profession. This process has been instilled throughout my education and has laid the foundations for the way I approach projects in my professional and personal life. Balancing academic experimentation with the practical and social grounding of real-life projects has been a challenging one throughout my four years of working in practice since graduating from the MArch Part II at the University at Westminster. I have mainly worked for Piercy & Company but I have also been an associate for Architecture Sans Frontières—both experiences being distinct in the way design research and the process of designing have operated in contrast to that at university.

Within the framework of DS11, during my two years on the MArch course, an emphasis placed on process, precedent and narrative, was to become the core foundation of my self-directed and self-critical design thinking. The studio's thematic framework at the time was focused on the manufacturing process and the city, which constituted a strong foundation for theoretical research and its implementation within the cultural context of site-specific urban fabric. The first semester oscillated between group and individual work, which developed my appreciation for collaboration—something inherent in my experience of professional practice. Intense one week exercises prioritised an efficient process of design research which correlated with practice where one is not afforded the luxury of time—informed decisions need to be made quickly both during design development and during construction on site.

The process of researching, travelling, interviewing, cataloguing and writing my MArch dissertation (in parallel with studio) on The Weavers of Bombay, was one of the most fulfilling projects I undertook whilst at university. Exploring an area of history that has barely been researched and recorded, for me highlighted the mutual importance of 'discovery' in the design process.

Since graduating, I have worked at two medium-large sized practices. At my current practice (Piercy & Company), collaboration is one of the key aspects of the design process since our team works very closely with fabricators, engineers and 'makers', and this dialogue is intrinsic to the ethos of the studio. The focused approach towards form, material and texture results in meticulous detailing and particular care taken over 'interfaces', whilst not losing sight of overall form and function. Over the last 3 years I have worked on the detailed design of a £30m commercial development in central London for Derwent London, taking the project to completion on site. The client has a history of well-made, design-led buildings, pioneering innovation and characterized by robust detailing. This definitively 'hands-on' approach has had a major impact on the design process through frequent design reviews during the early stages of the project. Initial research led to us to explore the rich history of Berners Street. This brought to light a historical narrative identified with the 'arts and crafts' and a legacy of manufacturing. Inspiration gained from cabinet, furniture, and musical instrument making, became a strong theme that informed the proposed overall aesthetic and detailing, which fitted well with the practices', the client's, and my own design ethos.

I believe that critical debate enriches the design process and I aimed to maintain the critical discussions we had at university, in my professional career. Soon after graduating, I was part of a team that co-founded a fortnight-long summer school in London for 25 students from over 15 countries to engage in a series of debates, lectures and workshops. Topics ranged from ethics to artificial intelligence and from parametricism to classical architecture. This informed my role as CPD co-ordinator in the company, and the creation of a programme that could inspire innovation in design— we have had in-house talks ranging from British weavers and furniture makers to community and political engagement strategists, and from pioneers in virtual reality techniques.

I started volunteering for Architecture Sans Frontières at the first stage of a project for post-earthquake reconstruction in a town in Nepal, and am now an associate for the organization (we are at Stage 3 of the project). I have found that connecting with others holding similar values, opens up different avenues of the design process than when working under the supervision of a tutor at university or a director within the workplace. Within the culture of a voluntary organisation there is less emphasis on hierarchy, research becomes more open, and the success of a particular project is more directly based on immediate impact.

The majority of the time spent on the typical ASF project is learning 'on the job', generating knowledge and expertise, and developing skills that need to be applied instantly but which are refined through feedback and collaboration. Whilst the charity has developed design methodologies in response to processes in the field, and participatory design tools, these are constantly being adapted and refined to suit the context and the specific needs of the space, people and culture involved in the current project. Inspired by the concept of narrative, place-making and material craftsmanship, I am passionate about critically thinking through and designing an architecture that situates itself within the wider landscape of social, economic and political agendas. I believe that stylistic preconceptions should constantly be re-examined in relation to contextual dilemmas and the requirements of the inhabitants and users of buildings. Looking to the past gives a foundation to forward thinking, and merging the 'intellectual' and the 'physical' into the process of design research, both at work and as a volunteer, has been a challenging but rewarding experience—and one that I will continue to redefine.

The contrast between the ideology of the 'master builder' inherent in the integrative model

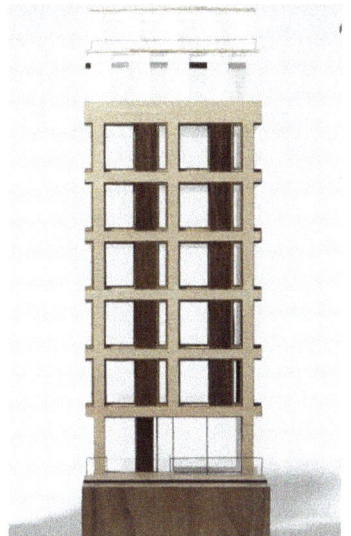

of architectural education and the architect's relative lack of influence within the building industry, has been widely discussed (and has been starkly apparent in my own experience). The erosion of the architect's traditional role has had a negative impact on design research and decision making, however the complexities which have led to niche markets have encouraged close collaboration with experts in specific areas of practice. I retain the belief nonetheless that inspiration is fundamental to architectural innovation, and that understanding precedent, though apparently self-limiting, can also lead to experimentation through a focused design research process.

MA (Hons) University of Edinburgh, MArch University of Westminter, PG Dip University of Westminster. Currently in practice (from October 2014) with Piercy & Company, and previous experience at Grimshaw Architects, Benoy and Fletcher Priest Architects. Associate at Architecture Sans Frontiere (ASF–UK) from February 2017

10/11
ANTWERP

RECOMBINANT ARCHITECTURE

Shane Bowen

Ellina Liana

Joseph Frame

Moss Lucy

David Pekovic

Robert Percy

Anthony Powis

Ognjen Ristic

Temitope Shoda

Richard Thebridge

Witts Matt

Sarah Borowiecka

Julianne Cassidy

Elizabeth Cook

Lucy Brooke

Charlotte Gallie

Gwenaël Jerret

Klementina Klocek

Georgie Robinson

Louise Scannell

Tong Scarlett

2010/2011

ANTWERP/GHENT:
LONDON TO FLANDERS

ANTWERPEN/GENT:
RECOMBINANT ARCHITECTURE

Landmarks:

GROTE MARKT/FARMERS' TOWER/
KATHEDRAAL/ONZE LIEVE
VROUWEKATHEDRAAL/GROENPLAATS
SQUARE/ROCKOXHUIS/STADHUIS/
ARCHIEF EN MUSEUM VOOR VLAAMS
CULTURLEVEN/BROUWERSHUIS/
DAGBLADMUSEUM/DIAMANTMUSEUM/
FILMMUSEUM/MODEMUSEUM/
MUSEUM SMIDT VAN GELDER/MUSEUM
VLEESHUIS/PLANTIN MORETUS MUSEUM/
STEEN MUSEUM/VOLKSKUNDEMUSEUM/
KONINKLIJK MUSEUM VOOR SCHONE
KUNSTEN ANTWERPEN/CAPPELLA
ARTE FALCO/JORDAENSHUIS ART
GALLERIES/KONINGIN FABIOLAZAAL/
KUNSTGALERIJ ISABELLA BRANT/MAYER
VAN DEN BERGH MUSEUM/MIDDELHEIM
OPENLUCHTMUSEUM/MUHKA
CONTEMPORARY ART GALLERY/MUSEUM
VAN HEDENDAAGSE KUNST ANTWERPEN/
MUSEUM VOOR FOTOGRAFIE/RAAMTEATER
OP ZUID/STEDELIJK PRENTENKABINET/
PLANTENTUIN/ RIVIERENHOF/
SCHRANSHOEVE SPROOKJESHUIS/
STADSPARK/ RUBENSHUIS/ ONZE-
LIEVE-VROUWEKATHEDRAAL/MUSEUM
AAN DE STROOM/ZOO ANTWERPEN/
PLANTIN-MORETUSMUSEUM/BEGUINAGE/
MODEMUSEUM PROVINCIE ANTWERPEN/
MUSEUM MAYER VAN DEN BERGH/MHKA/
FOTOMUSEUM ANTWERP/HET STEEN/
PARK SPOOR NOORD/PROVINCIAAL
RECREATIEDOMEIN DE SCHORRE/
MIDDELHEIM MUSEUM/CAROLUS
BORROMEUSKERK/ SINT-PAULUSKERK/
OPENLUCHTTHEATER RIVIERENHOF/
RED STAR LINE/VLEESHUIS/DE
RUIEN/STADSPARK ANTWERPEN/
VLAEYKENSGANG/ SINT-JACOBSKERK/
PALEIS OP DE MEIR/LETTERENHUIS/
ATELIERFLAT JOZEF PEETERS

Coordinates:
51°13′N 04°24′E

Region:
Vlaams Gewest

Area:
204.51 km2

Elevation:
219 m

Population:

1846	118,662	—
1866	156,441	+31.8%
1880	230,135	+47.1%
1890	310,424	+34.8%
1900	383.557	+23.5%
1910	455,422	+18.7%
1920	473,862	+4.0%
1930	525,041	+10.8%
1947	526,396	+0.02%
1961	547,350	+4.0%
1970	549.146	+0.03%
1981	501,261	−9.55%
1990	470,349	−6.57%
2000	446,525	−5.33%
2010	483,505	+8.28%

Demonym(s):
Antwerp(se)/(enaar)

Patron Saint:
Saint Walpurga

Recombinant Architecture
Questions of scale – the architecture of the miniature – indeterminate – architecture – mega-structure as architecture – logistical scale – proximity and place – working at a distance – ferrying – working 'on site' – port house – waiting room – maison du people – creative industries

Museum collective
Fashioning the museum – 'collections' and itinerary – Flemish School: the production of art and culture – education and industry – transporting culture: Thames to Scheldt – temporary contemporary

Social collective
Recombinant hybrid – waiting-room – surgery – co-op – communal space and public performance – architecture and the everyday – from indifference to utility and pleasure – the department 'store'.

This year we will be running two parallel programmes in the studio. The first is focused on the concept of the 'expanded museum' (or Museum Collective), and the second on the idea of social architecture (the Social Collective) viewed as an updated interpretation of the Maison du Peuple—architectural paradigm of the Flemish (socialist) co-operative movement during the late C19th and early C20th, but reinterpreted for the C21st. Our formal approach is to propose a recombinant architecture, to be investigated as a series of elements (or typologies) at different scales and proximities (from 'at a distance' to 'on-site'), which are subjected to hybridization at intervals in the development of the project.

Preliminary Projects
During the first term, we are setting out a framework for three design projects, following parallel themes (aesthetic and social) which alternate between individual and group work. The projects are not conceived as studies but resolved individual designs, which are subject to combination (and recombination) and constitute a vocabulary of elements with which to work subsequently.
Semester One
Recombination: these projects may be conceived in the abstract; may be sited in London, or instead at one remove in Flanders. As transactions between London and Flanders, and between the aesthetic and social, they are envisaged eventually to be presented in recombinant form within the terms of an architectural 'catalogue' (Diploma 2), or as a definitive hybrid model (Diploma 1).
Semester Two
Flemish Transpositions: the catalogue provides a framework for the development of an ongoing 'theses' (Diploma 2) to be taken 'on site' in visiting Antwerp and Ghent at the end of January. Diploma 1 in contrast will pursue a new project focused on production, process and the theme of 'bridging', for the remainder of the year.

04 YEAR ONE: FLANDERS HOUSE

05 YEAR ONE: BRIDGING GHENT

01 THE FLANDERS PANEL/
THE WAITING ROOM
001   flanders panel – icon/in-transit/installation
        waiting room – non-place/in-transit/interior
002   recombination

02 NARRATIVE SEQUENCE/
CO-OPERATIVE SPACE
001   narrative sequence
002   recombination

03 SCHOOL OF PAINTING/
PERFORMATIVE SPACE
001   gallery or acaemy – framework and identity
        public interface
        performative space
        interface
002   recombination

04 YEAR TWO: CATALOGUE

05 YEAR TWO: DESIGN THESIS

02 NARRATIVE SEQUENCE/ CO-OPERATIVE SPACE

001 narrative sequence
002 recombination

MULTIPLE SPACES

Select a museum, gallery or art collection, in Antwerp or Ghent (try not to repeat work on the same institutions as your colleagues - though some repetition is inevitable – and broaden your search within Flanders if necessary). Research and present whatever you can find out about the organization of spaces within the particular museum (its sequence and the itinerary of the visitor).

ITINERARY

While experience of a museum, gallery is constituted by a 'sequence', or 'matrix' of spaces, what may be deduced about the logic of 'passage' through or between them (via thresholds or lobbies)? What pattern of circulation or movement informs the visitor's choice of route to individual rooms or display spaces? Is this planned and 'directed', or down to a deliberate, or an arbitrary, individual choice? And how does this narrative correlate with, or affect (positively or negatively), the experience of viewing the artifacts on display?

What constitutes spatial narrative in a museum? An enfilade sequence from room to room, 'lines' of movement between rooms, or offset arrangements of rooms, alcoves or cabinets, accessed separately from continuous linear spaces. Consider the conventions of the 'room', 'gallery' and 'corridor' (or long gallery) and their inter-relationship. Is this narrative primarily about physical space or does it correlate with a chronological or periodic arrangement of artifacts (described in the format of a guided tour)?

DESIGN

Arrange a series or combination of rooms into a narrative sequence of gallery spaces (which recognizes museum typologies). These should be incorporated on two (or more) floors and should include double height spaces. Constitute a single 'threshold of arrival' and consider the lighting of both floors.

Define your own limits as to the extent of this aggregation or sequence of rooms (number, area and dimensions). It should constitute an identifiable architectural complex, element or building, which provides a hierarchy of at least three different scale spaces in which to display paintings or artifacts (the repetition of similarly conceived spaces doesn't rule out variation). Your previous Flanders Panel should be incorporated as a 'multiple' within this narrative sequence. You may treat the design as a ('un-sited') prototype, or locate your design on a site of your choice in London or Flanders.

FINAL PRESENTATION

Firstly, describe your composite gallery in 2D plans and sections, which discriminate between the volume and built form of the main spaces. Secondly, illustrate a related 'narrative', conventionally a sequential 'storyboard' employing sketches, diagrams, cartoons, montages, words or animations. While the precision of the representation of space and form, and threshold 'conditions' (openings, doors, windows, roof-lights), is paramount in the 2D drawings, the narrative 'sequence' may be more rhetorical, experiential or fictional, than strictly 'accurate'.

02 NARRATIVE SEQUENCE/ CO-OPERATIVE SPACE

■ 001   narrative sequence
   002   recombination

MULTIPLE SPACES:
What can be held to represent a 'co-operative space? Is the sense of communal experience induced by spatial arrangement or by the particular uses or activities occupying, intended for, or programmed into, individual spaces? Is it necessary to define the nature of the Co-op as an institution before designing a 'co-operative space'? You are asked to research and represent the range of spaces and different activities provided within a particular 'Maison du Peuple'. Visualise and explain the variety of uses and their interrelationship.

INSTITUTION
Your project should be envisaged in the context of a particular institution of your choice, whether historical (and updated) or contemporary. Consider building types that represent or serve a social collective (whether co-operative, collaborative or communal):

Association/Institute/Society/Club/Company/Guild/Lodge/House/Co-operative/Community Centre/Political Party

DESIGN
In the first instance consider the public identity and external 'face' of the type of institution you have chosen. Is it overt or covert about its presence in the public realm, being displayed for all to see or camouflaged in some way ('there' but 'not there'). Secondly choose an activity, or associated uses, within the institution, which epitomize the concept of 'co-operative space'.

Epicerie/Boucherie/Salle de Café/Jeu/Buffet/Magasins/Ateliers/Salle de Reunion/Bureaux/Salle de Spectacle   Tabacie /Reserve Bar/ Grand Terrasse   (Maison du Peuple, Brussels 1896)

Your design of the spaces supporting this activity (linked to the entrance) should elaborate and programme a spatial hierarchy (or set of distinct spaces) and discriminate between, 'public', 'social' and more 'private' spaces of different scales.

PRESENTATION

How is the identity of the institution to be represented in the character of its public entrance, façade, or logo? Design one of these.

Draw up 2D plans and sections, which discriminate between the volume and form of the inter-related spaces.

Describe the set of spaces occupied and 'in use'. Avoid computer generated abstract 'figures'.

02 NARRATIVE SEQUENCE/ CO-OPERATIVE SPACE

001 narrative sequence
002 recombination

Having made individual projects for a narrative sequence and co-operative space, the second stage of the project is, as previously, to collaborate as a group transforming this work into recombinant form. In contrast to the previous project, the procedure is to be viewed as a formal exercise where spaces and forms derived from the individual work are combined and re-combined (at least once) - and you are asked to demonstrate this process. Whether this is arbitrary or informed by a rational 'logic', the final 'product' should be constructed and represented with a high degree of architectural conviction.

PRESENTATION:
working in pairs as before but reversing responsibilities:

01 Construct a physical model of your recombination to a scale which conveys its sculptural quality as an object, but which also reveals interior space by cutting or sectioning the model.

02 Secondly, produce two representative drawings that place the external form of the recombination in context 'on urban location' in Flanders, and which explain how the two original programmes may be retained in some way, within the new formal configuration.

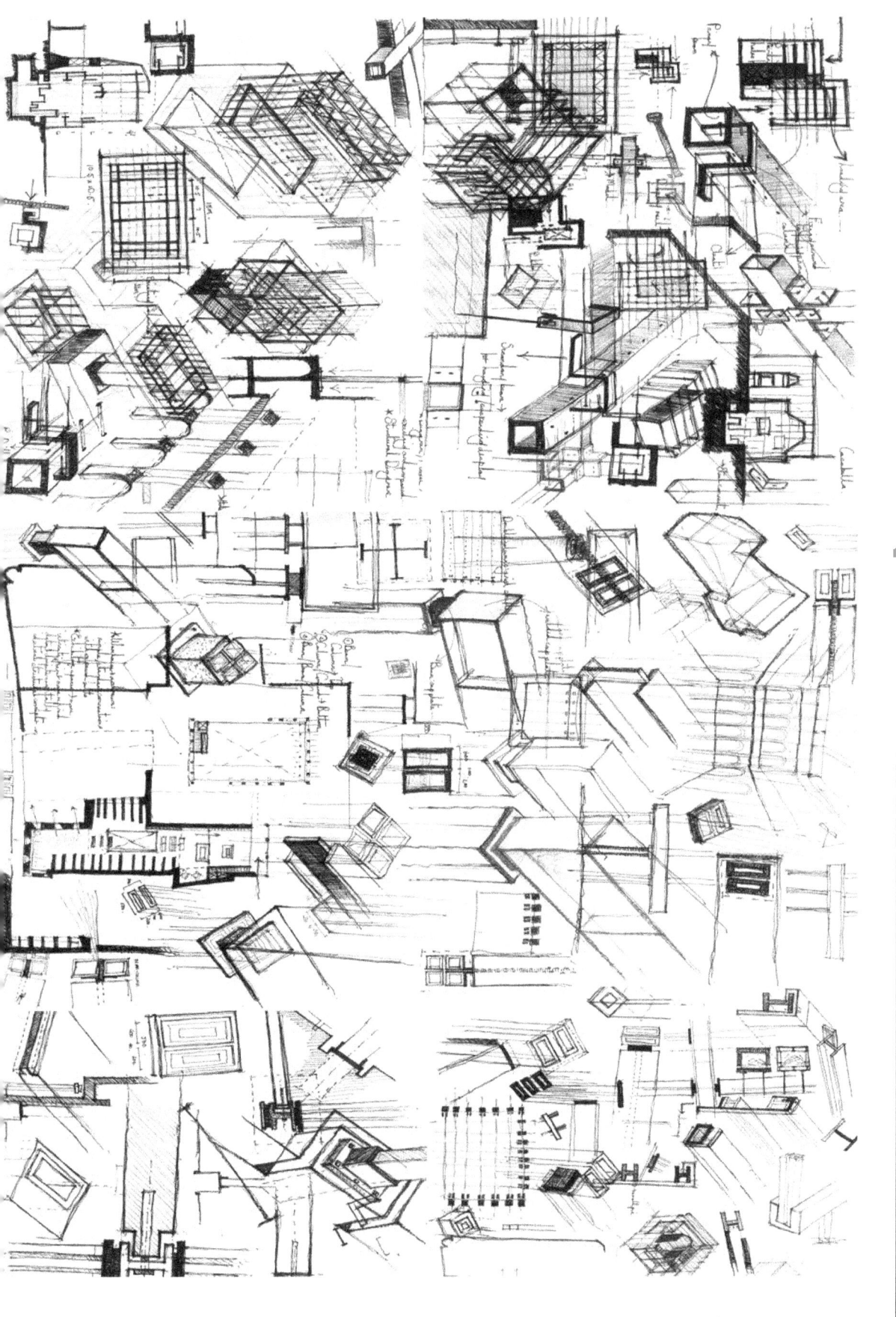

02_AP_S_008_002_031_P70_EP

02_AP_S_002_010_039_P70_C

02_AP_S_002_011_040_P71_C

02_AP_S_004_003_032_P70_IP

70

02_AP_S_003_004_033_P71_HP

02_AP_S_009_005_034_P71_M

02_AP_S_005_006_035_P71_IP

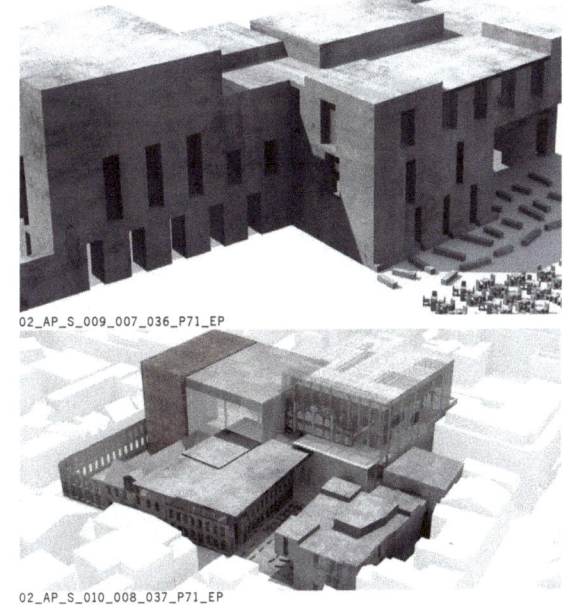

02_AP_S_009_007_036_P71_EP

02_AP_S_010_008_037_P71_EP

02_AP_S_011_009_038_P71_EP

02_AP_S_006_012_041_P72_IP

02_AP_S_007_013_042_P72_IP

02_AP_S_010_014_043_P72_M

02_AP_S_004_015_044_P72_HP

02_AP_S_004_021_050_P72_C

02_AP_S_003_022_051_P73_P

02_AP_S_008_016_045_P72_IP

02_AP_S_005_017_046_P72_HP

02_AP_S_012_018_047_P72_EP

02_AP_S_009_019_048_P73_IP

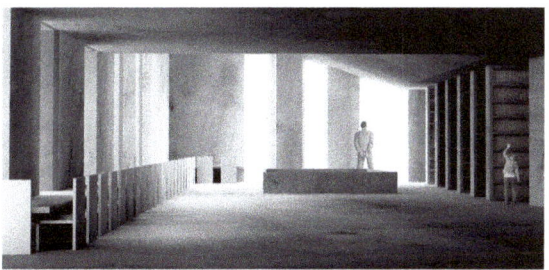

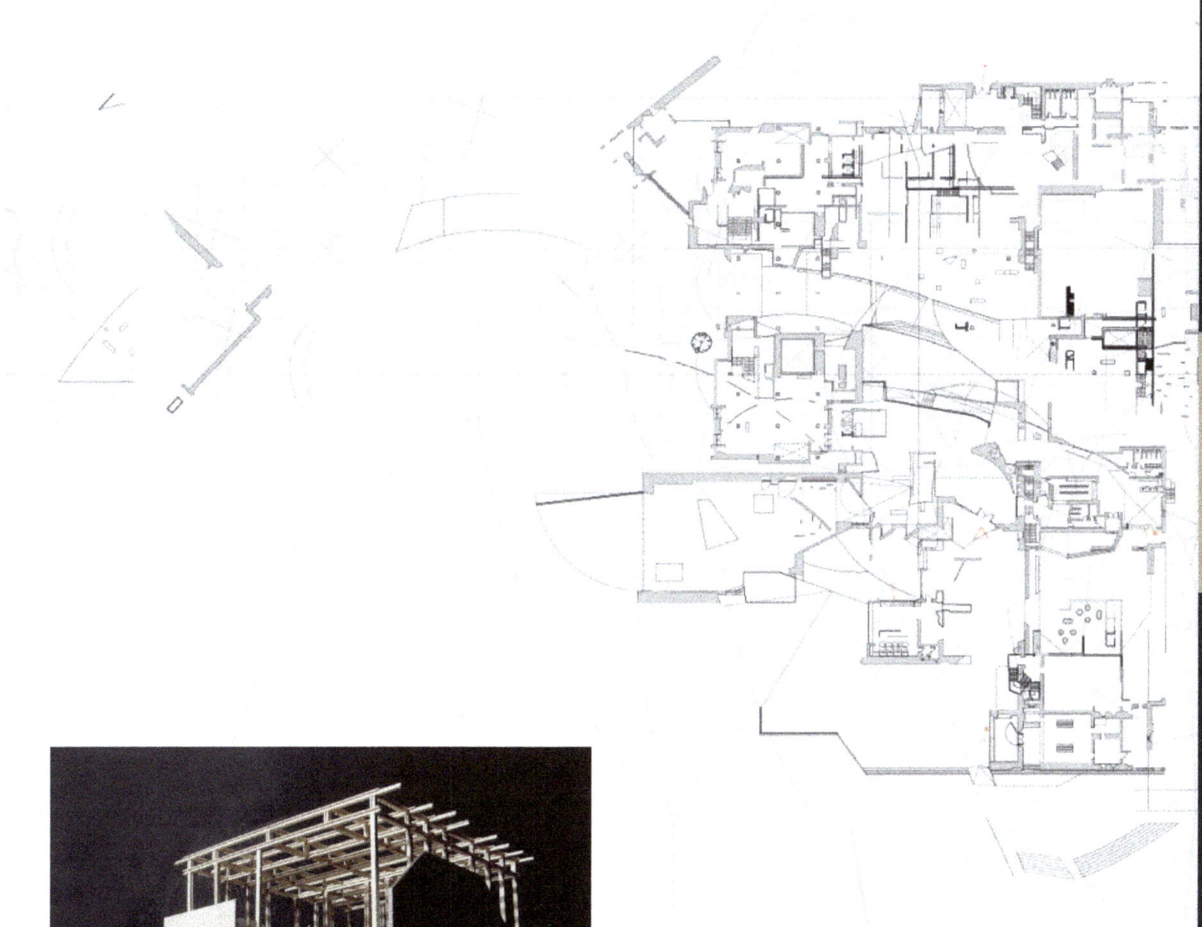

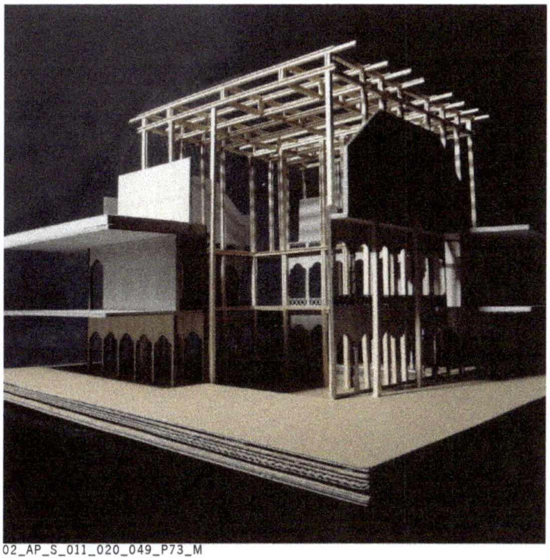

02_AP_S_011_020_049_P73_M

LOUISE SCANNELL

THOUGHTS ON PRACTICALITY AND COLLABORATION

The studio programme for my thesis year was set in Antwerp, Belgium. Initial week-long projects looked at the nature of performance spaces and explored how theatricality can be achieved through architecture. My subsequent research into Belgian theatre revealed the geographical and linguistic cleavages that exist across the country and which condition its cultural identity. This cultural division was further exasperated by a lack of common media, there were for instance no bilingual universities in the country (except the Royal Military Academy) and the lack of any major cultural (or scientific) organization in which both the main communities were represented. However, the forces that once held the Belgians apart—religion, and economic and political opposition or identification with the Dutch and French—had moderated. These cultural divisions were also apparent in theatre: with ethnically separate theatre groups and a lack of collaboration between companies from different regions; but these were complemented by theatre groups founded by immigrant communities—the Irish Theatre Company, the American Theatre Company (both based in Brussels) and the British and American Theatrical Society in Antwerp.

Theaterwerkplaats aimed to act as a platform for cultural exchange between different communities in Antwerp by opening-up the experience of theatre to the large immigrant community in the north of the city. The project considered the nature of different types of performance spaces, and investigated how they could be utilized to draw people into the development. Its design was intended to exploit an inherent drama inthe building and its interiors, given their integral relationship with the surrounding landscape—creating unexpected and exciting experiences for visitors and passersby. The theatre workshop was located at the west end of the then newly developed Park Noor Spoord in the north of Antwerp. Overlooking the docks—which were subject to major regeneration—the site was also adjacent to the district inhabited by the largest immigrant community. Here, the landscape rises from the park to the east providing access to the upper civic upper level of the building. Approaching the site from the west offered visitors entry into the 'experimental' undercroft space. Various circulation routes connected the two levels and form part of the theatricality of the building. The undercroft was intended to be a large, penetrable open space with an extended fly-system that could be used to create different spaces (and house workshops) to support various performance types. This open space aimed to give freedom to performers and artists by creating an informal setting intended to be

inviting to people unfamiliar with the theatre.Suspended in the deep structure above the undercroft two fixed theatres were located. These stood out as more visible to the public, set out on the upper level and clad in copper, showcasing longer running performances which were expected to attract larger audiences whose income was intended to subsidize the 'workshop' space. The project required particular technical consideration of acoustics, sightlines and the complexities of the back of house spaces.

In the six years in practice since completing my studies, I have worked in two large London-based offices where I have experienced a wide range of projects, including urban design, commercial and residential projects, all located here in the city. Over the past four years I have focused on residential-led projects, which have ranged from high-end private developments in central London; such as Eagle House near Old Street roundabout; to 100% social housing developments like the four schemes on which I amcurrently working as part of the London Borough of Southwark's 'New Council Homes' initiative. Some of the residential projects have included community assets, where for example the redevelopment of Dulwich Hamlet Football Club provided both a new pitch and facilities for the club and the local community, alongside residential redevelopment. As is to be expected in London, a number of schemes I have worked on have had complex relationships with heritage structures or transport infrastructure, Royal Mint Street for example as a housing scheme which straddled DLR tracks and cantilevered over Network Rail lines. These projects have offered experience across different work stages, although given the nature of the construction industry inLondon I have spent more time on earlier rather than later on-site project development. This has involved many projects at concept or strategic design stages, for example Church Street 'capacity studies' which looked carefully at the phasing of the proposed development, with due consideration of how existing residents could bere-accommodated and community uses could continue to function throughout construction. In addition, I have taken a number of schemes through the 'planning'process, in particular the Dulwich Hamlet Football Club development and the 'New Council Homes'initiative in Southwark. In contrast my responsibilities have included involvement in the detailed design and construction of individual projects like Eagle House (completed in 2013).

Working as an architect, requires an extremely wide range of skills which are reflected in the nature of the different stages of architectural education. Many of these are developed in the studio, however others can only be grasped through the experience of working in practice, and some abilities simply come more naturally to different people. Personally, the skills I developed from a studio education that are most directly reflected in my day to day work, are the process of design development, communicating proposals, and a strong work ethic. A crucial skill, less exercised in studio education, is that of teamwork. While I do think that the competitiveness of studio culture can be a positive force, driving students to achieve the best quality individual projects, it is also isolating. Contrary to this, professional life is to be part of a team—be it within the practice, or the wider remit of the overall project team. I feel that teamwork, especially with disciplines beyond architecture, would be beneficial to studio education. My own experience since completing my studies has been in large London-based practices, generally working on large projects, some high profile but mostly residential. I have no doubt my experience would be very different in a smaller practice.

The process of developing a design, from the brief through to a fairly detailed level, was for me the main skill developed throughout my Part II studio experience, and it now forms the major part of my everyday work in the office. The DS11 studio briefs established a strong base for design development–establishing themes rather than building programmes or typologies at the start of the year. These early themes covered varied aspects such as culture, and the history and politics of the city that had been selected for the year's project location. As we delved into this research we became aware of the city's characteristics; what had influenced city form and culture, and what factors were shaping its future. With this comprehensive knowledge, we developed projects that responded to the city, design decisions being rooted in this reasoning—whether towards an urban planning consideration or a detailed design element. This approach to design has been carried through into my work in practice. A thorough understanding of the site, the client, the local stakeholders, the political issues surrounding a project are vital to ensure that the scheme responds successfully to its particular set of challenges throughout the design process and the building's lifetime. Awareness of wider issues around the project are particularly important since the construction industry is extremely reactive to political and economic factors, and architects need to be responsive to these issues. Regular tutorials and 'crits' at university ensured that academic projects developed at a fair pace. Tutorials and 'crits'

fostered the practice of listening to and processing comments and criticism, while being sufficiently adaptable to either overcome a problem creatively or to make changes to the project. Critical thinking is a vital skill and one continually applied in practice. I have worked on professional projects when, many months into the design process, an unexpected issue has arisen (anything from unknown ground conditions to unanticipated feedback from a local planning authority) which requires considerable modifications to be made to a scheme. This requires careful judgement to assess whether the issue can be resolved through adaption, or if a more significant reconsideration of the overall design is required (evaluating what the knock-on effects might be). Of course, changes to an academic project only have a limited impact, whereas in the 'real' world cost constraints; assurances that might have been made to communities, and agreements made with local planning authorities, need to be taken into account.

Communication skills are clearly transferrable from studio culture to working in practice. Verbal presentation is only part of this, since architects are generally explaining physical proposals. 'Crit' presentations required convincing graphic and curation skills where each image contributed to the verbal narrative. Tutorials prompted different skills, in particular the ability to focus directly on the issue of the moment in order gain instructive rather than incidental advice; while with portfolio submissions the graphics and layout in themselves had to 'tell the story'. Almost every day in the office I am required to present designs to someone— whether a colleague, a consultant, a community group or planning authorities. Something that has

become more apparent in practice is that a variety of audiences require different kind of presentations and methodologies. Presenting a project to a group of local residents will require different drawing types and vocabulary, compared to presenting the same scheme to a group of architects at a 'design review panel'. This variation was not really an issue at university—presentations were only to fellow students and tutors or visiting practitioners. University projects would benefit from more interaction with the 'real world'. Responding to more realistic issues could develop the skill of communicating the nature of designs to a wider range of people; difficult to achieve however since university projects are generally speculative without the role of a real client.

The university architecture studio is a competitive environment which can be isolating, very stressful, and in some cases unconstructive. Personally, it raised my commitment to the project in hand and gave me the drive to develop the best quality project I could. I was fortunate to be surrounded by a great group of people in my studio, and having friends with whom to share the stressful process, certainly helped. In practice, the stakes are much higher. Your design decisions will likely be built and stand for many years to come, and will consequently directly affect people's lives. I feel a great responsibility to ensure that the projects I work on are a success, and work hard to achieve that. At my current practice, there is far more support than at university; working with a tight knit team who have different levels of experience and who each bring their own qualities to ongoing projects. Staff at all levels are encouraged to contribute to design workshops, fostering an inclusive environment where we can all learn from each other.

While I have focused on the positive links between studio and practice, there are many aspects of working in practice that the studio does not prepare you for: collaboration with other disciplines; business development; practice management, and the many challenges of live projects, such as budgetary constraints, buildability, difficult clients, and technical issues. However, with a few exceptions I don't think the studio is the best place for all these aspects to be addressed. Some are covered by the Part III course, others can really only be learnt 'on the job'. However more focus on teamwork, including working with other disciplines, would be beneficial in the studio. Endless industry reports reiterate that teamwork is the key to realising successful projects, and indeed it is such a major part of working in a practice. The studio programme did include short group projects, but these were often challenging—perhaps due to the lack of defined roles, timetabled as they were at the beginning of the year when there was not yet a clear intent for the work. In an office, generally individual roles are clear and respected, and except in unfortunate situations there is a mutual desire todo what's best for the project. Incorporating a degree of teamwork and coordination with other disciplines within work in the studio would not only benefit design and coordination skills, but integrate them with the skill of creative problem solving. Writing this short piece has required me to look back on my experience in studio. As the number of years since completing my studies increases, memories of the more stressful times of my studio experience have faded. What I remember most strongly was the wonderful opportunity to really immerse my self in my thesis project, enjoying concentrated research 'on site', and into

building typologies and related programmes. The luxury of time and focus that we had in studio (although it never felt like it at the time) does not exist in practice—decisions have to be made in quick order to meet ambitious time-frames, and 'designing' a project is only a part of day-to-day work, alongside 'coordination' with consultants, 'managing' a team and wider practice roles.

Louise Scannell: BArch University of Nottingham, DipArch University of Westminster. Currently in practice (from Sept 2016) with WestonWilliamson+Partners, and previously with Farrells LLP (2011–2016), Newtecnic and HeoStudio

15/16
GENOA

G

MODES OF EXCHANGE

2015/16

GENOA:
NORTH WEST ITALY

GENOVA:
MODES OF EXCHANGE

Landmarks:

PALAZZI DEI ROLLI/PALAZZO ROSSO/
PALAZZO BIANCO/PALAZZO REALE/
PALAZZO ANGELO GIOVANNI SPINOLA/
PALAZZO PIETRO SPINOLA DI SAN LUCA/
PALAZZO SPINOLA DI PELLICCERIA/VIA
GARIBALDI/BELVEDERE CASTELLETTO/
DUOMO DI GENOVA/PIAZZA DE FERRARI/
TEATRO CARLO FELICE/PASSEGGIATA
ANITA GARIBALDI/ACQUARIO DI
GENOVA/ABBAZIA DI SAN FRUTTOSO/
PALAZZO DUCALE/BASILICA DI SANTA
MARIA ASSUNTA/CATTEDRALE DI SAN
LORENZO/COMMENDA DI SAN GIOVANNI
DI PRÉ/SANT'AGOSTINO/SANTA
MARIA DI CASTELLO/SAN MATTEO/
SAN DONATO/SANTO STEFANO/SANTI
VITTORE E CARLO/BASILICA DELLA
SANTISSIMA ANNUNZIATA DEL VASTATO/
SAN PIETRO IN BANCHI/SANTA MARIA
DELLE VIGNE/NOSTRA SIGNORA DELLA
CONSOLAZIONE/SAN SIRO/SANTA MARIA
MADDALENA, SANTA MARIA ASSUNTA DI
CARIGNANO AND CHIESA DEL GESÙ/SAN
BARTOLOMEO DEGLI ARMENI/NOSTRA
SIGNORA DELLA GUARDIA/PALAZZO SAN
GIORGIO/LANTERNA/ PALAZZO BIANCO/
PALAZZO TURSI/PALAZZO GEROLAMO
GRIMALDI/PALAZZO PODESTÀ/PALAZZO
REALE/PALAZZO ANGELO GIOVANNI
SPINOLA/PALAZZO PIETRO SPINOLA
DI SAN LUCA/PALAZZO SPINOLA
DI PELLICCERIA/PALAZZO CICALA/
VILLA BRIGNOLE SALE DUCHESSA DI
GALLIERA/VILLA DURAZZO-PALLAVICINI/
VILLA DORIA CENTURIONE/VILLA
DURAZZO BOMBRINI/VILLA SERRA/VILLA
GIUSTINIANI-CAMBIASO/VILLA ROSSI
MARTINI/VILLA IMPERIALE SCASSI/
VILLA GRIMALDI/VILLA NEGRONE
MORO/VILLA ROSAZZA/VILLETTA DI
NEGRO/VILLA DELLE PESCHIERE/VILLA
IMPERIALE/VILLA SALUZZO BOMBRINI/
VILLA GRIMALDI FASSIO/CIMITERO
MONUMENTALE DI STAGLIENO/ALBERGO
DEI POVERI/ACQUEDOTTO STORICO
DI GENOVA/CASTELLO D'ALBERTIS/
CASTELLO BRUZZO/VILLA CANALI
GASLINI/MACKENZIE CASTLE/PALAZZO
DELLA BORSA/VIA XX SETTEMBRE/
STAZIONE MARITTIMA/ALBERGO

Coordinates:

44°24′25.87″N

Region:

Liguria

Area:

240,29 km²

Elevation:

19 m

Population:

1901	377,610	—
1911	465,496	+23.3%
1921	541,562	+16.3%
1931	590,736	+9.1%
1936	634,646	+7.4%
1951	688,447	+8.5%
1961	784,194	+13.9%
1971	816,872	+4.2%
1981	762,895	−6.6%
1991	678,771	−11.0%
2001	610,307	−10.1%
2011	608,493	−0.3%
2015	588,668	−3.3%

Demonym(s):

Genovesi/Zeneixi

Patron Saint:

St. Giovanni Battista

MIRAMARE/TORRE PIACENTINI/
ARCO DELLA VITTORIA/BISCIONE/
PORTO ANTICO/ MURA NUOVE/MURA
VECCHIE/GIARDINO BOTANICO CLELIA
DURAZZO GRIMALDI/ PARCO NATURALE
REGIONALE DELL'ANTOLA/PARCO
NATURALE REGIONALE DEL BEIGUA/
VILLA DURAZZO PALLAVICINI/

Genoa's historical legacy is as a city-state, a maritime power reliant on the trade, transportation and the currency of exchange that characterised the onset of a capitalist economy. Hemmed in from its Ligurian hinterland by adjacent mountains, urban districts are subject to the folds of the local terrain, the port now separated from the city at large by a raised autostrada. Local politics have encompassed ideological extremes of financial and social 'exchange'. There is the regulation of navigation, trade and immigration, and on the other hand the public communal discourse associated with a 'social' currency of exchange. A 'market' or an 'exchange'; whether a building, a concept, an activity or a place; incorporates both aspects.

The regulation of maritime trade has taken on a distinct ethical and political dimension in the context of mass immigration across the Mediterranean. A new Maritime Court and Assembly are proposed for Genoa, its civil and political jurisdiction being the coastal waters and marine borders of the EU.

In parallel the urban concept of an Exchange (of assets, commodities, information, goods) will be the focus a variety of 'thesis' projects addressing social space within the ambit of 'a general economy of architecture' (of infrastructure or restoration). Legislative codes of practice condition architecture, just as does the rhetorical interplay of space and form, or environmental 'exchange' and the recycling of ambient energies and materials.

When the Red Brigades arose in Genoa and elsewhere in the late 1970's and early 80's, they continued...(a)...Genoese tradition of pointing the way to change [...] Genoa led the rise of capitalism, slavery, and colonization in the Middle Ages, international public finance in the sixteenth century, poor relief in the seventeenth century, republicanism in the nineteenth century. (2)
(Steven A Epstein, Genoa and the Genoese)

GENOA CITY SURVEY

Trajectories across the city – five intervals sectioning the city – experiencing – sampling – walking – duration – 10 photographs: order and hierarchy – city as exchange survey themes: focussing on the interior – urban fabric – building locations – identities – community and everyday life – transport adjacencies – environment.

04 YEAR ONE: MARITIME COURT AND ASSEMBLAGE

01 ANCHORAGE
001 itinerant vessel
002 chamberwork

02 THE CURRENCY OF EXCHANGE
001 transactions
002 district and exchange type

03 YEAR 2: CATALOGUE
001 itinerant vessel
002 chamberwork

04 Two Themes
001 tectonic exchange
002 energy exchange

04 YEAR TWO: URBAN EXCHANGE

■01 ANCHORAGE

001   itinerant vessel
002   chamberwork

> All the ships in Jules Verne are perfect cubby-holes, and the vastness of their circumnavigation further increases the bliss of their closure [...] the Nautilus, in this regard, is the most desirable of all caves: the enjoyment of being enclosed reaches its paroxysm when, from the bosom of this unbroken inwardness, it is possible to watch [...] the outside vagueness of the waters, and thus define [...] the inside by means of its opposite. (3)
> (Roland Barthes, Mythologies)

When does an itinerant 'vessel' cease to be itinerant? What class of object is it? An artefact or a utensil, a maritime object, or an architectural object-type? According to the dictionary: a hollow receptacle, ship or boat, wooden duct or person. Obtain a 'vessel' and a 'chamber'. Pay particular attention to their configuration, scale and shape, and their form and surfaces. Model their enclosure and thickness.

Place one within the other (as container and contained) in three variants typically: 'below' or 'on the surface' or 'above'. Each chamber should be (partially) visible from the exterior. How is the chamber to be stabilised, foreclosed or anchored? Light: inside/outside, objective/subjective, shadow. to be stabilised, foreclosed or anchored? Light: inside/outside, objective/subjective, shadow.

INITIAL PRESENTATION:
OBJECT AND INTERIOR.

01 physical models
02 visualise in light
03 photograph their combination

01 ANCHORAGE
■ 001   itinerant vessel
   002   chamberwork

> When I went to examine the chamber, the light, the ambience where I would hang my painting [...] I first looked at the façade of the building, which I barely remembered, and once inside I felt as if I were moving around an inner façade which extended into walls, furniture, the faces of employees, carpets, black telephones, clear varnish, an even temperature, the clean smell of polished wood, a surface as opaque as a tiled façade rising three floors in a square which looks almost provincial. (4)
> (Jose Saramago, The Manual of Painting and Calligraphy)

Select the representative façade of an urban building in Genoa. Examine its characteristic order and aesthetic quality. Translate, rescale, abstract or return these qualities onto the constitution a fictional interior within: typically, the enclosure of a court, atrium, hall, galleria or other collective or public space. Taking the spatial form of the group's chambers as redolent of available sources, configure an ideal aggregation of rooms or spaces in relation to this interior space. Retain, transform, distort, flex or multiply. 'Plan' and 'section' a typical piece of this complex in articulating the transitions or thresholds between spaces. Consider a hierarchy of en filade relationships and the separation of poché space, or their modernist inversion characterised in asymmetry, layering and proximity. A social narrative (whether domestic, collective or public) should inform the nature of these spatial 'exchanges' between public social and private. Visualize the relationship between the inner spaces of different scales.

> The Palazzo Bianco was built in the 16th century and underwent numerous alteration beginning in the 18th century. From the late 19th century until its virtual destruction in 1942 by the Allied bombings of Genoa, the palazzo had variously housed a restaurant [...] painting, decorative arts, and a military museum. After the bombing [...] only the outer walls remained of the original structure. Reconstruction of the palazzo began in 1945 and was completed by 1949. (5)
> (Stephen Leet, Franco Albini: Architecture and Design 1934-1977)

FINAL PRESENTATION:
THE SPACE OF THE INTERIOR

01 strategic explanation
02 spatial narrative (plan and section)
03 social narrative (occupying the transition)
04 view from, or between the confines of, the interior

03_GA_S_012_001_059_P92_IP

03_GA_S_013_002_060_P92_IP

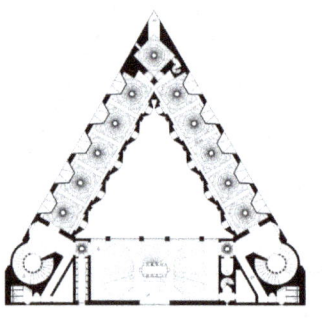

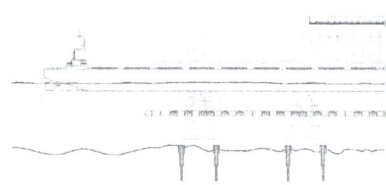

03_GA_S_014_003_061_P92_IP

03_GA_S_012_004_062_P92_M

03_GA_S_015_005_063_P92_IP

03_GA_S_017_006_064_P93_EP

03_GA_S_018_007_065_P93_EP

03_GA_S_019_008_066_P93_EP

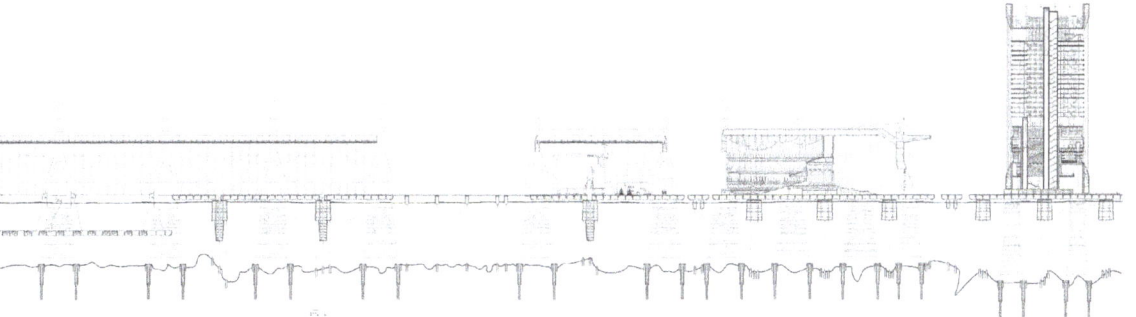

03_GA_S_016_009_067_P93_IP

03_GA_S_001_010_068_P93_DI

03_GA_S_003_011_069_P93_SP

03_GA_S_017_014_072_P94_IP

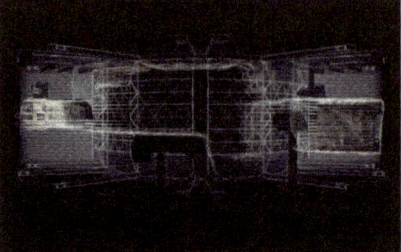
03_GA_S_002_015_073_P94_DI

03_GA_S_018_016_074_P94_IP

03_GA_S_001_017_075_P94_E

03_GA_S_002_026_084_P95_E

03_GA_S_003_027_085_P95_S

03_GA_S_003_018_076_P94_DI

03_GA_S_020_019_077_P94_EP

03_GA_S_005_020_078_P94_C

03_GA_S_019_021_079_P95_IP

03_GA_S_021_022_080_P95_EP

03_GA_S_020_023_081_P95_IP

03_GA_S_006_024_082_P95_C

03_GA_S_004_025_083_P95_DI

TOBIAS PLUNKET

STUDIO CULTURE

Only a year out of the education system and soon to return for my Part III; fortunate to find a job after a short summer break; the 'studio' and its attitudes are still very fresh in mind. With regard to studio culture; it is not my intent for these notes to be a definitive critique, but rather to encourage discussion, if also taking an opportunity for the occasional gibe at problems within the remit of architectural education.

Studio culture has become increasingly focused on the 'crit' which is something not to be ignored. It becomes the sleepless 'all-nighter', and represents a fundamental issue within studio culture, rarely perceived as what it claims to be: a mutually beneficial appraisal of work. That is the culmination of a long and emotional journey, which becomes the cause of much unnecessary angst and distress. Students often misinterpret what a good critique is. A student interviewed in the (2013) documentary 'Archiculture' describes it well:

[...] by definition it's a critique. It's a criticism. So, if you go into...[this]...critique, and all the critics...can do is blow hot air up your ass and tell you how great the projects look, to me that's not a good critique [...]

'Crits' are the most public display of design work and, naturally, the reception of one's project in a critical manner is going to cause distress—rightly or wrongly. But it is often the perceived project which causes the most anguish. To describe what I mean by 'perceived project', experienced when the last time you went to an open 'crit', an end of year show, or thumbed through a studio's catalogue and took the time to understand the ins and outs of the architecture, rather than just as if an unlearned observer gawking at illustrations. Maybe the greatest problem lies with the 'crit's' raison d'etre—that central and most cherished key drawing.
It is easy to be distracted by the hypnotic display of graphic prowess displayed at many end of year shows. But if you could turn off the Photoshop layers, hide the incidental lines and look past this veil (or those stereotypical trees and bird silhouettes), what you are left with is often not much of, well, anything. I am of as guilty of this as anyone else since my final year thesis (with DS11) comprised of an architectural archive located in an abandoned factory (imaged in 120,582 lines hosting 12,484,673 pixels).

Located in the post-industrial Italian city of Genoa: once a prosperous port and now a city caught in the critical doldrums between unexpressed potential and economic disaster—a superstructure split in two at its most delicate point, between the historic city and the waterfront—a city in need of re-appropriation.

My first step towards resolving this was to recognise infrastructure as a secondary cause, in the fragmentation of space. Employing Situationist theories, I undertook a series of psychogeographical journeys to

access these fragmented non-spaces which presented the opportunity to subvert, or détourne, the vernacular architecture of Genoa to better re-appropriate these spaces. Using the Situationist manifestoes as a starting point, the proposal became more technologically minded. The 'trompe l'oeil' façade popular in northern Italian architecture was documented through three-dimensional scanning. Using photogrammetry on an urban scale allowed for the direct subversion of these mappings through everyday anomalies; the slightest errors implicit in the scanning, caused distortion, mistruths and beautiful alterations akin to the contingencies of everyday life.

The resulting 'architecture' appeared much like a three-dimensional version of a pointillist painting produced by a documentation process which forms millions of points, orientated and arranged in space to form a series of impressionist façades. Its physical manifestation was an array of LED voxells arranged in a 3D matrix held within the main space of the Silos Granari Hennebique, which was intended to act in much the same way as the painted façades to create the illusion of a physical building. Essentially this created an experiential device which manipulated the 'found' precedent of painted Genoese facade, turning a tired typology into a heuristic device. The rhetorical scale of the proposal was intended to bind its individual elements together as a singular city-scale gesture.

Throughout my architectural education, I always wondered whether in masking the conceptual thinness of our projects with visual complexity, we actually deceived our tutors? Were our mistakes or lack of development well hidden by lens flare? Probably not, but it offered a certain satisfaction when the end of year show came around.

These images have become synonymous with university projects, and are often the first loss in practice. A self-indulgent design process, perhaps, implausible beyond the temporal idyll of an un-built 'studio project', contrasts with the reality of a 'building' schedule. Perhaps this is why the 'studio' is the way it is? The only time, in many of our careers, when the fantasy of the architect as artist is available to us (who become 'planners' in later life).

Personally, I found this visuality largely beneficial to my personal development. Fantastical projects provided the perfect opportunity to research, experiment and learn computer software I would never likely have discovered otherwise. DS11's foundations in the research catalogue and individual thesis proposal provided the opportunity to follow, within reason, whichever interest the student desired. As a result, a studio style was never really affected and it was left to the student to decide how he or she wished to characterize the project. As a whole, this led to much more engaging projects. Throughout my undergraduate study the design tutor was usually thought of as a surrogate client. However, during your masters, and in DS11 especially, they became more of a principal (or patron), offering free rein whilst keeping a watchful eye to ensure you stayed on track.

Although the studio syllabus primarily focused on individual projects, it was not an environment that conformed to individual learning. Instead what I found best about the studio, was how much one could learn from so many people in such a short amount of time - I learnt as much from my fellow students as my tutors. Studio may not prepare you to practice as an architect straight out of university, but it does provide you with the skills and ability to become one in practice. Having absorbed as much of everyone else's knowledge as I could I consequently went from designing Berkley homes-style toilets to working on new stadia for some of the world's most challenging environments and prolific events.

Throughout my architectural education, I was often told to treat the course like a 'professional' 9–5 job, which was bemusing since few of us had been subject to life in an architectural office until graduating from our degree course; even now, I await the experience of said 9–5 job. But did the studio prepare me for life after university? Or was I thrown into the deep end in struggling to get by? Architects severely undervalue and underestimate their time and its worth.

There is a stark difference between the architecture we have been exposed to throughout our studies, and the buildings on which most will be working fresh out of university. Since the fifties, the role of the architect has severely diminished, from all-round master builder, to a squint-eyed serf lurching from contract to contract to pay the bills. There must be a clear distinction in one's mind between the ongoing project and your aspirations, otherwise you will end up disheartened when the property developer looking to make a quick buck doesn't approve your bespoke kitchen and replaces it with a Howdens basic range fitting. As Ernesto Nathan Rogers famously put it: "Dal cucchiaio alla città" (From the spoon to the city), in description of the architect's role in society. Designing is not just of a building but engages the occupants' lifestyle. Well, that spoon has become the responsibility of the subcontractor and you have been novated from the 'city' after it has been 'value engineered' in favour of a design and build contractor who intends to squeeze as much money out of the project as possible, with no care for its architectural merit. This is a rather pessimistic and anecdotal impression of 'real life' as opposed that in the 'studio', yet it still begs the question whether architectural education needs to be updated for the twenty first century, as this world has not been covered in any syllabus I have experienced.

An archaic education system, then, and a paternalistic studio culture that has existed since the Beaux Arts, and an extended tripartite system still based on the model that emerged from a RIBA conference on Architectural Education in 1958 (the same year the hula-hoop was invented).

The RIBA is slowly coming to terms with this situation, admitting that 70% of workplaces and 80% of students feel their education didn't prepare them for professional life; instead promoting an outdated and parochial understanding of how design knowledge is acquired and produced, valuing expertise over synthetic knowledge and image production over process and practice. However, many universities are now embracing a sustainable orientation and encouraging state of the art technical advance in manufacturing and research. New options in education are also emerging like the London School of Architecture who, taking a step back to a time before the 1950s, advocate pupilage in the workplace.

Arguably students themselves are responsible for not taking advantage of what is on offer. Worried about their grades they often stick with what they already know, rather than risk the unknown. I felt under considerable pressure in switching studios, yet I learnt more than otherwise in drawing

together the wide range of disciplines that now inform my creative thinking. With the price of education rising, surely doing the same thing for two years is literally short–changing yourself? After all, when was the last time you were asked your grade at a job interview?

Whilst I shall not, or cannot (non-disclosure agreements) say much about the details of individual projects in practice, what I will say is how similar to studio culture practice has turned out to be, thankfully. Mine is a relatively young practice and there are more than enough opportunities to develop technical skills however you see fit, be that in detailing, management or computational design. Others reading this will have had a completely different experience of studio culture, but is that not what makes this sometimes daunting and inadequate experience so desirable?

Toby Plunkett: BA(hons) Kent School of Architecture/University of Kent, MArch University of Westminster. Currently in practice (from October 2016) with Pattern Architects, and previously with Darling Associates (2013-2016).

09/10
TRIESTE

T

COSMOPOLITAN 'REGIONS' / GLOBAL LOCALE

Reuben Barker

Lucy Brooke

Julianne Cassidy

Jerret Gwenaël

Fiona MacDonald

Louise Scannell

Tong Scarlett

Katherine Ashley

Cruse Stephen

Amelia Dickinson

Dyson Dean

Otman Gusby

King Robert

Alexandre Lou

Camilla Pitt

Chris Raeburn

Paul Richardson

Harriet Roderiques

Craig Rosenblatt

Edward Wood

2009/2010

TRIESTE:
NORTH EAST ITALY

TRIESTINITÀ:
COSMOPOLITAN 'REGIONS'/
GLOBAL LOCALE

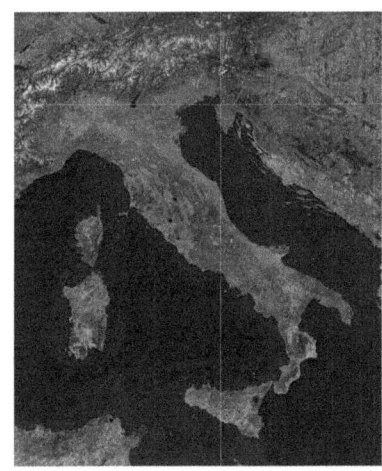

Landmarks:

CATTEDRALE DI SAN GIUSTO/ CHIESA SERBO-ORTODOSSA DELLA SANTISSIMA TRINITÀ E DI SAN SPIRIDIONE/CHIESA DELLA BEATA VERGINE DEL SOCCORSO/CHIESA DELLA BEATA VERGINE DEL ROSARIO/ CHIESA DI SAN NICOLÒ DEI GRECI/ TEMPIO EBRAICO - SINAGOGA/CHIESA DI SANTA MARIA MAGGIORE/LA CHIESA DI SANT'ANTONIO NEL BORGO TERESIANO/ CHIESA DI SANT'ANTONIO TAUMATURGO/ CHIESA DI SANT'APOLLINARE /CON GLI AFFRESCHI DEL PITTORE FORLIVESE POMPEO RANDI/CHIESA CATTOLICA PARROCCHIALE DELLA MADONNA DEL MARE, PIAZZALE ANTONIO ROSMINI/ CHIESA EVANGELICA LUTERANA DI CONFESSIONE AUGUSTANA/BASILICA DI SAN SILVESTRO/CHIESA EVANGELICA METODISTA/CHIESA ANGLICANA DI CRISTO/TEMPIO A MARIA MADRE E REGINA DI MONTEGRISA/CHIESA DI SAN PASQUALE BAYLON/CIMITERO MONUMENTALE DI SANT'ANNA/ CIMITERO EX MILITARE DI SANT'ANNA/ CIMITERO MILITARE AUSTRO-UNGARICO DI PROSECCO/CIMITERO MILITARE AUSTROUNGARICO PRESSO PROSECCO/ CIMITERO MILITARE AUSTRO-UNGARICO DI AURISINA/CIMITERO ANGLICANO/ CIMITERO EVANGELICO/CIMITERO GRECO-ORTODOSSO/CIMITERO ISRAELITICO/CIMITERO MAOMETTANO/ CIMITERO SERBO-ORTODOSSO/ BASILICA FORENSE/ CASTELLIERE/ VAL ROSANDRA/SAN GIUSTO/ARCO DI RICCARDO/ ANTIQUARIUM DI VIA DONOTA/ ANTIQUARIUM DI BORGO SAN SERGIO/ BASILICA PALEOCRISTIANA/TOR CUCHERNA/ CASTELLO DI MIRAMARE/ CASTELLO DI SAN GIUSTO/CASTELLO DI DUINO/CASTELLO DI MUGGIA/ FARO DELLA VITTORIA/LANTERNA EX PESCHERIA CENTRALE/PALAZZO DELLE POSTE/PALAZZO ECONOMO/PALAZZO GALATTI/PALAZZO DELLE FERROVIE DELLO STATO/PALAZZO LEO/PALAZZO DELLA LUOGOTENENZA AUSTRIACA/ ALAZZO DEL MUNICIPIO/OSPEDALE MILITARE/ PALAZZO MODELLO/

Coordinates:
45°38N 13°48E

Region:
Friuli-Venezia Giulia

Area:
84.49 km2

Elevation:
2 m

Population:

1921	239,558	—
1931	250,170	+4.4%
1936	248,307	-0.7%
1951	272,52	+9.8%
1961	272,72	+0.1%
1971	271,87	-0.3%
1981	252,36	-7.2%
1991	231,100	-8.4%
2001	211,184	-8.6%
2009	205,50	-2.7%
2013	204,849	-0.3%

Demonym(s):
Triestini

Patron Saint:
St. Justus of Trieste

PALAZZO CARCIOTTI/PALAZZO MARENZI/PALAZZO VIVANTE/ PALAZZO DEL TERGESTEO/ PALAZZO DEL LLOYD TRIESTINO/ STAZIONE MARITTIMA/ARSENALE DEL LLOYD/PALAZZO AEDES/ PALAZZO PANFILI/PALAZZO GOPCEVICH/PALAZZO PANFILLI/ CASA CATOLLA/CASA BARTOLI/ PIAZZA UNITÀ D'ITALIA/PIAZZA DELLA BORSA/CANAL GRANDE/ CAFFÈ SAN MARCO/GALLERIE ANTIAEREE KLEINE BERLIN/ TRENOVIA DI OPICINA/STORICA TRANVIA INAUGURATA NEL BORGO TERESIANO/VILLA NECKER/VILLA ECONOMO/VILLA COSULICHVILLA SARTORIO/VILLA ENGELMANN/ VILLA SIGMUNDT/VILLA HAGGICONSTA/VILLA REVOLTELLA/ VILLA GIULIA

This year's studio is focused on the 'Italian' city of Trieste, which paradoxically embodies a multi-ethnic cosmopolitan culture. Currently the city is proposed as the transnational capital of a new Euro-region (Veneto, Friuli Venezia-Giulia, Carinthia, Istria) encompassing parts of Italy, Austria, Slovenia and Croatia. 'Translation' (Joyce wrote Ulysses here) and 'transaction' (as port of the Austro-Hungarian empire) are identified as themes intrinsic to a city held, in its contemporary incarnation, to internalise many of the characteristics of globalization. How might this novel 'idea of the city' inform the architecture of new social, cultural and political institutions, and a revived economy of 'research' (enterprise zones and business parks)?

A parallel interest is to re-conceive the question of typology in architecture, rethinking the relationship between habitual models, abstract figures and the contingent occupation of generic space. The logic of planning has been increasingly marginalized in an architectural culture prioritizing sculptural fluency, generative form making and anecdotal characterization, which we aim to redress.

* * *

TRIESTE VISIT

mapping/multi-cultural, mediateque/zone
translation: linguistic and literary
language/oral culture/libraries/the city of the mind (myth)/literary culture and history of the city/literature on the city/language schools and labs/comparative literature/role of the translator/the other/new media/centre for translation and communication/between cultures/hybrid typologies/mediateque and centre for translation studies.

transaction: cultural and economic
city as market/warehouse/free port/trading-zone/banking and insurance/social transactions/economic migration/generating a new economy/business parks/industrial estates/development typologies and transformation (realism)/Karsk zone.

five intervals
documentation and sectioning the city/urban fabric/literary locations/identity, community and everyday life/transport adjacencies/environment

03 YEAR ONE: MEDIATEQUE AND CENTRE FOR TRANSLATION STUDIES TRIESTE ZONE

001 site and context: lost or found
002 landform or ideal territory
003 work in progress: modeling and formal figures
004 anecdotal or hierarchical detail (external)
005 social and economic parameters
006 endgame: representation and appearance, fragment or totality

01 MODELING TYPOLOGIES
001 object type
002 packaging or wrapping

02 FORCEFIELDS/
POLLUTION AND THE ART OF WEATHERING
001 dissection/re-modelling
002 itinerary/model transformations
003 type: occupation and re-cast

04 YEAR TWO: TRANS-NATIONAL: CITY REGION AND MICRO-COLLECTIVITIES
001 environmental interface/territory/programme
002 spatial/structural proposition

■ TRIESTE VISIT

While we are mapping out a framework for the survey, and identifying particular issues and themes for consideration, this is not intended to be unduly prescriptive, concerned rather with contextual documentation related to the topography of the city and available sites for your various projects. In order to confront the multi-cultural character (and history) of Trieste we have a strong interest in how you experience this aspect of the city and its communal everyday life.

What evidence do you come across of cultural solidarity on the one hand, and where is Triestinitá or hybrid ethnicity to be found? What is the architectural manifestation of this condition, evident perhaps in transformations of buildings, or neighbourhoods?

We are encouraging each of you to follow up your own preoccupations concerning the Mediateque or Zone (Dip 1) or your putative design 'thesis' (Dip 2), and visit Trieste with a clear agenda in mind. Try to avoid the unfocused gaze of the architectural tourist and determine what it is you intend to document, research and discover before we depart. It is not that we are uninterested in contingent experience, or unsuspected insights, but we expect a degree of focus on matters to hand. It is one thing to drift without intent, another to acknowledge the, albeit well worn, meanderings of the disinherited Situationist or urban flaneur as a deliberate choice.

■ 01 MODELING TYPOLOGIES

001   object type
002   packaging or wrapping

PRELIMINARY INVESTIGATIONS
This initial work touches obliquely on themes (translation and transaction) relevant to projects in Trieste, but more directly prompts an engagement with the question of typology in architecture: where generation of form comes to be represented within the conventions of orthographic projection, or conversely

CAD/CAM modelling techniques. The short studies, while setting out general observations and basic procedures, are not intended to be unduly prescriptive. Al-

though they do ask for particular outcomes, there are many ways to interpret them. Engage the questions raised and determine a productive interpretation of each exercise in bringing a degree of sophistication and intentionality to your understanding of the issues raised. The initial study involves selecting and packaging three-dimensional artefacts.

OBJECT TYPE

How to choose, make or fashion an object as a 'type'? A series of characteristic objects or the repetition of a particular object? Is this an object type or a prototypical artefact? More straightforwardly are they typical objects of some kind? If so, from this series (or family) of similar objects, identify the most representative.

Collect two 'found' or 'fabricated' object(s): one (model 01) seen as authentic or 'original', and the other (model 02) being a variant, copy, surrogate or imitation of (having resemblance to or sharing characteristics with) the original. Record both in high quality detailed photographs. The objects should be chosen for their precision, intricacy and complexity, and be of a sufficient scale and substance (preferably 150 x 150 x 300mm) to enable them to be 'worked', cut or manipulated.

PACKAGING OR WRAPPING

You are subsequently asked to package each object separately, as if for postage or transport. Consider protective material and the external layer, finish or structure of the 'package'. Record the process of protecting, wrapping, containing or crating up the objects. Each package should be 'identified', labelled for delivery to Trieste, and its carriage specified. Photograph both packages for posterity.

■ TWO THEMES

TRANSLATION:
Linguistic and Literary

Language, Oral Culture, Libraries, The City of the Mind (Myth), Literary Culture and the History of the City, Literature on the City, Language Schools and Labs, Comparative Literature, The Role of the Translator, The Other, New Media, Centre for Translation and Communication, Between Cultures, Hybrid Typologies, Mediateque and Centre for Translation Studies.

TRANSACTION:
Cultural and Economic
City as Market/Warehouse, Free Port, Trading-Zone, Banking and Insurance, Social Transactions, Economic Migration, Generating a New Economy, Business Parks, Industrial Estates, Development Typologies and Transformation (Realism), Karsk Zone.

CITY SURVEY:
Below radar from sea to borderlands
Five intervals (group-work)

Between groups parcel out a survey of five 'intervals' through the city from the seafront to the Carso, across the Karsk and, in principle, to the Slovenian border. The width of the interval is for you to determine in order to make a comparative survey. Each section should be self-explanatory being more or less at a tangent to the shore, though you may need to angle or deflect the route relative to the urban configuration of your sector. Consider six primary aspects of each interval.

01 Porto Vecchio—Piazza della Liberta—Università—Trebiciano

02 Piazza Ponte-Rosso—Ospedale Maggiore—Boschetto Park—Timignano

03 Piazza Unita D'Italia—Castello—Villa Opicina District (two urban 'islands')

04 Punta Franco Nuovo—Hippodrome—Housing Block (Viale Pasteur)

05 (Muggia)—San Sabba—S.Anna Cemetery—New Hospital

DOCUMENTATION AND
SECTIONING THE CITY

Given the topographical context of Trieste, situated between the shoreline and Karsk plateau, draw two sections through city and its hinterland. One should be scaled geographically, the other limited by the urban fabric and its extent. Consider spot-heights, relative levels and vantage or viewpoints— mapping representative views, as they are relevant to your experience of the city. The scale(s) of your survey, and what you choose to register (in more or less detail), should be determined independently by each group.

URBAN FABRIC
Produce an edited figure-ground plan of the territory covered by your interval.

LITERARY LOCATIONS
Research the location of libraries, and university buildings that might be associated with the Mediateque. Determine and document potential library sites (and consider literary associations with particular places).

IDENTITY, COMMUNITY AND EVERYDAY LIFE
Taking your cue from our introduction, document community identity and transactions as you experience them 'on the street'.

TRANSPORT ADJACENCIES
Transpose connections to transport infrastructure (roads, docks, terminals, railway lines and stations, tram/bus routes) against each interval to determine strategic parameters, particularly with regard to the periphery of the city and the adjacent border. Register flows of people and goods. Locate a potential development zone outside the city.

REGARDING THE ENVIRONMENT
Consider whether the architecture of the city may be seen to respond to prevailing environmental conditions, and what impact this has on your perception of its materiality.

DIPLOMA ONE
Mediateque and Centre for Translation Studies

Compare notes concerning potential sites within your interval. Return with sufficient descriptive survey information regarding adjacent buildings and facades as the context for a suitable site.

DIPLOMA TWO
Trans-national: City Region and Micro-collectivities

Bearing in mind our introductory notes at the beginning of the year you should now have defined the focus of your 'thesis project', so that you return from Trieste armed with relevant material. We have suggested a range of plausible themes and programmes, which we suggest you relate to your own particular interests. Remember the particular emphasis we have put on theoretical cogency and an environmental agenda.

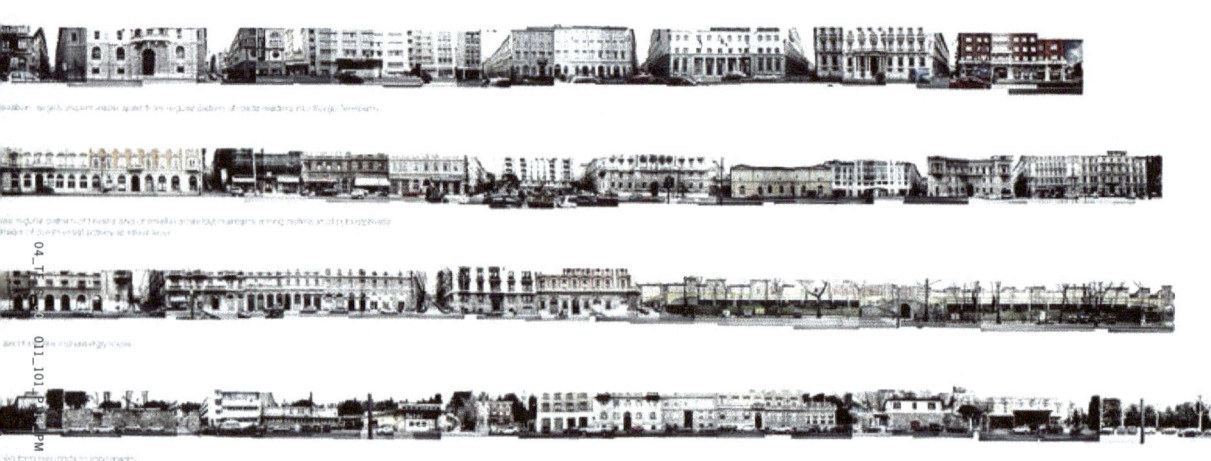

04_TE_S_024_001_091_P114_EP

04_TE_S_013_001_092_P114_M

04_TE_S_022_001_093_P114_IP

04_TE_S_004_001_094_P114_S

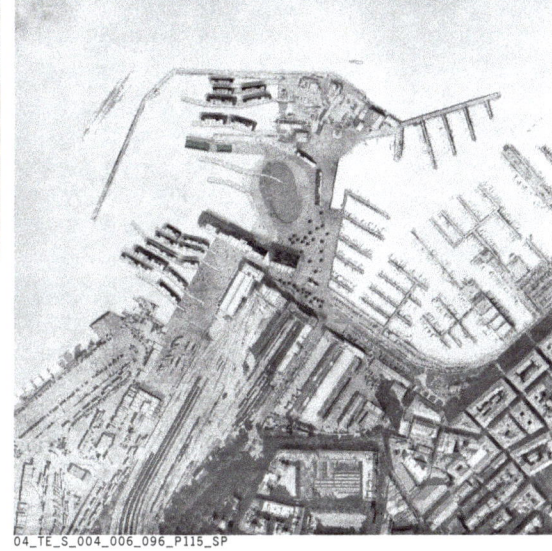

(J.Morris, *Trieste The Meaning of Nowhere*)
[..] HERMAN BAHR, ARRIVING THERE IN 1909, SAID HE FELT AS THOUGH HE WAS SUSPENDED IN UNREALITY, AS IF HE WERE 'NOWHERE AT ALL' [...] (6)

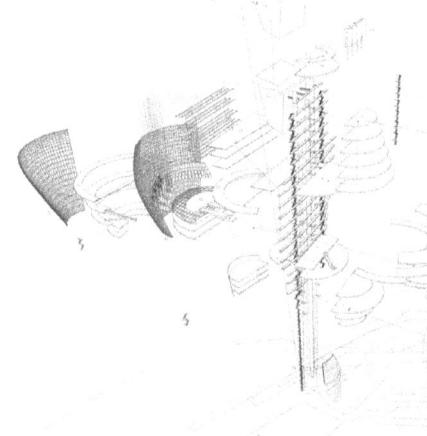

04_TE_S_029_018_108_P117_EP

04_TE_S_024_019_109_P117_IP

04_TE_S_004_020_110_P117_E

04_TE_S_008_021_111_P117_S

04_TE_S_003_022_112_P117_PM

04_TE_S_008_023_113_P117_HP

04_TE_S_009_024_114_P117_S

JULIANNE CASSIDY

GLOBAL COUNTERPOINTS

Since beginning my architectural education as an undergraduate in 2005, I have experienced two projects which have significantly shaped my evolving architectural philosophy or ethos. The first, a fictitious museum, was concerned with the transformation of an 18th-century Belgian Stock Exchange into a display, and exhibition space, and was pursued in a purely academic context while studying Diploma studio at the University of Westminster in London; and the second, a 325,00 m2 40-storey mixed-used development located in the Chinese city of Xiamen—currently under construction and due for completion in 2019 was undertaken whilst working in China for Farrells' Shanghai office. Although diverse in nature, scope and typology, and distinct in their differing potential for realisation (as represented or constructed), comparison of these two projects provides a means to assess the value and relevance of the conjectural 'design studio' project in cultivating or fostering meaningful architectural skills and thinking. Various elements affecting the way in which each project developed have been loosely identified as one of two types: the processes or 'design research techniques' used for development of the primary objective, and the contrasting effect of 'external influences' on these development processes..

INITIAL MOVES

The 'Museum for Displaced Collections', located in the city of Antwerp, was undertaken during 2010–2011 as the programme for my thesis design project. The focus of the year was to devise an architectural proposition which would positively improve a particular urban condition, pursuing a series of investigations (both remote and on-site) as generative devices. The final 'model' programme was arrived at following a thorough cataloguing of Antwerp's existing museums and galleries, and the subsequent realisation that the city was lacking temporary display spaces for collections displaced from their permanent 'homes' (for one reason or another). The Xiamen Financial Centre (XFC) project, in contrast, was awarded to Farrells' Shanghai office in 2015 following a successful competition bid within the auspices of a government programme to develop a series of international business 'zones' over the next decade. These 'hubs' would be underpinned by unique tax and trading laws intended to further boost China's ability to trade and deal in the global financial market. Although distinct in typology and outlook, the studio project and the live project are nonetheless comparable in their core raison d'etre - namely the identification of a social/cultural/economic need, to which the development of an architecture can conceptually respond.

DESIGN RESEARCH

The two projects developed from their initial briefs over several months of design development and refinement, via diverse methods employed at various points in the process: hand-drawn sketches, 3D digital models, 2D drafting, physical models and digital rendering. Both projects were subject to regular objective scrutiny and review (scheduled from the

beginning of both programmes) through which amendment and improvement would evolve. In order to allow for more effective review and reflection, the research carried out during the development of both projects was captured at pivotal moments in a hardcopy format (particularly in the early stages while the briefs were being developed or interpreted). Within the terms of the university project, this took the form of a 'research catalogue', and on the live project a series of 'end of stage' reports. The core structure and evolution of both projects (from a purely design perspective) was therefore derived from the same logic of 'trial and error' through applied design research techniques, which were summarised at key stages in the form of 'catalogues' of accumulated research on which review and reflection could be based.

RULE AND FREEDOM

Both projects were guided by a predefined set of parameters, outlined in respective 'project briefs' from the outset of each project. However, a key distinction between the two scenarios was the manner in which the content of each brief was composed and controlled. The structure of the Diploma course required the specifics of the project briefs in the final year to be constructed by the students themselves, whereas the brief for the XFC project was laid out as a set of legally-binding contractual conditions before the commencement of work. The university project brief inevitably remained flexible, amending and adapting to the developing needs of the project and the preference of the designer as work progressed. Conversely, the practice project brief was much less interpretive: creative expression would often be restricted by 'external' influences, whether regular in-house review feedback or the need to satisfy the client. Participating in the XFC project, it became apparent that in reality the client had a major influence on the direction in which the design was steered, on occasion to the detriment of the architectural design (in the opinion of the design team). This factor is little-considered in a university context. The studio project and the practice project therefore differ in the presence or absence of an omnipotent and hugely influential client, and in the impact that this figure has on the development of the architectural design and on the autonomy of the designer. It is worth noting that in China the 'client' tends to be represented by a single powerful, influential individual, as opposed to a relatively more democratic negotiation with a 'client team' in the UK.

BUDGETARY CONSIDERATIONS

An extension of the notion of client 'control' as a notable external influence on design is epitomized by the 'budget' (alongside other pragmatic considerations such as political, legislative, and bureaucratic influence). These were alluded to but little-considered in any detail at university. The 'business' or 'money-making' aspect of the profession is definitely the one with which I have struggled most since leaving education, having been required to create, first and foremost, a profitable 'product' as opposed to an idealistic, fanciful creation in the context of the design studio. Although these notions are explored more thoroughly during the Part III course, the Part I and Part II courses are distanced from reality in their tendency to focus strongly on utopian or romantic aspects of project design.

TEAMWORK + STUDIO CULTURE

Collaboration and a team spirit were necessities in both the context of university and in practice, and undoubtedly key external influences on the design research trajectory. The concept for the Museum for Displaced Collections was derived from a series of six short group projects undertaken at the beginning of the semester, in order to pool research resources and generate ideas for potential development towards a thesis proposal. By comparison, Farrells' XFC project team was 12-strong and spread across two offices (one in Shanghai and one in Hong Kong), often with additional temporary staff supporting output at busy periods. In both scenarios, various project tasks were identified, listed and delegated among team members, and regular monitoring by a designated individual would take place in order to ensure deadlines be met by all parties. Ultimately, though, the university project necessarily becomes a solo endeavor, the focus being to assess and rank one student against the next, whereas the practice project tends to be a truly collective effort from beginning to end. Unlike the academic project, the success of the professional practice is attributed to the design group as opposed to the individual, with the precise nature and structure of this group differing dramatically between individual projects and offices, and therefore influencing design decisions in different ways. On entering the world of practice, this culture certainly requires a distinct shift in thinking and outlook compared to that generally fostered at university.

CONCLUSION

It is clear from the above analysis that both projects utilised a combination of almost identical 'design research techniques' in the search for the optimum architectural proposition (modelling, rendering, sketching, review, reflection and cataloging of design research undertaken). The freedom accorded to the designer in order to interpret the outcomes of these techniques, however, differed between the two projects, largely as a result of the presence or absence of additional 'external influences' (budgetary considerations, bureaucracy, legislative requirements and hierarchical team structures). Although not outlined here in any detail, in the particular scenario outlined above, the geographic location of the XFC project resulted in the presence of a key external influence which would unlikely be an issue if working on a UK-based project, namely a variation of working cultures between practice in different countries. Rather fittingly, issues relating to the displacement of cultures were also touched upon in the university museum project, perhaps hinting that the notion of fluctuating, fluid, or variable project contexts and frameworks, could well become an important aspect of future live architectural projects in general. As international practice becomes more and more common, and the movement of global workers becomes less stagnant, the nature and effect of external influences on design decisions made will necessarily become more difficult to presume and emulate in the university studio context. Arguably, then, it is much more valuable to emphasise and invest effort into nurturing the internal logic of design research techniques in the context of university, leaving unpredictable additions to be discovered and better understood when encountered later in the practice context.

Julianne Cassidy: BA(Hons) University of Manchester, DipArch University of Westminster. Currently in practice with Farrells Shanghai (since October 2015), and previously with HPP Shanghai, Newtecnic and Stride Treglown.

13/14
TRIESTE/REVISITED

T/r

CITY AS MEDIUM

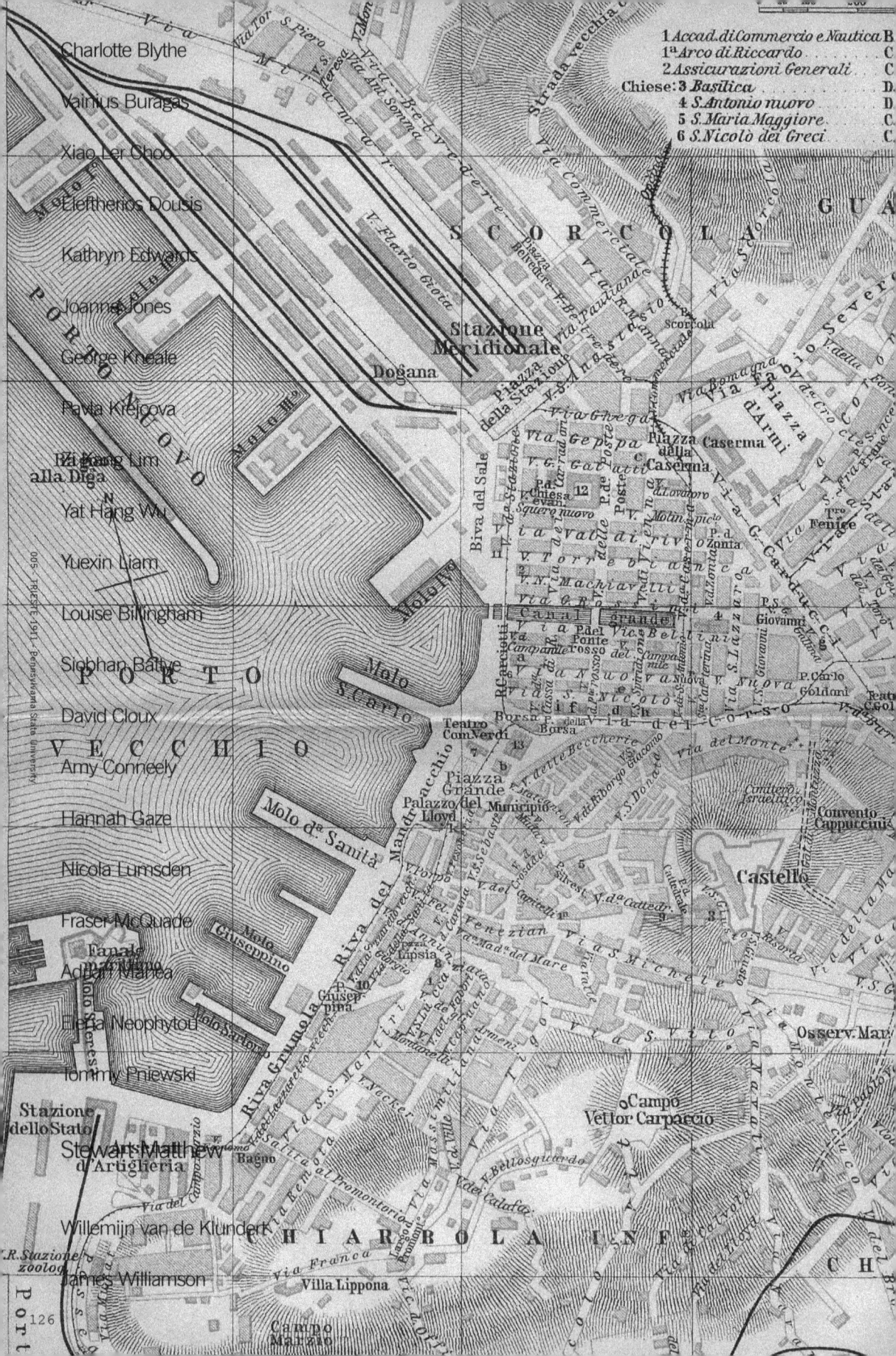

2013/2014

TRIESTINITÀ:
CITY AS MEDIUM

The 'Italian' city of Trieste paradoxically embodies a multi-ethnic cosmopolitan culture yet also a deeply conservative 'heritage': mediating between the limestone landscape of the Carso / Karst plateau and the Adriatic; between topology and fluidity, and between the stasis of 'investment' and the flux of economic change and migration.

Proposed as the trans-national capital of a new Euro-region encompassing different parts of Italy, Austria, Slovenia and Croatia, 'translation' (Joyce wrote Ulysses here) and 'transaction' (port of the Austro-Hungarian empire) are themes intrinsic to a city held, in its contemporary incarnation, to internalise many of the characteristics of globalization. How might this fictional 'idea of the city' inform the architecture of new social, cultural or political institutions, and a revived economy of 'research' (attached to enterprise zones and business parks)?

Our primary focus concerns the relationship between stability and instability. On the one hand the city has a fluid historical identity and on the other the material reality epitomised by the stolid stone construction following the Theresian quarter's severe grid. Beneath surface appearances there is the realm of the urban interior and the fissures and voids of the Carso's underworld (literal and metaphorical) on land, while the undersea realm of the marine environment may be captured in the aquarium. One does not visit Trieste to view iconic buildings but rather to experience the medium of the city: a built archive of aesthetic material, or alternately a complex of social, psychological or psychic agencies, mediated by a contemporary culture and marked by contrasting environmental conditions.

Trieste's past as an imperial port, underpins its banking and insurance institutions, and heritage-based if not hedonistic, tourism, but also the now largely empty dockyards. A certain vacancy prevails in the central districts, while the intermediate urban area includes variable examples of inter-war historicism and rationalism. The periphery evidences scattered post-war developments from the 60's and 70's schools, social housing and isolated institutions. Bracketed between the plateau escarpment and the sea, environmental extremes of summer and winter climate impact on the city as a maritime threshold, as does the seasonal and notorious Bora wind. The engineering of this interface, set between the geological topology and conditions below ground, and the transience of a volatile environment, is of particular interest.

TRIESTE VISIT

Sea view/city as medium/intervals/documentation-sectioning the city/urban fabric/locations/everyday life/transport adjacencies/environment
Technical Agencies
Detail and materiality/experiencing/constituting enclosure/opening up/narrative/viewing/environmental conditioning/ground/interface/weathering/force fields

04 YEAR ONE: AQUARIUM OF THE ADRIATIC MARINE INSTITUTE

01 CUSTOMS HOUSE
001 agency/situation/room
002 strategy/context/plan-section-narratve/view from the interior

02 DEMOLITION OR *LA NUOVA DIMENSIONE*
001 model/photo/urban intent
002 model as artefact/contextual/repetition-reproduction/city at large

03 YEAR ONE: ADRIATIC TRANSNATIONAL ECOLOGIES
001 configuring the Adriatic/undersea-viewing/Gulf of Trieste: ecology/landform-limestone
002 sitework/interface

03 YEAR TWO: CATALOGUE RAISONNÉ
001 Inventories/treatise/handbook/composition/programme

04 YEAR TWO: ARCHITECTURE AS AGENCY

02 DEMOLITION OR
LA NUOVA DIMENSIONE

001   model/photo/urban intent
002   model as artefact/contextual/repetition-reproduction/city at large

INTRODUCTION

This is the second two-week project and follows the pattern (individual and collective) of the first. Our intention was to introduce the concept of the city as an agency or a mediating social fabric, and subsequently in this second project to consider the drama of intervention, whether within or beyond Trieste's constituent form and configuration. You are invited to question the heritage culture and urban 'stasis' prevailing in the Theresian quarter (and elsewhere in the centre of the city). Rather than imagining and drawing, this project is focused on 'modelling':

> *If the model crystallizes within an object the thoughts of the architect, it thus permits the manipulation of the form through the use of the senses. (7)*
> (Pierre-Alain Croset, 'Microcosms of the Architect')

A model is a physical artifact but also an ideal proposition. We are concerned both with models that demonstrate a process (as work in progress) and those that are, by contrast, definitively complete (iconic as if for an exhibition). Both require thought to be given to the manner of their presentation: placed on a plinth, a stand or within a frame or cabinet, or positioned attached to a surface (floor, table or wall-plane). Consider the choice of material from which the model is to be made and the procedure of making (cast, cut, burnt, stacked or dispersed). Is its nature associative, tactile or symbolic? Is it figurative, abstract or purely material, in a sculptural process that may be subtractive, additive, homogeneous or fragmentary?

The fixity of the models stands in marked contrast to the meaning of the Latin word ruina: a collapse, or rather a collapsing– that is, a process. Using a three-dimensional model to depict actual destruction with shifting piles of rubble, unstable facades in danger of collapse, and the omnipresence of dust [...] is a material paradox. Years of labour go into making a permanent image of something that was itself impermanent. This paradox is nothing if not arresting. (8)
(Helmut Puff, 'Ruins as Models')

02 DEMOLITION OR *LA NUOVA DIMENSIONE*

■ 001 model/photo/urban intent
002 model as artefact/contextual/repetition-reproduction/city at large

In the first instance, you are asked to choose either the concept of demolition or the ideal of a novel (and in Trieste unfamiliar) form of urban intervention - la nuovo dimensione. Within each group individuals should address both approaches.

DEMOLITION

Construct a sculptural model that enacts a process of demolition (or series of demolitions) analogous to within the urban fabric of Trieste. The nature of this process might be destructive or controlled, being about breakage, cutting, smashing or sculpting. This could constitute a form of polemical 'erasure' or in contrast a partial, circumscribed or limited form of 'removal' or disassembly. Consider the question of scale, and major or minor demolition. The model should epitomise a material process and incorporate (or collect) accumulated debris, the by-product of demolition. Your particular demolition(s) may be associated with an urban district or quarter, multiple or singular urban blocks, a particular building or series of buildings, in creating or revealing new urban 'interiors' or sites for intervention. Whatever your intentions or attitude towards demolition (which should be unequivocally stated) your model should present the opposite process to that of 'construction' (yet not the theoretical 'deconstruction' of the recent past). There is inevitably something ambivalent about the construction of a model that traces or presents the consequences of destruction. In principle a negation, yet in this form the process acquires a positive intent (note the Futurist foray into Trieste). What has been coined the 'natural history of destruction' is generally associated with warfare or revolution, but here is considered as a means *to question an uncritical assumption of conservation or renovation, as representative of the 'status quo'. Demolition may also be a personal matter, polemically destroying things you do or don't value, in order to question the shibboleths of architectural culture, where an inquisitive intent or a critical agenda might produce unsuspected value.*

LA NUOVO DIMENSIONE

In contrast, model the explicit construction of an urban ideal or singular object or building type, one without precedent in Trieste. This might be constituted as a self-contained utopia, a singular one-off object or an ideally constituted urban framework or plan. There are many precedents in the history of ideal cities and urban planning, both utopian and dystopian, hence our contemporary wariness towards the concept of the urban ideal, whether traditional, avant-garde or 'virtual' in character. Both the former concepts have an uneven track record in the C20th, disowned in the more recent rhetoric of a networked 'information society' (or service economy), where virtual space and (embodied) interactivity displace conventional urban space (or places) in a hyper-dense, or dispersed, accumulation of activities. Without necessary recourse to paradigms of 'urban planning' (historical, modern or contemporary); the 'cloud' or 'ground-scraper', the tower or slab, and the extremes of scale or juxtaposition, all take issue with the urban homogeneity and consistency of the Austro-Hungarian grid, and 'familiar' scale of Trieste's 'old town'. What novel typologies or extreme conditions might be introduced at odds with the normative condition of the different districts of Trieste? The sometime fascist neo-Italian interventions of the interwar period around the inner city, and the large-scale projects of the later C20th on the periphery, in different ways conspire to construct an alternative urban architecture. What contemporary type, typology or alternative may be envisaged?

INITIAL PRESENTATION:
MODELLING PROCESS

01 model (process, object or framework)
02 photograph
03 urban intent (polemic: diagram–statement)

02 DEMOLITION OR
LA NUOVA DIMENSIONE

001 model/photo/urban intent
■ 002 model as artefact/contextual/repetition-reproduction/city at large

In the second week, each group is asked to develop two contrasting strategies in further detail, inverting the logic of the earlier work as a serial, or a singular, urban intervention, now set definitively in the local context of the city. Understanding this context should include addressing prevailing environmental conditions or factors, which are either resisted or accepted as acting on (or transforming) the 'model' artifact. The proposition concerned with demolition, originally contingent or quite possibly arbitrary in nature, should be reconstituted into an ideal proposition that requires a degree of perfection in its application to a selected site. Conversely the abstract ideal model of a nuovo dimensione should be moulded, compromised, tarnished, distressed or transformed in its concrete application to a locality, a prevailing environment and a more specific programme.

FINAL EXHIBITION:
DEFINITIVE MODEL

01 model as artefact
02 contextual elaborations
03 repetition or reproduction
04 from the city at large

(L. Bialasiewicz, *Europe as/at the Border*)
IN TRIESTE [...] 'GEOGRAPHIES OF ABSENCE' MADE UP A COSMOPOLITAN URBAN CULTURE THAT FAR FROM BEING 'LACKING' WAS, INDEED, CHARACTERISED BY ABUNDANCE: A CITY THAT WAS, AT ONCE, 'BOTH MANY PLACES AND UNIQUELY ITSELF' [...] (9)

05_TR_S_026_005_125_P135_I

05_TR_S_027_007_127_P135_IP

05_TR_S_014_006_126_P135_M

05_TR_S_005_008_128_P135_E

05_TR_S_005_009_129_P135_SP

05_TR_S_034_010_130_P135_EP

05_TR_S_011_012_132_P136_HP

05_TR_S_015_013_133_P136_M

05_TR_S_028_014_134_P136_IP

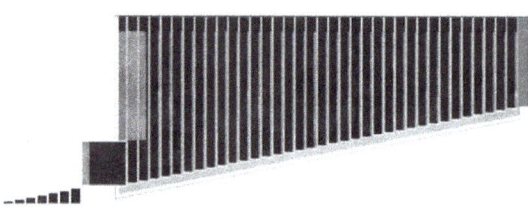

05_TR_S_007_024_144_P136_P
05_TR_S_014_025_145_P136_S
05_TR_S_006_026_146_P137_E
05_TR_S_008_027_147_P137_P

05_TR_S_006_015_135_P136_P

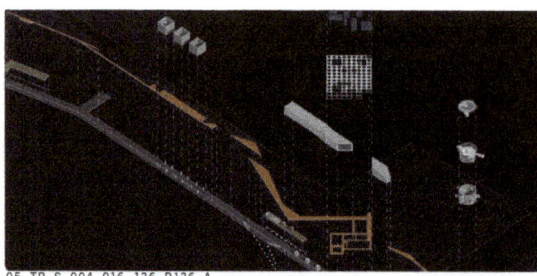
05_TR_S_004_016_136_P136_A

05_TR_S_029_017_137_P136_EP

05_TR_S_012_018_138_P137_S

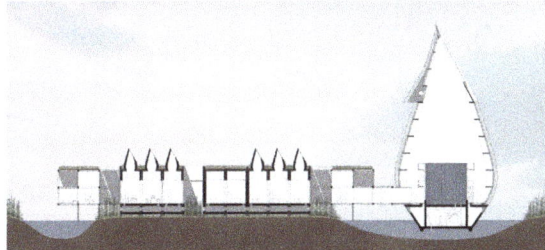

05_TR_S_013_019_139_P137_S

05_TR_S_029_020_140_P137_IP

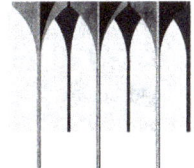

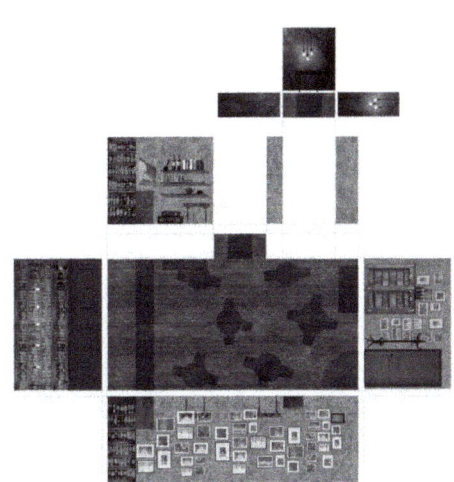

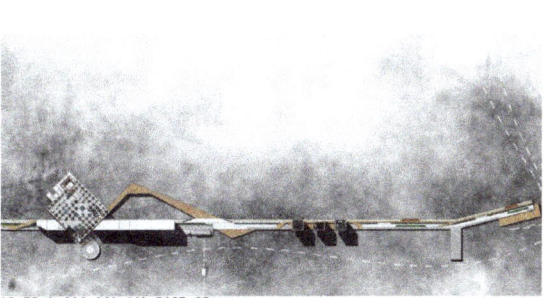

05_TR_S_006_021_141_P137_SP

05_TR_S_030_022_142_P137_IP

05_TR_S_012_023_143_P137_HP

HANNAH GAZE

EXPERIENCES IN THE STUDIO

The merits of the design studio remained a mystery to me during my Part I studies and I found it to be an intimidating, daunting and competitive place full of 'wrong' answers. I was much more comfortable in the lecture hall, in small groups listening to tutors, or in the library, researching books and architectural magazines. Perhaps this more structured way of learning was more familiar to me coming from a traditional school environment, however, I still feel that I was not ready for what studio culture offered so early on in my architectural education. It was not until my Part II studies that I began to realise the individual studio's potential for testing out concepts and for exchange and experimentation with ideas introduced from elsewhere. During those years, the studio became the centre of my studies, firm friendships were made, skills were honed and my confidence increased exponentially. I now feel that the design studio is a unique and important place, particularly at Part II level, where students have much more sense of themselves and of the kind of architect they wish to become. That said, I believe that this environment must be 'structured', but in an unrestrictive manner. Complete freedom can be paralysing so the art, I believe, is to encourage experimentation and the growth of personal skills and knowledge through open ended but directed exercises. Consequently, and with hindsight, my view now is that I was well suited to the DS11 studio, where the setting for a design project in a specific city, offered an exceptionally open framework, but one with many potential threads of research awaiting discovery. Intensive short studies were carried out at the beginning of the first semester. I was initially sceptical of the value in these projects, impatient to move directly into the design thesis. In fact, they allowed the studio group to take its first tentative steps towards collectively amassing a breadth of research in a short space of time through studies that encouraged exploration without a predetermined research agenda. In my view this represents the true value of studio culture, where students are freed from the competitive constraints of trying to seize on an 'idea'; instead fruitful, valuable and engaging conversation ensues and a shared knowledge is realised, to the benefit of all. DS11 subsequently, asked its students to produce 'a catalogue', a useful technique designed to allow each individual to curate this abundant shared knowledge and tease out individual ideas and interests. Students approach this in a variety of creative ways but for me this became a somewhat mechanistic process of recording and analysing the mass of ideas partially formed in the first few weeks. By doing so I was able to identify patterns and overlapping interests inherent in non-linear thinking, and a programme began to reveal itself. From this point, my thesis project progressed in a relatively straightforward manner; the catalogue provided a useful reference document to return to when my ideas appeared conflicted or cloudy, and served as a reminder of the ambition for the project. The studio left me with the skills to interrogate a conceptual or formal 'idea' and to have confidence in the 'testing phase' which is an essential part of the design process; through conversation and the exchange of ideas this leads to resolution, even if that is not always immediately clear. It has left me with enthusiasm for research and an appreciation of analysis and rigour with which I have always identified. My thesis project developed to reveal an ongoing interest in community architecture and public buildings and projects, which I was keen to pursue in practice.

I currently work for Walters&Cohen Architects, who over twenty years have built up a portfolio of public, educational and cultural projects. I remain passionate about projects of this nature, but what I have come to appreciate more directly in practice is the design studio's attitude to its body of collective work. Walters &Cohen passionately believes in research and each project is seen as a new opportunity to learn from, and in turn test out, ideas developed previously. Two projects stand out for me in how they shaped the practice's 'research' ethos. The Department for Education's (DfE) Building Schools for the Future initiative provided an opportunity to study how children learn, and design a model school based on this research. The ambition was to design an inspiring, flexible and innovative learning environment. The key is a central space, the 'heart' of the building: a multi-purpose linking space, generous and dynamic, available for gathering, presentations, and display and project based learning. It is intended to be a space that can be tailored to the individual needs of the school, creating a unique identity.

The design influenced policy guidance on 'learning spaces' and its key principles have been successfully implemented in several primary schools. Ten years later, the practice was approached by The Scottish Futures Trust to research and design a reference school that can be scaled up, or down, for use across Scotland. This was a useful reminder of the principles developed in the DfE model school and highlighted the progression of the practice's ideas and experiences. The practice places particular importance on the early RIBA work stages; thorough client consultation enhances and guides research, and the way that a client uses existing space is analysed to build a comprehensive understanding of the brief. Collaborative workshops are encouraged and occur regularly throughout the design process; all members of the team are listened to, including the client who is viewed as an essential part of the team. Ultimately this process makes for better buildings, something which is often acknowledged in post-occupancy assessments. For myself, it is wonderful to feel that the design of the schools I am involved with not only support the individual client and the particular needs of one school, but

also that my participation contributes to something wider: a knowledge base created in embodied research. I can see many parallels with the academic design studio here. While naturally the all-embracing freedom of the studio cannot completely translate into practice, given the realities of project constraints, the principles of an open dialogue and the exchange of ideas and research translate well. I feel that it is important for the architectural studio to recognise this and to encourage these practices.

Hannah Gaze: BArch University of Sheffield, DipArch University of Westminster. Currently employed at Walters&Cohen Architects (2014 –)

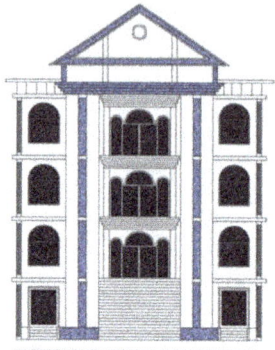
FIG A

FIG B

FIG C

FIG D

FIG F

FIG E

FIG G

FIG H

FIG J

FIG I

Romani Palaces

FIG L

FIG K

A STUDY OF THE ROMANI PALACES OF BUZESCU, HUEDIN AND SINTESTI, ROMANIA

MATTHEW STEWART

STUDIO: MYTHS OF A RECURRENT PRESENT

Coming from a regional university with a localised, green architectural agenda, studying in London at MArch level began as a bewildering experience. Previously 'baptised' through the 'year system' and a 'one size fits all' approach towards design projects during BArch, where the merits of top-down oversight and tight control of the curriculum gave way to rigid conformity, the first day of the March course felt an altogether different beast. Formally introduced to the studio system through a series of 'pitches' from respective tutors, what immediately stood out was the lack of a school style, demonstrated in the range of research interests, studio themes, exotic field-trips and representational techniques on show. The sheer diversity of output from each studio was dizzying, and so we're told, testament to the health and vitality of architectural education at Part II. There's an approach for everyone, whatever your creed or disposition. But the excitement soon gives way to a feeling of being overwhelmed as you are expected to make immediate studio choices and your day suddenly becomes a trip to Westfield. Do you choose the hand-drawing studio or the parametric one? The one that's interested in digital craft, or the anti-architecture studio? Can you realistically afford the tour to south China or is south London more practical?

Looking back, the anxiety inducing spectacle of that first day where studios were sold as if commodities, lies the heart of architectural education today. Almost every school of architecture has taken Alvin Boyarsky's Architectural Association market based model as a standard at Part II, finding its expression through end of year shows, catalogues, books, blogs, awards and ceremonies. A structure with its roots in 1970s radicalism and a reaction to the bureaucratic tendencies of modernist education, is today an all-encompassing behemoth across the country. Counter-culture has morphed into a dogmatic establishment. The argument for the studio or unit system is one of pluralism, autonomy and competition: by offering more choice to students, they are exposed to a variety of diverging positions and encouraged to specialise. Ignoring the uneasy coupling with the forced marketisation of the increased need to attract funding and students, is this really the case?

Recently I found myself reading Tristes Tropiques, Claude Levi-Strauss' travelogue and informal primer of structuralism; one passage stood out, concerning the myth of the absolute where he argues that human societies fail to create 'absolutely' and that the customs of any culture on the contrary may be defined in a hypothetical periodic table. Could the contemporary culture of architectural education be read in a similar vein? Levi-Strauss' idea of an inner structural logic challenges assumptions of unbridled progress. It suggests that a fixation on pluralism should be countered with equal attention to the hidden structures that govern and bind architectural culture together. Applied to the nature of the studio, this could encourage us to think beyond the apparitions of studio individualism, with its own customs and inevitable focus on the 'now', promoting a wider scope in order to recognise the recurrence of unresolved themes within architectural history that lurk beneath the surface. It might examine critically studio themes that are pursued through advanced technology and innovation— data driven design, algorithms and scripting digital fabrication— identified with an 'output' that takes for granted more traditional forms of functionalism and the urge for efficiency, a trust in technological utopianism or a romantic faith in the role of natural systems. It may also question the renewed thirst for making, 'doing' and craft, promoted by studios; not a wildly new phenomenon, but one rooted in the nineteenth century guise of romanticism's opposition to utilitarianism. By stressing the links between studios, rather than celebrating difference it might reveal a setup as begrudgingly predictable as the year system it replaced.

But demystifying the studio also serves a wider purpose. If certain themes appear and reappear at particular times, it is important to understand the conditions that influence this cycle as one both intellectual and material. In doing so, we shed light on our own cultural predicament. The objective reality where these conditions can be seen to take a material form, and therefore be analysed, is the urban. And it raises the question of how urbanity is approached: studios often affect to jostle with the issue—either directly by treating the city as object or indirectly through the 'context' of architectural proposals, or indeed by consciously rejecting the urban altogether. Today, it has become an unfortunate truism—if not a cliché—to say that the city is marked by distinct winners and losers. Countless articles, over the years, have been written about accelerated urban restructuring: the loss of public assets, displacement and precariousness; the privatization of public space; austerity and gradual institutional decline; gated condominiums, cupcake communities and gentrification; rapid technological change and the slow environmental apocalypse. Education seems very distant from this reality on the ground.

Since graduating from Westminster I have witnessed these phenomena both personally and professionally, as will countless of others working as architectural assistants in London. This became particularly clear working in the housing sector for two years, laying bare the paradox of practicing architecture after university: we work on projects that we will never

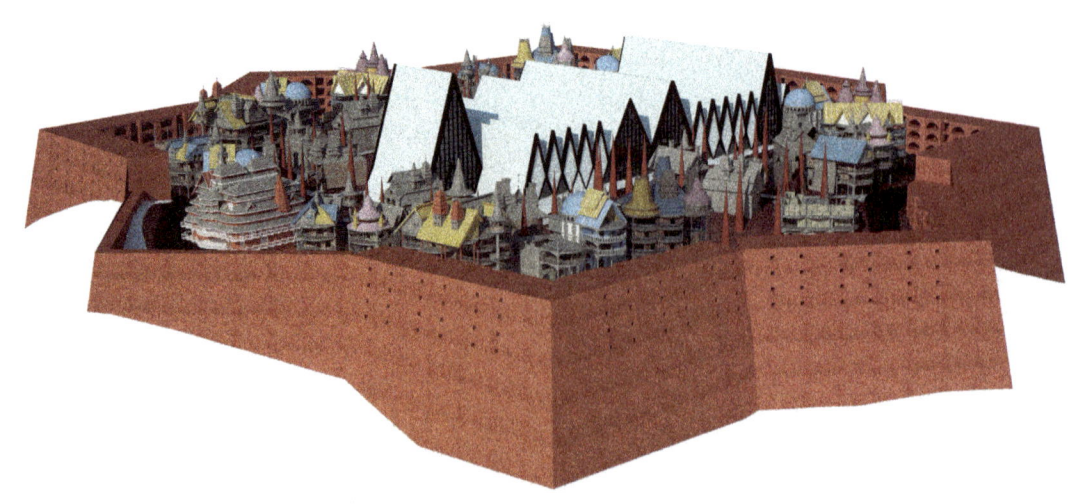

be able to afford to live in, for clients who have no stake in the city, while simultaneously fuelling the fire that makes the city increasingly unaffordable. Yet we still inhabit a privileged position—a reality-check emphasised while briefly working with housing activists fighting estate 'regeneration'. Discovering the role architectural practice's have played, and continue to play in this process; the contrast between the disregard shown to residents and the kudos attached to award nominations for the 'effort', was striking. But if myth hides the customary nature of studio education and its disconnection from real life, it is enforced by a wider separation of design studio teaching from the study of architectural history. The autonomy of each studio to set its own agenda; to disregard, adopt, misuse or pillage the relics of history for their own cause; creates a lack of accountability as to what serves as relevant discourse. It feeds a culture identified with the 'end of history' as if there is no alternative, further robbing us of an understanding of our own historical specificity. Time grows out of 'sync'; the present plays on a loop, and the past and future are put on hold.

Matthew Stewart: BArch University of Kent, MArch University of Westminster. Currently teaches first year on the BA Architecture course at UoW while working as a freelance designer and writer. Previously worked in practice with Studio Mcleod, Byoung Soo Cho Architects and Approach Architecture Studio, and as a researcher with URBZ.

16/17
BUDAPEST

B

ARCHITECTURES OF STASIS AND FLUX

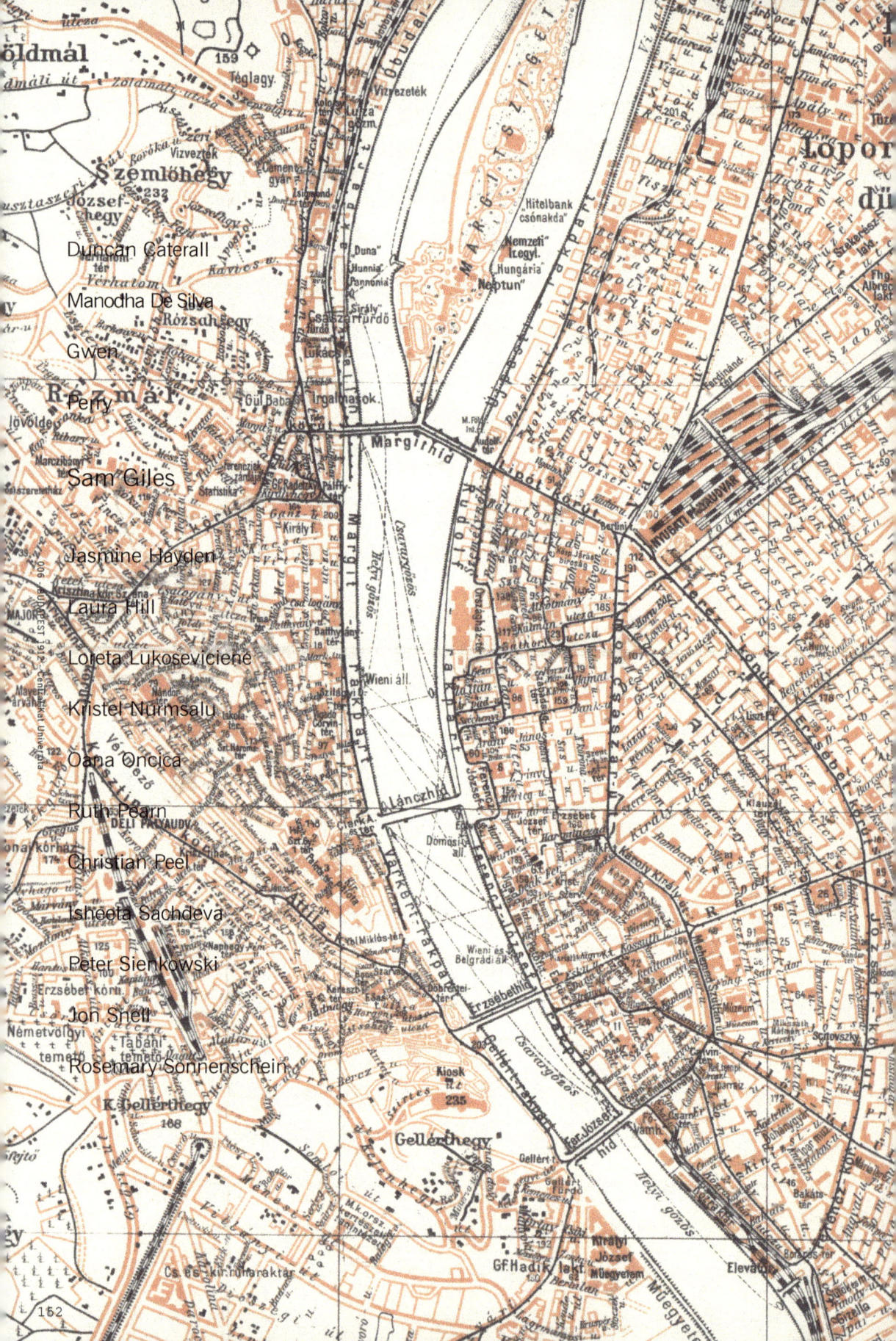

2016/17

BUDAPEST:
NORTHERN HUNGARY

BUDAPESTI:
ARCHITECTURES OF STASIS AND FLUX

Landmarks:

MAGYAR TUDOMÁNYOS AKADÉMIA/ AQUINCUM MITHRAEUM/BUDAVÁRI PALOTA/FŐVÁROSI NAGYCIRKUSZ/ CITADELLA/VÁROSLIGETI MŰJÉGPÁLYA/ VÍGSZÍNHÁZ/VÁRSZÍNHÁZ/DUNA PALOTA/ ERZSÉBET-KILÁTÓ/MAGYAR ÁLLAMI OPERAHÁZ/RÁKOSI-BUNKER/ HALÁSZBÁSTYA/LISZT FERENC ZENEMŰVÉSZETI EGYETEM/GELLÉRTHEGYI KÁLVÁRIA/GELLÉRTHEGYI-BARLANG/ CAFÉ GERBEAUD/ÜVEGHÁZ/GOZSDU- UDVAR/NAGYVÁSÁRCSARNOK/GRESHAM- PALOTA/MAGYAR NEMZETI BANK/HUNNIA/ KRISZTINA TÉRI ISKOLA/SZABADSÁG- SZOBOR/ PESTI MAGYAR SZÍNHÁZ/ MÁTYÁS KÚTJA/MŰVÉSZETEK PALOTÁJA/ NAGYTÉTÉNY/ORSZÁGOS SZÉCHÉNYI KÖNYVTÁR/NEMZETISZINHAZ/ÚJÉPÜLET/ ORSZÁGHÁZ/PETŐFI CSARNOK/SÁNDOR- PALOTA/BUDAPESTI ÉRTÉKTŐZSDE/ TSCHÖGLHAZ/VAJDAHUNYAD VÁRA/ VIGADÓ/FŐVÁROSI ÁLLAT- ÉS NÖVÉNYKERT/KIRÁLY FÜRDŐ/GELLÉRT FÜRDŐ/RUDAS FÜRDŐ/SZT. LUKÁCS GYÓGYFÜRDŐ/SZÉCHENYI-GYÓGYFÜRDŐ/ ÁRPÁD HÍD/ERZSÉBET HÍD/SZABADSÁG HÍD/MEGYERI HÍD/MARGIT HÍD/ SZÉCHENYI LÁNCHÍD/RÁKÓCZI HÍD/ PETŐFI HÍD/ASTORIA/HOTEL GELLÉRT/ FŐVÁROSI KÖZGYŰLÉS/FŐRENDIHÁZ/M1 A FÖLDALATTI/ANDRÁSSY ÚT/DEÁK FERENC TÉR/ OKTOGON/VÁCI UTCA/VÖRÖSMARTY TÉR/SZENT ISTVÁN-BAZILIKA/ RUMBACH UTCAI ZSINAGÓGA/GÜL BABA TÜRBE/ SZILÁGYI DEZSŐ/ VÁRKÁPOLNA/MÁTYÁS- TEMPLOM/ BUDAPESTI EVANGÉLIKUS EGYHÁZAK/DOHÁNY UTCAI ZSINAGÓGA/ NAGY ZSINAGÓGA/ VÁROSLIGET/ ÓBUDAI-SZIGET/ MARGIT-SZIGET/ NÉPRAJZI MÚZEUM/MAGYAR FÖLDTANI ES GEOFIZIKAI INTÉZET/MAGYAR TERMÉSZETTUDOMÁNYI MÚZEUM/ MAGYAR MŰSZAKI ÉS KÖZLEKEDÉSI MÚZEUM/FŐVÁROSI SZABÓ ERVIN KÖNYVTÁR/MAGYAR NEMZETI MÚZEUM/ SZÉPMŰVÉSZETI MÚZEUM/HŐSÖK TERE/ MŰCSARNOK/VAJDAHUNYAD VÁRA/ BUDAPEST-NYUGATI/BUDAPEST-KELETI PÁLYAUDVAR/HADTÖRTÉNETI INTÉZET ÉS MÚZEUM/DÉLI PÁLYAUDVAR

Coordinates:

47°29′33″N 19°03′05″E

Region:

Közép-aMagyarország

Area:

525.2 km2

Elevation:

96-527 m

Population:

1880	402,706	—
1890	560,079	+39.1%
1900	861,434	+53.8%
1910	1,110,453	+28.9%
1920	1,232,026	+10.9%
1930	1,442,869	+17.1%
1940	1,712,791	+18.7%
1950	1,590,316	-7.2%
1960	1,804,606	+13.5%
1970	1,945,083	+7.8%
1980	2,059,226	+5.9%
1990	2,016,681	-2.1%
2000	1,777,921	-11.8%
2005	1,697,343	-4.5%
2010	1,721,556	+1.4%
2016	1,764,263	+2.5%

Demonym(s):

Budapesti

Patron Saint:

Szent István király

The choice of Budapest as the location and focus of our studio projects this year relates to an initial interest in the constitution of twin cities, where 'twinning' as a theme might be understood at different scales: from the transnational context to that of the city itself, its urban districts, buildings and interiors. If 'twinning' denotes similarity, then 'singularity' promotes contrasts and conditions the dialogue between extremes suggested by our central theme: 'architectures of stasis and flux'.

Budapest originated in two settlements on either side of the Danube. Buda set against hills rising from the river and Pest developed from the medieval city as grid-planned districts on the wider Hungarian plain. The experience of circumscribed density and interiority in Pest, contrasts with the open panorama of the view from Buda's neighbouring hills. Budapest's largely C19th infrastructure existed within the shadow of Vienna as capital of the Austro-Hungarian Empire; whether as a twin, a copy, a simulation or a duplicate. The empire's identity, just as that of the EU, was confounded by emergent national identities, paralleling the schism between a metropolitan modernism and a provincial postmodernism. Consequently the culture of Budapest remained ambivalent, paralleling the modernist culture of 'Vienna 1900' upriver, but distinct in the details and iconography of its architecture, its own 'school' of psychoanalysis, and its own hinterland set in the wider context of rural Hungary.

As the second city of the empire Budapest retained a characteristic identity as Vienna's 'other' but with its own national credentials: twin cities separated by the 'iron curtain' of the Cold War, their fabric conserved in the west and eroded in the east. With the fall of Communism, the city has experienced renovation and development, focused inward as a tourist icon of Mitteleuropa but one subject to the global flux of neoliberalism. The contrasting eddies and flows of the Danube are indifferent to 'history', yet remain fundamental in isolating the political history and the contemporary post-industrial condition of Csepel Island to the south. Flows which areanalogous perhaps to the correspondences and transactions between separate parts of the city. Numerical districts incorporate the routines of everyday life, while subject to the vagaries of the city's tourist economy. How do we view Budapest, contrary to the logic of Brexit, located at the intersection of transnational regions and part of the infrastructure of the Danube? A 'post-dated', if cohesive, urban fabric whose C21st credentials will be tested in projects that, as interventions, recognise, incorporate or reject, the culture, themes, form and history of the city, as intrinsic aspects of their various architectures.

There are two ways of describing the city of Budapest: you can speak about 'the form of the city', that is about its topology, the relationship between centre and periphery, kernel and outskirts, working-class and upper-class districts, about nature and culture (in the city), and all this would be no different from those images we see with half-shut eyes after long and aimless days of roving, and which we might call geometric fantasies...

There is another Budapest. In the mirror of the Danube...Not everything that seems valuable above the mirror maintains its force when mirrored. The twin cities are not equal, because nothing that exists or happens in Budapest is symmetrical: every face and gesture is answered, from the mirror, by a face and gesture inverted, point by point. The two Budapests live for each other, their eyes interlocked; but there is no love between them. (10)
(Peter Esterházy, The Glance of Countess Hahn-Hahn)

04 YEAR ONE: RECONFIGURING THE BATHS

01 THE WORLD OF THE INTERIOR
001 recess
002 psychoanalysing the room

02 TAKING (TO) THE WATERS
001 Danubian
002 the pleasures of stasis

03 WATER TABLE
001 reclaiming the underground
002 geothermal conditions

03 CATALOGUE
001 hierarchy and construct

04 YEAR TWO: ARCHITECTURE OF STASIS AND FLUX

02 TAKING (TO) THE WATERS
001 Danubian
002 The Pleasures of Stasis

INTRODUCTION

This is the second two-week design project. The theme is conceived as metaphorical rather than literal in unlocking the potential of the stair, lift and escalator, to exceed their functionality in an imagined fluidity. Conversely the image of the static pool epitomises the inner logic of quiescent space, but equally at any 'threshold of arrival' space is momentarily anticipatory, and directional movement paused.

The next programme repeats the pattern of the first two weeks, working individually then collectively. The theme focuses on the relationship between Budapest and the Danube, city and river, in terms of the opposing qualities of stasis and flux as 'natural' phenomena, in architectural space and form, and in the realm of urban fabric and city life. The intention is to examine in what way these qualities have a metaphorical relationship with an urban architecture, where a diverse fluidity of assembly and arrival in the public realm, is tempered by a rationality that controls movement and access to anticipatory spaces from which the audience, spectators, or participants, are finally released into the space of the event (meeting, spectacle or performance).

AQUEOUS HUMOR

As a concept employed to conceptualise the fluid spatial qualities of Le Corbusier's architecture, the term may also be associated with the concept of undifferentiated or peripheral urban space (terrain vague), subject to the flux and flow of the urban economy and social life. In direct contrast, the concept of a 'corridor' (or 'bridge') channels movement in a directional 'connectivity', whether domestic, institutional or urban, often associated with the separation or zoning of activities and uses, endemic to the rigours of functionalism.

THE URBAN CORRIDOR

A straight and narrow street, arcade, or wider avenue, may function as a corridor. Equally a linear swathe of urban space or infrastructure; the product perhaps of demolition, redevelopment or urban landscaping; constitutes an urban corridor of different kind. If the use of the corridor in buildings is associated with an instrumental mentality, it has also been conceived as the space of unsuspected meetings and events beyond the frame of its institutional connotation.

Conventionally stasis (or entropy) in architecture is associated with the concept of a 'reflective' space, but for the purposes of this study / project it is conceived differently. That is as a momentary condition, pause or threshold space, between arrival and departure. In a classical tradition this would be associated with the formality of the 'ante-chamber'; in certain institutions with the generic 'waiting room' and, more generously in a cultural context, with the anticipatory nature of a public 'foyer'. Just as the empty theatre awaits a performance, these different spatial types anticipate an appointment, a meeting, an event or spectacle.

Whatever one's attitude to the relation between stasis and flux in the occupation and use of buildings, or conceptions of fluidity and redundancy, our interest here is how the instrumental and the un-programmed may be folded in on each other, as in the dis-functional corridor, the potential sociability of the waiting room or the ambivalent character of the foyer.

02 INTRODUCTION TAKING (TO) THE WATERS

■ 001 Danubian
002 The Pleasures of Stasis

Budapest's identity is at one with the Danube, its waters, histories and mythology, its ferries, barges, cargos, industries and technologies of transportation, just as urban buildings require their systems of movement and channelling of people coming and going. In the 'theoretical' city persistent biological metaphors link the functionalist 'discipline of the route'; informing patterns of 'circulation' in modernist buildings; to digital rhetoric about connectivity, spatial flow and flux (whether aesthetic or neoliberal).

Your initial study is to investigate the threshold between the city and the river, based on two themes: the aesthetic and the functional. Choose between a focus on experiencing the river from the city, or alternatively on the transfer or transport of people and goods between the two.

Bring together three modes of movement associated with the stair, and the two mechanisms of the lift (crane or hoist) and the escalator (travelator or conveyer belt). The stair may celebrate 'movement' in its static form, design, detailing and configuration, but it is as often a mundane service element, providing empirical access and egress, as a *repetitive utilitarian presence. The service or public lift comes as a mechanical package whose housing, interior, signage and momentary threshold or point of entry and exit, is habitually connected to the anonymous office, or hotel, lobby or corridor. The escalator as a mechanism is designed to convey the expectant flow of people between levels, but in a retail environment it is sometimes deployed to create a surrogate conviction of accessibility to otherwise marginal spaces.*

You are asked to create a 'infrastructure' that interrelates the three elements (repeated as you see fit). This may incorporate a directional surface (wall/plane, floor/ground, roof/ceiling) or the notion of a wider 'envelope' or enclosure. Essentially this is the design of a threshold that heightens experience of city and river and/or functions as a transfer mechanism. Any 'accommodation' included should be limited to a single room or container (of any scale –but which might be related to your previous project). We are looking for you to exceed normative arrangements and to design a rhetorical architecture of movement.

INITIAL STUDY

01 experience or transfer
02 three elements
03 infrastructure
04 directionality or fluidity
05 piece or fragment

PRESENTATION

01 axonometric or model
02 representing continuity plan/section
03 detail 1:10
04 on location

02 INTRODUCTION TAKING (TO) THE WATERS

001 Danubian
■ 002 The Pleasures of Stasis

Budapest is a city of bathhouses (Roman, Ottoman or C19th) and the pool, whether single or an aggregation with different characteristics, remains traditionally a static space of intimate reflection or communal sociability. This has been transformed into a spectacle of hedonistic leisure in its contemporary manifestation, with roots in the C19th spa and the growth of health tourism in 'taking to the waters'

Rather than asking you now to design a bathhouse, we are instead proposing you design a 'space of assembly' (of any scale: communal, local or XL), but one that incorporates a threshold condition as the precursor to 'an event space' (or an 'assemblage' of spaces). The particularity of the threshold is juxtaposed with the received typology of the main space (or spaces) which is conceived as a generic type (copy and paste). In contrast the threshold will be the main focus of your detailed design. Your conception of 'assembly' may be social, political or cultural; permanent or temporary; but equally technological or industrial as in an 'assembly line' (or indeed a craft 'production' process). A cultural variant would view an exhibition as an assembly. The overall agenda is open to your group's interpretation, but the architectural moves are intended to be more specific.

Your design of the threshold: foyer, waiting room, ante-chamber or concourse, will likely relate to wider external public spaces, but it is the currency of the 'in-between' that interests us: stair(s), passages, lifts, linkages, bridges, or escalators, all of which are part of a 'threshold of arrival'.

The proposal is to be conceived as a direct intervention in one the districts of the city adjacent to the river. Each group is asked to select one of the following five areas in which to locate their 'assembly':

Upstream N/NW
(II or island)
Upstream N/NE
(V)
Central E
(IV)
Downstream S/SW
(XI)
Downstream S/SE
(IX or Csepel)

Delineate the boundary of the particular district in relation to where the 'assembly' is located, typically at a representative sub-centre, one that gravitates towards, or is connected to, the river in some way. The notion of an 'urban corridor': as an existing condition; fictional or abstract concept; experiential route or proposed urban transformation; should link the 'assembly' to the riverside where one of each group's infrastructures should be relocated. It is not expected that the assembly itself be in direct proximity to the river (but that may be the case).

DESIGN PROJECT

01 district location
02 assembly
03 threshold of arrival
04 stasis and movement
05 urban corridor

FINAL PRESENTATION

01 district site plan
02 interface (generic figure/space of arrival)
03 sections/view into assembly/configuration
04 patterns of movement
05 urban connectivity

06_BT_SS_007_001_157_P164_SP

06_BT_SS_041_002_158_P164_EP

06_BT_SS_005_003_159_P164_A

06_BT_SS_009_004_160_P164_E

06_BT_SS_008_014_170_P164_A

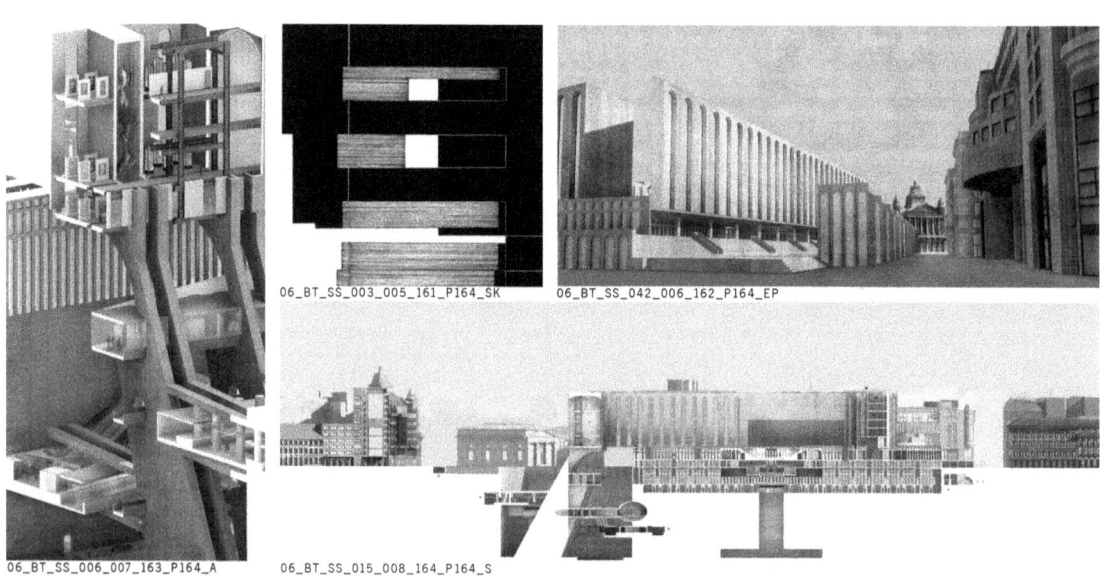
06_BT_SS_003_005_161_P164_SK

06_BT_SS_042_006_162_P164_EP

06_BT_SS_006_007_163_P164_A

06_BT_SS_015_008_164_P164_S

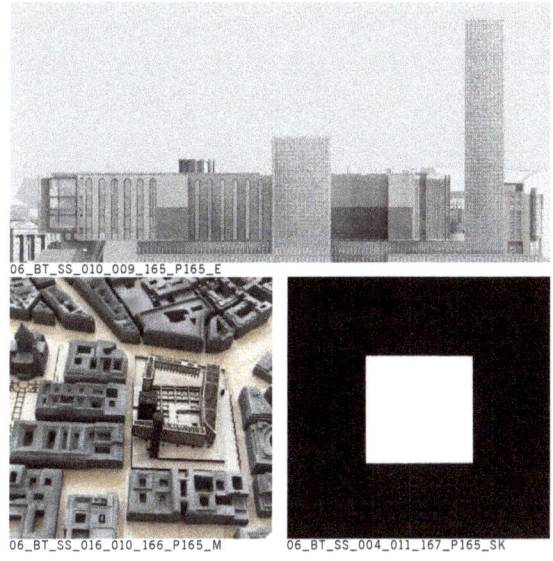

06_BT_SS_010_009_165_P165_E

06_BT_SS_016_010_166_P165_M   06_BT_SS_004_011_167_P165_SK

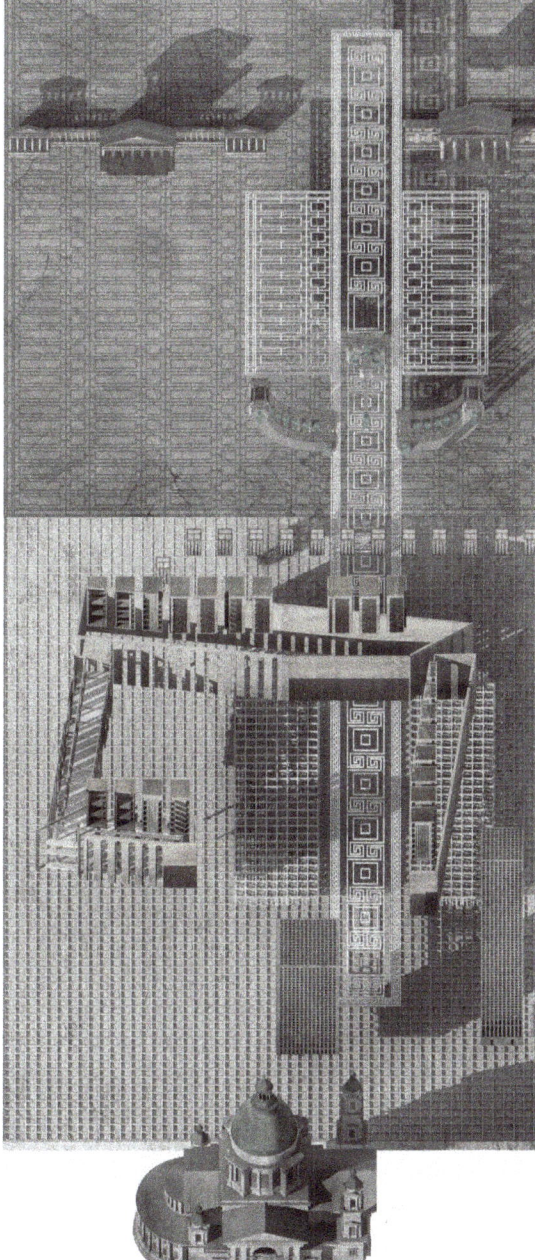

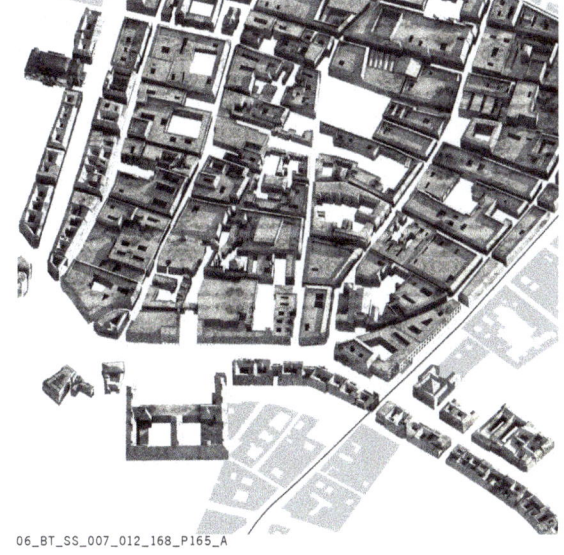

06_BT_SS_007_012_168_P165_A   06_BT_SS_007_013_169_P165_C

SAM GILES

PLUS ÇA CHANGE

I have less than fond memories of fumbling through Part 1 deadlines, reviews, tutorials and external examinations that provide a useful reminder of the necessity of coming-up-short. The inevitability of being caught out by the realisation you are not quite as clever as you half-thought, remains one of the more valuable lessons learnt in the studio. Reminiscences ingrain an otherwise inadequate sense of humility, a sort of ritual in itself, initiated through the 'crit'. In its various forms, the pinning up of work reveals the currency and limitations of the best you have managed to do; so shortcomings turn into personal failures and assaults on pride occasionally turn into tears. It remains fashionable to bemoan the cruel-to-be-kind culture of critting, but less so to 'celebrate' the first time an academic failing comes to so direct a point. The receipt of a piece of paper, codified with letters from the alphabet (or is it numerical now?) just doesn't force re-appraisal the same way a thirty second bout of silence does. And so it was, when I left Cardiff University in 2013, that I received a piece of paper codified with the digits '2.2', An outcome that had by then long been prophesised by a string of silences that I could unfortunately call my own.

Why do I mention all this? Four years later I could boast another piece of paper, bearing a more positive outcome, those silences replaced by occasional applause. From far less than ideal circumstances I had been accepted into Westminster and provided with a chance to redeem the benefits of what was now a much thicker skin. With all this in mind, it was easy hope for immediate success to follow, but there has of course been another layer of ritual humiliation that all aspiring architects must endure. It is that inheritance of the 'crit' – the much dreaded architecture 'interview'. Faltering presentations and floundering tutorials, with the dispiriting looks of boredom and frustration that follow, never really stay at the studio door. In the bubble of architectural practice a smiling receptionist and complimentary cup of tea might furnish an illusion that you are somewhere else, perhaps in the lofty world of construction. The formalities, however, of failing to convince the stranger across the room continue their hold on one's psyche. A meeting of personalities, tastes, expectations and evidence of ability (or lack of) combine to furnish a deeply personal experience (unavailable to many other professions). My own stories of enduring the admissions process furnish an additional layer of experience invaluable to a continuing grasp of how the profession operates beyond design and detailing. 'Admission', when viewed at either end of the stages of graduation, remains markedly similar in conduct, exemplifying the translation of studio culture into the seemingly less insular world of professional practice. It is, needless to say, a painful education.

Cast eyes back to 2015...

ROYAL COLLEGE OF ART
PART II STUDY
MARCH 2015

Royal College of Art - Part II Entry

My younger self arrives at 3:40, 20 minutes in advance for an interview scheduled at 4:00. Apparently, there is a slight delay...

Interview commences at 5:40,

The Panel consists of a Part II student, head of year Alex De Rijke and tutor Konstantinos Grigoriadis. All look exhausted.
AdR welcomes me to the RCA and notes that there are only 20 minutes to conduct the interview given that time is short.

AdR: "We are low on time so we would only like to see one project that you consider to be your most important".
SG: "Yes..[caught off guard]...I..." Proceed to explain project involving protest and designing a space for the activity in Parliament Square, and mention my tutor was Peter Salter in a bid to impress.

AdR "Is this all you have?"
SG: "For now...yes"

* Silence - roughly 10 seconds *

Pt.II: "So...[struggling]...what do you think protest means in this country?"
SG: "Well...this is a country that doesn't do revolution, we wait until the very last moment until change is necessary..." Begin to talk too fast, then panic slightly when AdR/KG fail to make eye contact. Discuss the 1832 Reform Act, 1867, 1884, forget to mention the 'Occupy' protests, and subsequently increase speed of delivery, Pt.II looks confused or slightly concerned, unsure. AdR, now flicking through portfolio book, looks bored.
AdR - [interjecting] "Well, yes I suppose you are right, this is not a reactive country...[pauses, pushes work aside, then looks up]...have you ever seen the movie *If?* ?"
SG: "The movie whose lead actor was in clockwork orange?"
[AdR finally allows a slight smile, KG continues to gaze vacantly, having not asked anything yet]"...I remember the scene with the motorbike, where they steal it and joy ri...
AdR - [interjecting] "Well yes, obviously, the bike and the girl represent freedom and the desire to escape" - proceeds to link scenes of nudity with protest.
SG: "I was actually thinking about the ending, where they revol...[LOUD BANG]

* BANG BANG BANG *

AdR - "Ah! Okay, well, sorry, that knocking means 20 minutes is up, was there anything you wanted to ask us?"

* Silence - roughly 10 seconds and 30 seconds packing up, KG stands...*

KG: "Thank you for your time".
AdR: "Yes, thank you. We will let you know shortly".

Rejection Letter arrives 3 weeks later

ARCHITECTURAL ASSOCIATION
PART II STUDY
MARCH 2015

Architectural Association - Part II Entry

Arrive at 2:20, confidence slightly dented following RCA experience. No delay this time, multiple panels operating, lead to the corresponding room by friendly AA assistant. Settles nerves.

5 minutes waiting, am informed the interviewer just needs a quick break. Door suddenly opens, step back, and Konstantinos Grigoriadis exits, pauses and stares.

KG: "Oh...it's you again".

* Silence - 7 seconds *

5 more minutes of waiting, then proceed to enter with Benjamin John Reynolds who was also waiting. He explains that due to time constraints he would only like to discuss what is considered my most important project.
SG: "Yes..[speaking too fast]...I recently redesigned my third year project..." Proceed to re-explain project involving protest and designing a space for it in Parliament Square, consciously emphasising that Peter Salter, formerly of AA and currently of Walmer Road Houses fame, was my tutor. Still a chance to impress, good stock and all that. Bid ends.

Silence - 5 seconds *

BJR - "Is this all you have, do you have any larger drawings?"
SG: "Well, I have these..." Provides drawings already set out on table

* Silence - 5 seconds *

BJR - "Do you not have anymore at all?"

* Silence - another 5 seconds, maybe *

SG: "Well, these are my most important drawings..."

* Silence - 10 seconds, definitely *

BJR - [Sighing] "Well, could you tell us why you decided to apply to the AA in particular?"

SG - [Shakey] "Well, I have fostered connections here for some time now, this is a unique place, but...of course...you don't need me to explain that...[evidently]..." 5-10 minutes of improvisation follow, BJR looks suitably uncomfortable, KG ambiguously inquires 'what do you hope to receive from the AA?' Why do neither of them seem to be smiling?

Taking 5 seconds to look at watch

BJR - "I think we'll have to leave it there. Was there anything you wanted to ask us?"
SG: "Um, no, I think that was everything".

* Silence - roughly 5 seconds and 60 seconds packing up, both say "thank you", KG stands up... *

KG - [slight smile] - "Well, pleasure to see you again" - [awkward chuckle].

Rejection letter arrives 1 week before the RCA's does.

WESTMINSTER UNIVERSITY PART II STUDY MARCH 2015

University of Westminster - Part II Entry

RCA/AA fates still unknown, waiting interviews to be held collectively in the Robin Evans Room, causing slightly nervous looks across to the table concerned. Allocated as last in my slot.

A fellow student on the interview list claims to be writing a book on Passivhaus, which dampens my confidence and returns after 20 minutes, dejected or maybe defeated, unsure - "He just stared at me. When I told him about my book he asked what use it was here?" Now feeling mildly ill, soon to be left in the now empty room, last on all lists as it turns out. Name called. Step up to desk, interviewers are Part II student and grinning tutor named Andrew Peckham.

AP: [shuffling notes] "so you're... Sam...Giles are you?"
SG: "I am...yes"
AP: [now smiling] "Ah yes, you're an interesting one Sam. I've read your application very carefully...you know we don't tend to give interviews here to people with 2.2s."
SG: "...I"
AP: "Well it's nearly lunch-time, can we just get straight to your most important project."
Proceed to re-re-explain project involving protest and designing a space for that in Parliament Square, consciously emphasising that Peter Salter, still formerly of AA and currently Walmer Road houses fame, was tutoring it. This may hel...
AP: [grimacing] "Peter Salter, God, they put you with him?"
Pt.II: "Who?"
AP: "One of these AA types, [mumbles, inaudible], unbearable. [adjusts expression] Did you bring one of these essays we asked for, I suppose we should take a look".
SG: "Yes, I did" Proceed to present paen to Tadao Ando, entitled 'How do we reintroduce a sense of meaning to contemporary architecture'.
AP: "So what is that exactly?"
SG: "Well, it talks about phenomenology, Heidegger, Norberg Schulz and compares that to Tadao Ando's writings on his Rokko Housing..." Explanation lasts all but 2 minutes.
AP: [Grimacing] "Do you buy all this stuff about phenomenology?"
SG: [Sweating] "In what way..."
AP: [Grinning again] You are aware Heidegger was actually an Nazi?"
SG: "Not Really".
AP: "Everyone obsesses over him, no one seems to know, they had that 'New School of Phenomenology' in Cambridge. [now giggling] I guess you didn't know either."

* Silence, 8 seconds *

AP: "So you read?"
SG: "All the time, yes"
AP: "Anything in particular?"
SG "Richard Sennet?"
Read on the advice of an existing student of course: "it's on their reading list, read it and they'll love you. Make sure to read the tutor's books as well - they always love that."
SG: The Fall of Public Man
AP: [Grinning] "Ah yes..."
SG: "Though my favourite..."
AP: "Aha!"
Remaining conversation a blur, though the conversation draws to a cordial close.
AP: "I guess that will do, was there anything you wanted to ask us?"
Before parting, one last trick, based on further advice: "Be sure to leave a small version of your portfolio, so they remember who you are at the end, they love that."
SG: "No, I think that's everything".
AP: "Well, we'll let you know shortly, you're certainly an interesting person".
SG: [Taking out A5 portfolio] "I wanted to leave you with this in the meantime, just so you could resample my work?"
AP: [Grimacing] Ah yes! Very tactical. Very clever". [Giggles]

* Silence, swift exit, swift response, and the rest is history *

There remains a consistent pattern to these (albeit abridged) memories even though their outcomes were unpredictable. My experience in applying for professional positions following graduation is notable for demonstrating how prevalent the experiences of the studio remain afterward graduation. There is much said about the bubble of academia and the reality of practice, yet these offshoots of studio culture remain consistent in both worlds.

The demands change yet the underlying philosophy, meant to 'foster' collaborative practice, is learnt and adapted from the studio. This is one link that tethers the two, another is where a school and its collective alumni may in effect form a relationship more akin to a franchise, where attitudes to a singular approach to design continues to follow and inform one another. The end result of this crossover is to institutionalise certain philosophies in the development of professional and intellectual maturity, and key to this phenomenon remains the 'humbling process'. The 'pin-up' mutates in form but its core values subsist as a powerful reminder of the underlying rules. At least, my own development; as of yet in its early stages; owes much to these patterns of learning that have continued, and will continue, to play their part beyond the peculiar silences of formal education.

FOSTER + PARTNERS PART II POSITION JULY 2017

Foster + Partners - Part II Position

Interviewer asks for a colleague, Doug (last name omitted), UCL graduate, to join and provide a second opinion. Explain recent graduation project and a reading of Budapest. Table awash with A1 drawings in no particular order.

SG: "Was there anything else you wanted to ask?"

D: "Not really, I'm a little concerned actually, you don't strike me as particularily compatible to what we are trying to achieve here."
SG: [Caught off guard] "In what way do you mean?"
D: "Well look, what we do here is experiement, we study and advance on what we know. We push materials, technology, structure, none of this [pointing at portfolio] strikes me as having any of that."
SG: "In what way?"
D: "What evidence do you have of material experimentation? There isn't any evidence of it here. We like to experiment with materials. We used new masonry composites for our Bloomberg Office for example. We're always pushing and expanding on our expertise, it's not just about the product. Our Maggie's Centre is another example, we took the decision to use timber and push the boundaries of our task from the perspective of construction. How do you challenge structure? What do materials mean to you? How does your architecture speak for that sort of thing. There's none of that here!"
SG: "Well.."
D: "There's no need to answer, I'm just telling you."

* Silence - 5 seconds *

SG: [panicking] "Well my work wasn't really about materiality, I wanted to explore history and how the original and contemporary Budapest might intersect?"
D: "How does that work?" [Points towards the scheme's archive tower] "This is basically the Casa del Fascio in Rome" [refering to Mussolini's Palazzo della Civiltà Italiano] "I mean I was there the other week! This is fascist form".
SG: [Attempting to be lighthearted] "I trust you are not accusing me of being a fascist?"
D: "I mean, look, I just haven't seen drawings like this since...well, for years." [pointing to worms-eye perspective] "This is basically the sort of thing we liked to do in studio in the 80's. What's contemporary about it, it's just Postmodernism?"
SG: [Rising to reach for another A1] Well, maybe I can explain fur..."

* Silence - 5 seconds *

D: "This isn't an opportunity for you to prove me wrong, Again, I'm just telling you."

* Silence - another 5 seconds *

SG: [Still standing] "Well, let me explain to you anyway, I have influences from Koolhaas...which were in my Catalogue" [begin reaching for catalogue and A1 sheet in tandem] "I could also show you my dissertation?"
D: [Staring]"I don't want to see that."

* Silence - 15 seconds, fail to find relevant page, interview sours to a close *

SG: "Was there anything else you wanted to ask...again?"
D: "I think that was everything... Right, well collect your things and I'll come to see you out. But lovely graphics by the way!" [slight smile]

Exit, shake hands; hold head in hands

Rejection letter arrives 1 week later

Sam Giles: BSc Welsh School of Architecture and MArch Part II (Distinction/Silver Medal nominee) University of Westminster. Currently employed with KTB architects, previously with Darling Assosiates as a Part I Assistant. Invited critic UoW BArch.

SILESIAN FIELDS

08/09
WROCŁAW

W

RECOVERING WROCLAW / CITY AS PALIMPSEST

Stephen Cruse

Amelia Dickinson

Frances Edwards

Filipa

Fonseca-George

Robert King

Camilla Pitt

Craig Rosenblatt

Chris Raeburn

Sait Saitoglu

Edward Wood

Edward Checkley

Paul Cowling

Darren Furniss

Tom Honeyman

Sophie King O'Neil

Jamie Mayers

Helen Misselbrook

Tom Soper

Ashish Sudra

Marion Ware

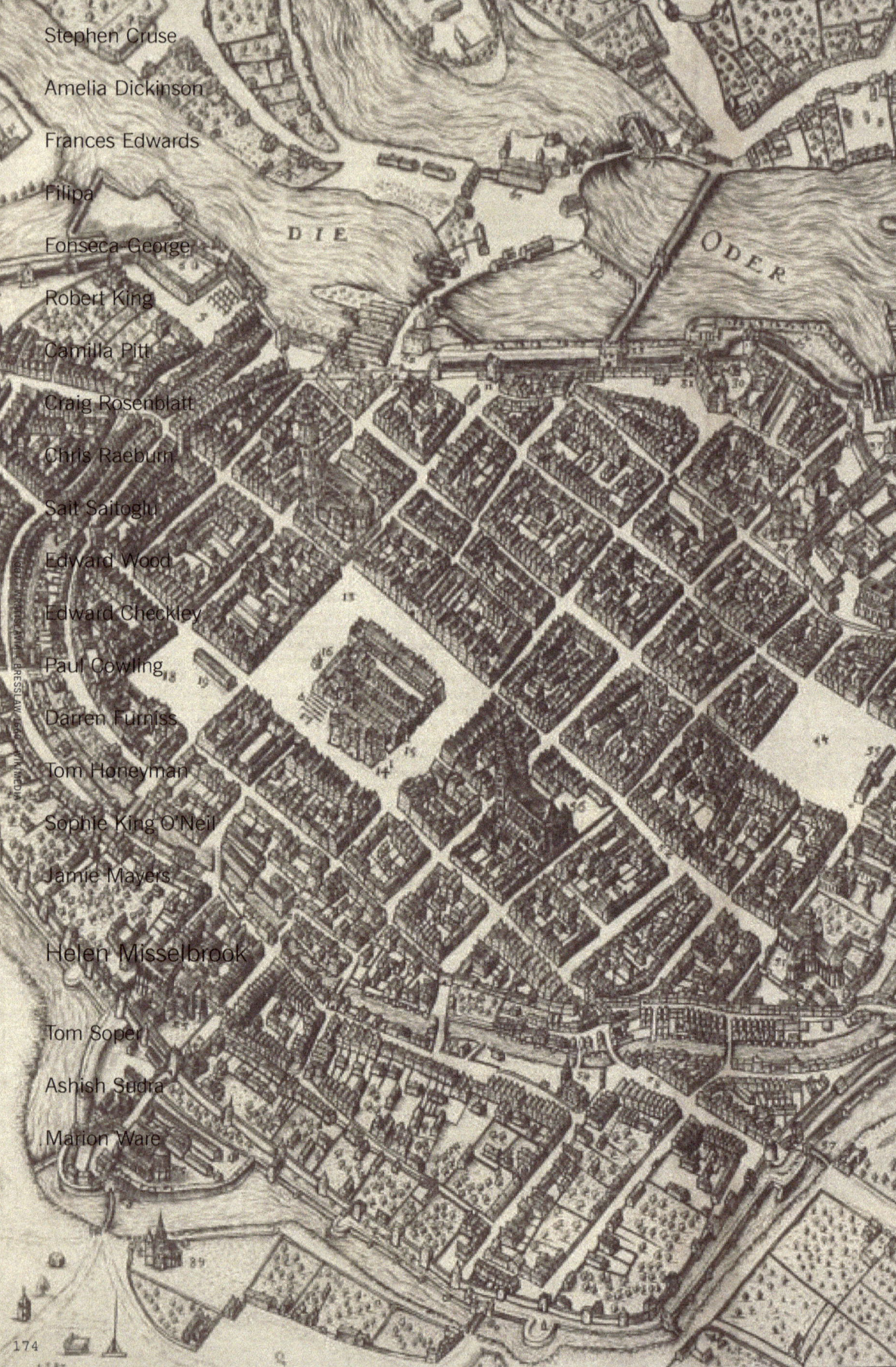

2008/2009

WROCŁAW:
WEST POLAND

WRO:
RECOVERING WROCLAW/
CITY AS PALIMPSEST/
SILESIAN FIELDS

Landmarks:

PLAC SOLNY WE WROCŁAWIU/STARY RATUSZ/HALA STULECIA/KOŚCIÓŁ ŚW. MARII MAGDALENY/KUCZCI ZWIERZĄT RZEŹNYCH/BAZYLIKA ŚW. ELŻBIETY/ARCHIKATEDRA ŚW. JANA CHRZCICIELA/OSTRÓW TUMSKI/ RYNEK/OGRÓD ZOOLOGICZNY WE WROCŁAWIU/ WROCŁAWSKA FONTANNA/ SZCZYTNICKI PARK/ WRÓBLEWSKIEGO STREET 9/OGRÓD BOTANICZNY WE WROCŁAWIU/ STADION OLIMPIJSKI/ STADION MIEJSKI WE WROCŁAWIU/ SKY TOWER/KOLEJKOWO/HYDROPOLIS/ UNIWERSYTET WROCŁAWSKI/KOŚCIÓŁ IMIENIA JEZUS WE WROCŁAWIU/ WIEZA CISNIEN/PAŁAC KRÓLEWSKI/ SYNAGOGA POD BIAŁYM BOCIANEM/ STARY CMENTARZ ŻYDOWSKI/ CMENTARZ ŻOŁNIERZY WŁOSKICH/WROCŁAW GŁÓWNY/OPERA WROCŁAWSKA/KOLEJ GONDOLOWA 'POLINKA' WE WROCŁAWIU/ ŚLĄA/PIERZEJA ZACHODNIA/ŁNOCNA PIERZEJA/PIERZEJA WSCHODNIA/ KAMIENICA/RATUSZ WIDZIANY Z PLACU SOLNEGO/MAŁA IGLICA/TARG KWIATOWY NA PLACU/CHRISTKINDLMARKT/ PIWNICA ŚWIDNICKA/MUZEUM PANA TADEUSZA/MUZEUM NARODOWE WROCŁAW/MUZEUM ARCHITEKTURY/ ORKIESTRA FILHARMONII NARODOWEJ WARSZAWIE/SZCZECIN PHILHARMONIC/ POWSZECHNY DOM TOWAROWY RENOMA/ PRĘGIERZ WE WROCŁAWIU/TEATR LALEK/ KOŚCIÓŁ ŚW. ELŻBIETY

Coordinates:
51°6′N 17°2′E

Voivodeship:
Lower Silesian

Area:
292.92 km2

Elevation:
105-155 m

Population:

1921	239,558	—
1931	250,170	+4.4%
1936	248,307	-0.7%
1951	272,522	+9.8%
1961	272,723	+0.1%
1971	271,87	-0.3%
1981	252,36	-7.2%
1991	231,100	-8.4%
2001	211,184	-8.6%
2009	205,507	-2.7%
2013	204,849	-0.3%

Demonym(s):
Vratislavian

Patron Saint:
Święta Jadwiga Śląska

This year's studio is focused on the Polish city of Wroclaw. Our particular interest is in the historical transformations and fluctuations of its Polish and past German identity (as Breslau), and its peripheral status as a city in post-war Eastern Europe. In parallel with the fluctuating borders of Poland at different historical junctures, the city has been subject to periodic change, characterized by its devastation at the end of WW2 and its current revival within the auspices of the EU (post 1989).

Thematic Studies: Production and Reproduction

Working in small groups of students from each year, two initial parallel studies will begin to develop an initial engagement with Wroclaw 'at a distance' before visiting (when the city will be studied in its full range of urban conditions, everyday life and sites of production). The formal variants produced will be sited within three different conditions of urban landscape: the interiority of the 'old' town, the disjunctive central periphery, and the wider Silesian 'field' which is construed with an ecological connotation.

Diploma One: Exhibiting Practices

The logic of collecting / the nature of installation / re-arrangement, composition and repetition

Diploma Two: Wroclaw: Vortex of History

Excavating the past / from Wolkenkratzer to Silesian Fields / three urban interventions

1920's and 1930's Wroclaw

Your research will also focus on the modernist culture of Wroclaw in the 20's and 30's which, arguably, was second only to that generated in metropolitan Berlin or the Bauhaus in Dessau and Weimar. Significantly the city's administration itself appears to *have promoted modernist trends, both in terms of town planning and urban architecture, rather than this simply being generated by local academies. Iconic buildings by Max Berg, Eric Mendlesohn and Hans Scharoun, have survived the traumatic events of 1945, though like most 'modern' buildings of that era they have become 'heritage' sites (whether renovated or derelict). Consequently, their contemporary status and condition (now) is often anomalous and requires a degree of historical reconstruction for their objective value to be understood. With this in mind, consider that the 1920's conception of the modern city was identified with the paradigm of the Wolkenkratzer (or cloud-scraper) which, in the functional view of city planners at the time, synthesized the vertical Hochhaus (high-building) within the wider horizontal low-rise planning of the city at large.*

WROCŁAW VISIT

Visiting Wroclaw, we will consider two current international competitions for the city; the first as the main project for the year, and the second as a prompt for the design thesis:

Diploma One: Wroclaw Museum of Contemporary Art (MOCA)

A second reciprocal programme for a new Polish Cultural Institute in London will follow during the Second Semester.

Diploma Two: The Agency of Production

Final year students will establish their own framework for the' thesis' project, initially considering the urban design competition for the environs of Wroclaw's main railway station. This acts as a threshold condition located in a 'central periphery' accessing both the 'old town' and the outer margins of the city. All three territories offer an interface with different sites of production and manufacturing which will constitute the main focus for the development of individual 'thesis' projects. The two competitions themselves provide alternative scenarios.

04 YEAR ONE: WROCLAW MUSEUM OF CONTEMPORARY ART

05 YEAR ONE: PCI: POLISH CULTURAL INSTITUTE

Y1 - 01   **THE LOGIC OF COLLECTING**
001   copy, replica and re-production

Y1 - 02   **THE NATURE OF INSTALLATION**
001   exhibit reproduced object

Y1 - 03   **RE-ARRANGED,**
                   COMPOSITION AND REPETITION
001   integrate into the city

                   Y2 - 01   **EXCAVATING THE PAST: FOUND OBJECTS**
                           001   city as palimpsest
                           002   process of excavation
                           003   autonomous object

                   Y2 - 02   **FROM WOLKENKRATZER TO**
              SILESIAN FIELDS: REPRESENTING THE CITY
                           001   three objects
                           002   material identity
                           003   form and substance original copy
                           004   replica
                           005   the reproduction

03   **THREE INTERVENTIONS; HISTORIC CENTRE,**
       CENTRAL PERIPHERY AND EDGE CITY
001   'found objects' reconstituted within contemporary Wroclaw

04 YEAR TWO: **THE AGENCY OF PRODUCTION**

05 YEAR TWO: **DESIGN THESIS DEVELOPMENT**

| Y1 - 01 | THE LOGIC OF COLLECTING |
| 001 | copy, replica and re-production |

| Y1 - 02 | **THE NATURE OF INSTALLATION** |
| 001 | exhibit reproduced object |

| Y1 - 03 | **RE-ARRANGED, COMPOSITION AND REPETITION** |
| 001 | integrate into the city |

> The complex Silesian cultural cross-pollination and the city's own confusing history still determine to this day the mentality of Wroclaw's inhabitants, who have to live with a past that is not their own. (11)
> (Christian Welzbacher, 'Wroclaw: Europe's Open End')

Our intention is to address the dual theme of 'reproduction' and 'production' before visiting Wroclaw. The concept of reproduction is bound up with the identity of the city literally rebuilt after WW II, providing, in the reconstruction the old city centre, a curiously neutral historical authenticity (rather than a problematic reformulation of Breslau). Arguably acting as 'roots' for a displaced population from Lvov to the east, this historical simulation has avoided an overt identification with either a Polish national architecture or its Germanic origin. In post-millennial terms it has assimilated the expansion of tourism and opportunities for marketing the city.

REPRODUCINGARCHITECTURE:
The Culture of the Copy
This sense of up-rootedness among the imported inhabitants of Wroclaw should be seen as the real driving force behind the reconstruction of the city:

> [...] the hitherto German Breslau was lovingly rebuilt down to the last detail. Thus a large part of the historical built substance is back where it was, as though nothing had happened. (12)
> (Christian Welzbacher, 'Wroclaw: Europe's Open End')

The practice of imitation and the culture of copying may be viewed as a positive practice or a negative condition. Imitative design is a derogatory term viewed in terms of the canons of 'creativity', yet typological repetition is a positive conceptual aspect of rationalist architecture. Repetition is endemic to both *architectural practice and the material production of architecture. The precedent study, while a necessary thing, is however tainted with associations with an unthinking application of things past. We envisage a more open agenda.*

COPY, REPLICA AND RE-PRODUCTION

Consider the distinct implications of each term: a mechanical process lacking intentionality; an authentic appearance that is perfect but lacks the original substance; and a transformative process or methodology (remaking or representing the original in a changed form).

Y1 - 01   THE LOGIC OF COLLECTING
001   copy, replica and re-production

Y1 - 02   THE NATURE OF INSTALLATION
001   exhibit reproduced object

Y1 - 03   RE-ARRANGED, COMPOSITION AND REPETITION
001   integrate into the city

Consider the theme in the context of the proposed programme for a Museum of Contemporary Art (MOCA), where the issue of cultural reproduction is well established in the tenets of C20th artistic practice. This study is intended to engage the characteristics of display spaces, but should be viewed as a primarily artistic, rather than functional, exercise.

01 THE LOGIC OF COLLECTING

Each pair of students is asked to form a 'collection' of ten everyday, aesthetic or historical objects, which are later to be exhibited or installed in prototypical exhibition spaces (rooms or enclosures). It is for you to determine the thinking behind your choice, whether they are conceived as a 'family' of similar or related things, or contrastingly a range of distinctly different objects. How they are collected, and in what form they are presented, depends on your own perspective. Three of the objects should be surveyed in order to be precise about their dimensions and form. Take one and reproduce it materially, visually or conceptually. This process should produce three forms of the object: copy, replica and reproduction (according to your interpretation of these categories), each to be set out in the context of the collection as a whole. Presentation: collection, dimensioned objects and a reproduction

02 THE NATURE OF INSTALLATION

The second phase of the study is to design an exhibition for, or installation of, one form of the reproduced object. The space in which the exhibit is placed should be conceived in terms of viewing and experiencing the object. This should have a bearing on how it is conserved, protected, illuminated and conditioned. The proposal for a single installation should be conceived autonomously in the own terms without contextual implication as an ideal prototype. Presentation: object and installation.

*03 RE-ARRANGEMENT,
COMPOSITION AND REPETITION*
In the final phase of the study, following our visit to Wroclaw, a series, a set or an aggregation, of the model installation designed previously, should be fully integrated into the fabric or landscape of the city. The urban consequences of this arrangement (or composition) are to be explained clearly in visual terms. Each of the three interventions should be conceived at a different scale (from accommodating the 'collection' to exhibiting a single object), and the ideal form of the original installation adapted to changing circumstances (from centre to periphery). Presentation: urban multiples.

Y2 - 01   EXCAVATING THE PAST: FOUND OBJECTS

001   city as palimpsest
002   process of excavation
003   autonomous object

Y2 - 02   FROM WOLKENKRATZE TO SILESIAN FIELDS: REPRESENTING THE CITY

001   three objects
002   material identity
003   form and substance original copy
004   replica
005   the reproduction

*Cultures are edifices with countless room, corridors, balconies, and attics, all arranged, furthermore, into such twisting, turning labyrinths, that if you enter one of them, there is no exit, no retreat, no turning back. (13)
(Ryszard Kapuscinski,* Travels with Herodotus*)*

In this initial study we are primarily concerned that you should engage the culture and history of the city of Wroclaw as this is of architectural consequence. To read the available histories of the city is one thing. It is another to engage material 'evidence' as it exists in maps, representations, photographs and other documentation. In a sense we are asking you to engage in a process of archaeological excavation and reconstruction. And while you may come across complete pieces of evidence from different periods you will often be confronting fragments of this and that. In the first instance it is your own ability to represent this process as much as make direct use of the material which interests us, since a degree of self-consciousness is a marker for the theoretical development of your design 'thesis'.

CITY RAILWAY STATION TRANSFORMATION

Essentially this study is intended to provide you with a 'grounding' in the culture of the place, before our visit, as you begin to formulate your own interests and framework for studio this year. It represents a threshold of investigation if you like, much as the existing central railway station provides a threshold of arrival on the central periphery of the city, giving access both to the 'historic' town centre and to the outlying areas of social housing, industry and suburban development. Wroclaw had five major railway stations by 1900, and major railway sites remain outside the centre. Tangible evidence, perhaps, of the how the history of the city can only be understood in relation to its external political, cultural and economic relationships.

The competition to transform the environs of the current city station is merely put forward as a 'retrospective' starting point for your individual projects, not simply as a site but in its 'connective' implication. The competition will be concluded by the time we visit. It is primarily with other sites in mind that our initial moves are set out, though you may wish to return to the station (with a critique of the competition in mind).

There is a certain correlation between the rapid development of the city in the late C19th (railways, banks, hotels), typical of the period, and events post 1989 with the demise of the Iron Curtain. It seems the post-industrial service based economy has similarly transformed the city (banks, retail shopping, hotels, service industries) in its role as administrative capital of Lower Silesia, while it still occupies a strategic location in terms of road and rail infrastructure and transportation.

INITIAL STUDIES

These are structured in three stages, which move from a loosely visual and material emphasis towards a transformative formal, social, and finally a potentially ecological agenda. You are expected to bring your own logic to this sequence or progression.

01 EXCAVATING THE PAST:
Found Objects
City as Palimpsest - the Process of Excavation and the Autonomous Object

For the first stage of the study we are asking each pair of students to trawl through, or systematically survey if you prefer, available documentation of the urban development of Wroclaw in order to excavate three 'found objects' (not necessarily object buildings). What has the city produced in terms of historical or contemporary 'products'? The city represents the 'ground', which you are excavating, and it may be that these objects are only gradually divested from it. Excavations take the form of a material 'cross-section' through time, revealing the accumulation of historical material. There is the spoil and waste produced by this process. Bear in mind that an archaeological mentality is as much conceptual as material.

You should present the logic (or otherwise) of how you went about this work, elaborating your process of 'excavation' in visual terms. The particular choice of objects or buildings should have a connotation with which you identify. Bear in mind the concept of 'layers' of history, the stratification of an excavation, and the manner in which 'finds' are presented as if specimens, categorised as evidence, labeled, numbered and tagged. We are looking for an artistic 'representation' (through a process of painting, montage or digitisation) of this process and an identification of the objects before they are cleaned and their character fully revealed. The procedure adopted should treat the object as something to be scrutinised, but also understood as an artifact 'produced' by the process of excavation. Presentation: excavation of three 'found' objects .

Y2 - 01   EXCAVATING THE PAST: FOUND OBJECTS

001   city as palimpsest
002   process of excavation
003   autonomous object

Y2 - 02   FROM WOLKENKRATZE TO SILESIAN FIELDS: REPRESENTING THE CITY

001   three objects
002   material identity
003   form and substance original copy
004   replica
005   the reproduction

02 FROM WOLKENKRATZER TO SILESIAN FIELDS
Representing the city. The next move is to process the three objects to clarify their material identity, form and substance, in bringing each object into a sharp focus. Unlike the archaeologist you are actively re-deploying the objects, rather than exhibiting them in a museum (unless that is how you view the city). The degree to which you transform or remake the objects is a relative decision. Whatever the procedures you adopt, the objects should be re-presented and placed relative to the everyday life of the city without reference to their original location (or source).

You are asked to represent the essential qualities of each object, however you interpret them, and place the objects in a new social relationship to the city from which they have been taken. We would emphasise this is not to relocate them on physical sites but to re-contextualise the objects in relation to the backdrop, skyline or cityscape of Wroclaw. The Raclawicka panorama presents a potential spatial model for this presentation. Bear in mind the concepts of the 'original copy' and replica, and the notion of a reproduction. In setting the objects in a new relationship to the city as a fictional exercise, we are interested in two extremes: the vertical city of the 'cloud-scraper', and the 'grounded' horizontal city, which we have identified with the term Silesian 'field'. This evokes a landscape or space 'beyond' the city (its hinterland viewed as an ecological or spatial field), but also the concept of the city itself as a landscape. Presentation: essential objects and everyday life.

03 THREE INTERVENTIONS: HISTORIC CENTRE, CENTRAL PERIPHERY AND EDGE CITY

001 'found objects' reconstituted within contemporary Wroclaw

03 THE 'HISTORIC' CENTRE, THE CENTRAL PERIPHERY AND EDGE CITY

The final stage of this study, ideally pursued after visiting the city, is to embed the three transformed 'found objects' back into the structure of contemporary Wroclaw, associated with one of the three territories we have categorised as centre, central periphery and edge city. Equally parallel territories could be construed as city 'islands' (whether physical or perceptual). The logic of the interventions should imply a coherent urban strategy. The forms, dimensions, outlines or contours of each object should be convincingly integrated into the urban fabric or the lie of the land. Each intervention should be precisely located, sited and persuasively represented to look as if it has always been there. The 'objects' should be identified with a particular programme but with a degree of artistic license in functional terms (studio complex, data or media park, and industrial site, are merely suggestions). Presentation: island city—embedded objects.

07_WW_S_032_003_175_P190_IP

07_WW_S_013_002_174_P190_HP

07_WW_S_033_015_187_P190_IP

07_WW_S_009_004_176_P190_C

07_WW_S_004_005_177_P190_PM

07_WW_S_044_006_178_P190_EP

07_WW_S_014_007_179_P190_HP

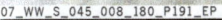

C. Welzebacher, *Wroclaw: Europes Open End)*

THIS SENSE OF UP-ROOTEDNESS AMONG THE IMPORTED
INHABITANTS OF WROCLAW SHOULD BE SEEN
AS THE REAL DRIVING FORCE BEHIND
THE RECONSTRUCTION OF THE CITY. (14)

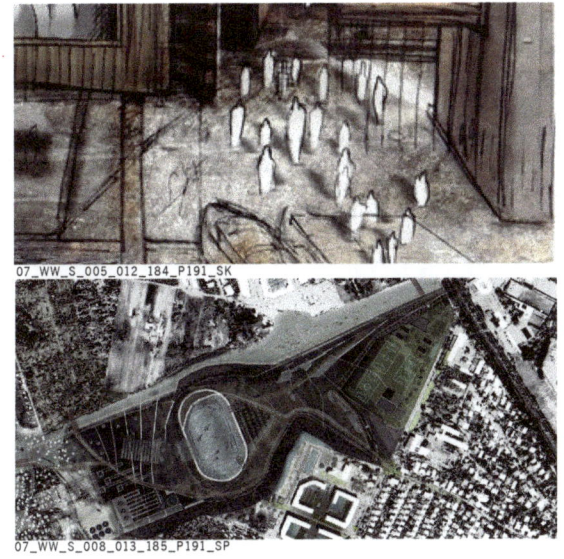

(I. Wiblin, *Recovery Territory: The Spectral Cities of Bresslau and Wroclzw Photographically Revisited*)

I KNOW THIS PLACE, BUT I DO NOT KNOW IT. BEING IN THE PRESENT IN WROCLAW GRADUALLY UNLOCKS A PAST. I READ CLUES OUT IMPRINTED IN THE FACADES OF BUILDINGS. I SEE THE OLD CITY MAPPED OUT IN COATINGS THE DUST. (16)

(N. Davies & R. Moorhouse, *Microcosm*)
NOTHING BETTER ILLUSTRATES WROCLAW'S
PREDICAMENT THAN [...] 'THE EXPLOITATION OF BRICKS'
[...] IN 1949 [...] (DOM) WAS CLOSED DOWN [...] INSTEAD OF BEING REBUILT,
WROCLAW WAS TO BE KNOCKED DOWN IN THE MOST CALCULATED
AND CYNICAL WAY [...] TO COLLECT UNDAMAGED
BRICKS FOR THE RECONSTRUCTION OF
WARSAW. (15)

07_WW_S_021_022_194_P193_M   07_WW_S_034_023_195_P193_IP   07_WW_S_015_024_196_P193_HP

HELEN MISSELBROOK

THE AGENCY OF ARCHITECTURE

Our final design thesis project was situated in the Polish city of Wroclaw, the capital of the Lower Silesian Province of Poland. Themed design briefs were focused on 'the agency and logic of production and re-production'; investigated the notion of 'city as palimpsest', and sought a corresponding ecological 'recovery' of the Silesian landscape. Wroclaw is one of the country's main economic, scientific and cultural conurbations situated on the river Oder, rich in mineral and natural resources, and consequently includes key industrial sites.

The design briefs were subdivided into a series of group survey studies and individual design tasks in order to establish a strategic framework incorporating three characteristic territories: the 'old town' centre; the 'central periphery', and the outer margins of the city—identified as 'Silesian fields'. All three territories offered an interface with various 'sites of production', both industrial and cultural, with potential for the development of our individual thesis projects set within the legacy of the city's disturbing C20th history. Our engagement with Wroclaw began with an initial study to excavate an object from the historical landscape of the city. I chose a tin of caviar to represent a population whose displaced 'potential' was transported from east to west...for me this acted as a dark reminder of the forced migrations of people throughout WW II, as well as a celebratory metaphor of the free movement of people following Poland's membership of the EU gained in 2004. The river Oder is now an infertile environment for sturgeon, while Poland itself has emerged as one of the world's most notorious black-markets for poached caviar in Europe. A second study required us to transform the 'object' and re-contextualise it within the cultural landscape of contemporary Wroclaw. I physically separated out each sturgeon egg and carefully placed it in bubble wrap to alter our perception of a mass consumption packaged product in order to suggest an individual investigation of each egg as a potential life-form. Our third task was to redeploy the transformed object within the cultural city-scape of Wroclaw. I chose to transform the caviar into a luxury face cream, to be sold globally, in order to highlight the macabre lengths that people go to preserve their youth. On our visit to the city, detours out to the periphery took my friend Sophie and myself to experience 'epic' industrially scarred landscapes; located at the termination of major arterial railway lines and disfigured with monumental stockpiles of discarded metal. A perfect metaphor for the contamination of the ground with heavy metals from a Silesian industrial past, with their problematic impact on the immune systems and fertility of Polish residents (cultivating state owned allotments for food production). At a 2008 iCSi Conference in Budapest P. McDonald noted that: 'Demographic change is one of the three major forces now remodelling Europe', beside the effects of globalisation and technological transformation. Poland along with Slovakia apparently had the lowest fertility rate in Europe, well below the critical restoration level. At the time of our visit in 2008/09 it was estimated that one in every five Polish couples experienced infertility. IVF assisted reproduction was then legal in Poland, but only available privately, the state refusing to subsidize treatment, given the strong and emotive influence of the pro-life Catholic lobby. The health minister at the time Ewa Kopacz opened a Pandora's box by proposing state funded IVF treatment for low-income families. Poland's Catholic Church opposes IVF calling it 'a sophisticated method of abortion'.

To regulate the IVF market at the time the bio-ethics team at the prime minister's chancellery drew up a new parliamentary bill aiming for a compromise: to maximize 'protection of human life', but on the other hand 'to make this procedure accessible to couples who cannot afford it'. It was this debate that informed my final thesis project which proposed a 'Site of (Re)-production', whose programme aimed to right an injustice and provide state-funded fertility treatment for families denied the chance of children by their economic situation.

Phase One—proposed the decontamination of urban allotment land in removing the heavy metals of the Silesian industrial past which, to this day, have had a detrimental impact on the immune and fertility health of Wroclaw's inhabitants who use the allotments to grow food. My thesis project aimed to create safe landscapes, as a city-wide 'natural fertility pharmacy'. Urban gardens and orchards would cultivate free produce containing folic acid, vitamins, zinc, selenium, carnitine and beta carotene, all linked to increased fertility. Future parents within the community could actively participate in the cultivation of these therapeutic landscapes. Using a process called 'GeoMelt' Vitrification the contaminated soil would be melted to form a glass-like material, similar to Basalt rock, impeding further leaching of the pollutants into the ground water supply.

Phase Two—orchestrated the excavation of vitrified allotment soil and the fabrication of the inert glass-like material to form cladding for the Fertility Research Centre and its debating chamber. The Centre was to be located on an island site adjacent to the Medical University and provided laboratories and research facilities to be occupied by the Embryology

Department. The programme included a debating chamber to facilitate debate on matters of policy. A series of community based fertility retreats were intended to provide natural and holistic methods of fertility treatment. Phase 3—was to be implemented once legislation allowed the provision of state-funded IVF treatment to Polish couples. A cemetery would be created on the island site, as a permanent resting place for the frozen embryos collected, but unable to be used, in state-funded IVF treatment (in accordance with Catholic beliefs).

The conceptual and polemical nature of my final design thesis was steeped in 'design research'. It was an opportunity to highlight what I felt was an injustice in formulating a city-wide strategy and a responsive architectural proposal. The DS11 design brief sought a response to the cultural, historical and architectural city-scape of Wroclaw, but I felt that the political, theological and geo-political 'landscape' was also vital to put forward an expanded conception of what constituted the 'site'. All too often the design research ethos cultivated at university; which encompasses macro-scale approaches to the city; becomes gradually eroded or abandoned in daily architectural practice. Sites are circumscribed by the notional topography of a red line on a planning application, severing our ability as architects to create the urban visions which are promoted in the academic design studio. Does architectural practice dull the political engagement of 'design research', now placed under the auspices of commercial enterprise? Having graduated from Westminster in 2009, at a time of economic downturn, I started my own architectural business in a climate where my peers were being offered unpaid internships. Together with my partner Caine MacNeil, and aside from our architectural practice, I launched a website in 2011 which acted as a free architectural recruitment site. This aimed to end unpaid internships in the architecture industry (now banned for chartered practices) and was supported by the then president of the RIBA Angela Brady. Once again, I had found myself in the midst of a 'design research project', in this case designing a website targeting an injustice. I am currently 'masterplan design guardian' on the £100m Circus Street development in Brighton. We are turning a derelict municipal market into part of an urban 'innovation quarter'; a powerhouse for regeneration in the city centre. In the process, we aim create a sustainable, productive, healthy model of city life, with public spaces, a lively creative atmosphere, and a real sense of community.

In this mixed-use partnership with Brighton and Hove City Council and South East Dance, we are providing a programme of accommodation that will galvanize the surrounding area: 142 new homes; 450 student apartments; 'The Dance Space', a new base for the internationally acclaimed South East Dance company; a community hub with a fresh injection of business and start up spaces, and future plans for a new University of Brighton library, and an academic building. This involves 'greening' a space that's offered little of ecological value in the past; building accommodation around two large, green urban squares; encouraging the growth of fruit and vegetables in allotments (on a site where fresh produce was once sold); planting disease resistant elms and taking steps to nurture bio-diversity. Common sociological and ecological themes current in my final thesis project have been threaded into my architectural work in practice. I am currently Director of Helen

Misselbrook Architects working as a consultant for shedkm Architects on the Brighton project for developer U+I. My hope is that running my own business will give me a strong sense of independence and the basis from which to reinvigorate my political voice. An authentic voice emboldened by those design research projects with DS11.

Helen Misselbrook: BA Hons Int Arch UWIC Cardiff, LTS Architects, Dip Arch University of Westminster. Currently director of Helen Misselbrook Architects, masterplan design guardian for U+I Developer/Consultant at shedkm Architects (on Circus Street masterplan, Brighton). Previously with LTS Architects and Resolution Architecture. Remains responsible for Studio World (free recruitment site).

11/12
KRAKÓW

K

DUAL IDENTITIES

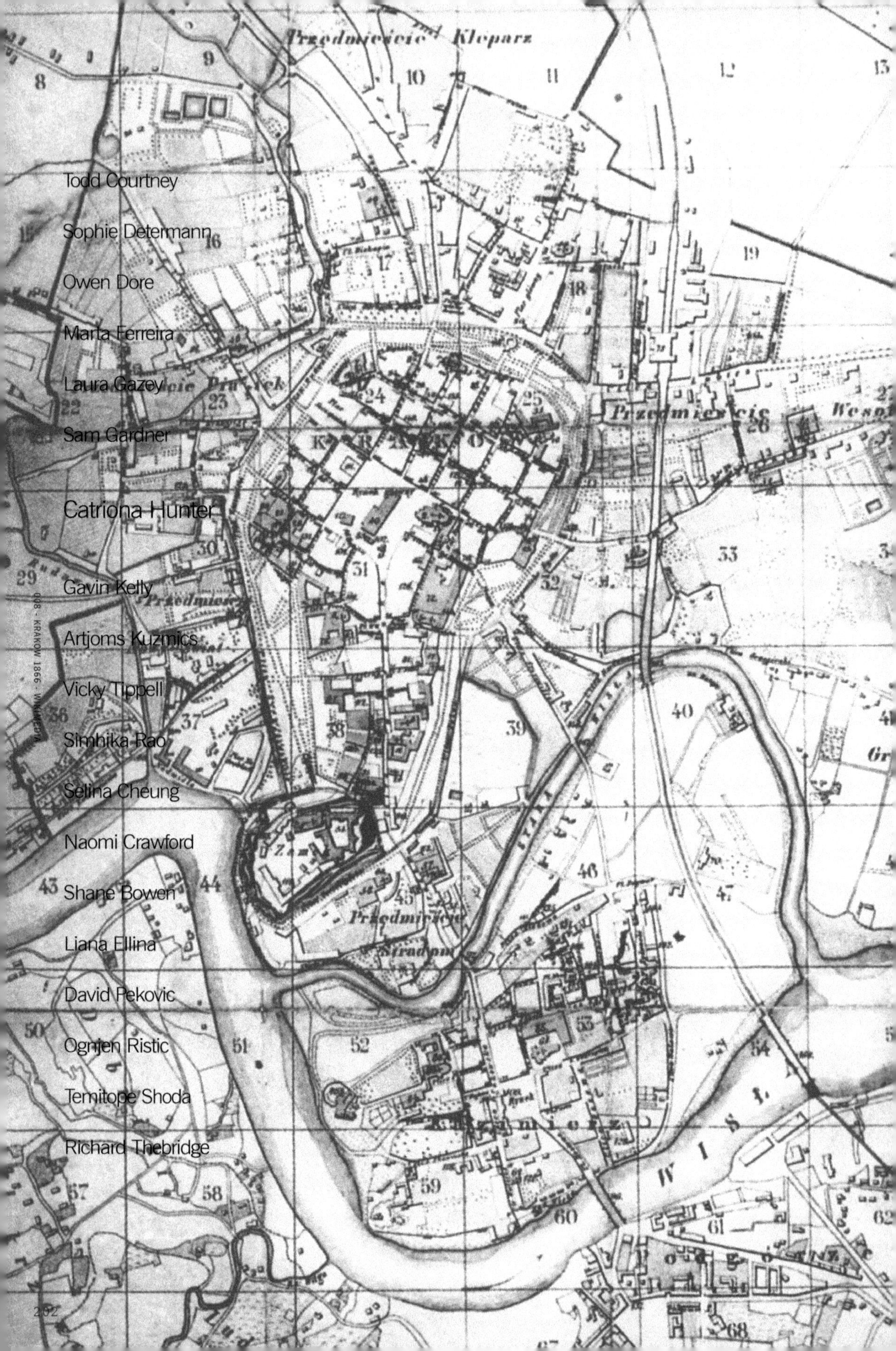

Todd Courtney

Sophie Determann

Owen Dore

Marta Ferreira

Laura Gazey

Sam Gardner

Catriona Hunter

Gavin Kelly

Artjoms Kuzmics

Vicky Tippell

Simhika Rao

Selina Cheung

Naomi Crawford

Shane Bowen

Liana Ellina

David Pekovic

Ognjen Ristic

Temitope Shoda

Richard Thebridge

008 - KRAKOW 1866 - WIKIMEDIA

2011/2012

KRAWKÓW/KATOWICE:
MINING THE SEAM

SILESIAN TERRITORIES:
DUAL IDENTITIES

Landmarks:

KOPALNIA SOLI WIELICZKA/WAWEL/
OJCOWSKI PARK NARODOWY/RYNEK
GŁÓWNY/SUKIENNICE/KOŚCIÓŁ
WNIEBOWZIĘCIA NAJŚWIĘTSZEJ MARYI
PANNY, KOŚCIÓŁ MARIACKI/ KRÓLEWSKA
BAZYLIKA ARCHIKATEDRALNA ŚŚ.
STANISŁAWA I WACŁAWA NA WAWELU/
DROGA KRÓLEWSKA/BARBAKAN
KRAKOWSKI/KOPIEC KOŚCIUSZKI/
WIEŻA RATUSZOWA W KRAKOWIE/
SYNAGOGA KUPA/SYNAGOGA POPPERA/
SYNAGOGA TEMPEL/SYNAGOGA REMUH/
SYNAGOGA DAWNA W ZAMOŚCIU/MUZEUM
LOTNICTWA POLSKIEGO W KRAKOWIE/
MUZEUM KSIĄŻĄT CZARTORYSKICH
W KRAKOWIE/OGRÓD BOTANICZNY
UNIWERSYTETU JAGIELLOŃSKIEGO/
SMOCZA JAMA/MUZEUM NARODOWE W
KRAKOWIE/KOPIEC KRAKUSA/KOŚCIÓŁ
ŚW. WOJCIECHA/TYNIEC, ŚWIĘTOKRZYSKIE
VOIVODESHIP/POMNIK ADAMA
MICKIEWICZA W KRAKOWIE/MUZEUM
HISTORYCZNE MIASTA KRAKOWA/OGRÓD
ZOOLOGICZNY W KRAKOWIE/SKAŁKA/
KOŚCIÓŁ ŚW. FRANCISZKA Z ASYŻU/
MANGGHA/ŻYDOWSKIE MUZEUM GALICJA/
UROCZYSKO LAS WOLSKI/KOŚCIÓŁ ŚŚ
PIOTRA I PAWŁA W KRAKOWIE/BAZYLIKA
BOŻEGO CIAŁA/BRAMA FLORIAŃSKA/
FABRYKA EMALIA OSKARA SCHINDLERA/
BŁONIA/MUZEUM SZTUKI WSPÓŁCZESNEJ
W KRAKOWIE/BIELAŃSKO-TYNIECKI
PARK KRAJOBRAZOWY/TENCZYŃSKI
PARK KRAJOBRAZOWY/MUZEUM
ETNOGRAFICZNE IM. SEWERYNA UDZIELI
W KRAKOWIE/ŻUPNY/SYNAGOGA STARA/
IZAAK JAKUBOWICZ

Coordinates:
50°4′N 19°56′E

Voivodeship:
Lesser Poland

Area:
326.80 km2

Elevation:
219 m

Population:

Year	Population	Change
1791	023,591	—
1835	036,000	+52.6%
1870	049,800	+38.3%
1900	085,300	+71.1%
1910	137,592	+61.3%
1921	184.300	+33.9%
1931	219,300	+19.0%
1945	298,500	+30.1%
1955	428,231	+43.4%
1965	520,145	+21.4%
1975	684,600	+31.6%
1985	740,120	+8.1%
1995	744,967	+0.06%
2005	756,629	+0.15%
2015	762,508	+0.07%

Demonym(s):
Cracovian

Patron Saint:
Stanislaus of Szczepanów

Our primary interest is in two themes: the relationship between the historical city and its industrial or proletarian 'other', and that between the processes of excavation and of manufacture, whether understood in literal or metaphorical terms. In Kraków, Nowa Huta a Stalinist satellite and ideological steel-town has long since been absorbed by suburbanization and become part of the city at large; whereas Katowice's development was part and parcel of C19th industrialization and an economy of manufacturing fuelled by adjacent coal mines. Under Communism the latter's proletarian character was consummated as Stalinogrod, only to be subsequently denigrated as an environmentally pernicious legacy of polluting heavy industries. How may a contemporary architecture mediate or stand outside the historical legacy of these transformations, and in what sense can the paradigmatic 'processes' of archetypal heavy industry; of smelting, casting, forging and machining; be revisited in the form of the high technologies with which we are more familiar? And what architecture appropriately frames the new forms of socialization endemic to a contemporary networked economy played out within the residues of a socialist past (and acting as a potentially socialist future)?

Preliminary Projects

As an introduction during the first term, we are setting out a framework for three design projects. Following parallel themes (formal, environmental and social) they, initially, alternate between individual and group work, working towards a mutual or personal conclusion. The projects are not conceived as 'studies', but each rather constitutes an architectural 'design'. They engage dual identities and constitute a vocabulary of elements with which to frame a building complex, or an architectural thesis: 01 Form-work, 02 Environmental Register, and 03 Social Affiliations.

Semester One:
Social Assemblage and Constituting an Inventory
The formative content of the initial projects is intended to be consolidated in the design of a representative social assembly (or event space) to be located in Krakow (Year 1), or in drawing up an 'inventory' that catalogues their content (Year 2).

> [...] the SEM (Silesia Ecological Movement) met regularly in Katowice's central market square, or rynek [...] as a place to deliver public performances which sought to dramatise the environmental problems of the city through symbolic theatre [...] collectively these protests [...] have given rise to...a grey ecologies movement...(which)...emphasises the move away from environmentalism [...] towards a new concern for urban ecologies. (17)
> (Mark Whitehead, Between the Marvellous and the Mundane)

Semester Two:
Silicon Topologies and the Organisational Complex
The Year 2 inventory provides a framework for the developing a design 'thesis' to be taken 'on site' in visiting Krakow and Katowice towards the end of January. In contrast Year 1 will interrogate either city with respect to a focused brief for an innovative administrative and manufacturing centre.

KRAKÓW VISIT

A particular force field from the following conditions: sound (noise) pressure (wind / ground compression) radiation or other forms of energy (light/heat/electromagnetic/atomic) temperature variation (freezing / melting) movement (traffic/geological) ideological conviction (left or right)

05 YEAR ONE: CONSTITUENT ASSEMBLY ORGANISATIONAL COMPLEX

01 EXCAVATING TYPE/SMELTING AND PURGING
001 form-work
002 procedural subject

02 FORCE FIELDS/ POLLUTION AND THE ART OF WEATHERING
001 force fields
002 pollution and the art of weathering

03 MANUFACTURED COMMUNITIES/ THE COMMUTARIAN PRESENT
001 manufactured communities
002 the communitarian present

05 YEAR TWO: CATALOGUE RAISONNÉ
DESIGN THESIS

02 FORCE FIELDS/POLLUTION AND THE ART OF WEATHERING

■ 001　force fields
　 002　pollution and the art of weathering

FORCE FIELDS

Working individually choose a particular force field from the following conditions: sound (noise)　pressure (wind / ground compression)　radiation or other forms of energy (light/heat/electromagnetic/atomic)　temperature variation (freezing / melting)　movement (traffic/geological)　ideological conviction (left or right)

This list is not scientifically precise, but the general categories should be clear. You may wish to be more specific in technical terms about the precise parameters of the force field selected.

VISUALISE IN SPATIAL TERMS

The intensity and action of this force or energy field (which may be active and energetic, or passive and slow acting). Employ characteristic imagery or animation techniques that highlight its volatile or steady state. Refer to scientific or technical information and documentation but present this knowledge in aesthetic terms and at a scale that encompasses the spectator. Visual rhetoric should persuade us of the action of this 'force'.

TRANSFORMATIVE LOCATIONS

Identify a physical site on which to intervene, in Kraków or the neighbouring region, that is likely to be exposed in reality, or as you conceive it, to an intense force field at a particular moment in time (present, seasonal, historical).

CONTEXTUALIZATION

Identify a building type or model (be specific about formal typology or programme of occupation and use), whether from previous work in your group (or others), to locate on the site you have chosen. Alternatively select an existing building with which to work. Demonstrate its context with conviction in plan and section (or perspective).

These representations of the building should be to scale and be shown convincingly integrated into the force field that is acting on the surrounding terrain or territory (whether this is realistic or invented).

*INDIVIDUAL PRESENTATIONS
Visualisation, Plan, Section or
Perspective in Context.*

02 FORCE FIELDS / POLLUTION AND THE ART OF WEATHERING

001   force fields
002   pollution and the art of weathering

*As late as 1994, the heavy industries of Katowice were producing daily, ambient concentrations of black smoke in the winter which were six times higher than the permissible European Union standards [...]. (18)
(Mark Whitehead, 'Between the Marvellous and the Mundane')*

Select the proposal in your group that is best visualised in relation to its local force field. Consider in detail how the building you have chosen reacts to, or is acted on by, the environmental pressure to which it is subjected, and how to dramatise this effect. This obviously involves elaborating the design of the overall building making best use of all your available skills. Research the problem of environmental pollution endemic to Kraków and Katowice (and the surrounding region). Does this pollution; air-born, liquefied, or accumulated in the ground (topology) or terrain (landscape), interface with the action of the force field on the building concerned in any way? If not simulate a response to one form of pollution. Depending on the environmental performance you seek for the building consider transforming the structural, or enclosing, elements of the chosen building type, model or existing building you have chosen, in response to environmental considerations in any way you feel appropriate. You might transform what is light to become heavy, what hard to soft or what is open / transparent to be closed / opaque (for example).

*EROSION AND
MANIPULATION*

Working once again in pairs confront two different passive and active aspects of what might be described as an environmental interface at 1:10 / 1:5 / 1:1.

Once detailing suggested the coming together of disparate materials [...] Today it stands for transient couplings that wait to be undone or unscrewed, a temporary embrace that

none of the constituent parts may survive. (19)
(R. Koolhaas, H. Foster 'Junkspace')

For me, detailing means exercising the utmost care at the junctions between different materials or different elements of a building [...] the best details are usually those that are not consciously perceived'. (20)
(A. Siza, 'On Materials')

IMPACT DETAILS
First: describe in 'details' how the relevant force field impacts on the form, structure, enclosure or surroundings of the building? How will it deform, erode and change over time? Can the building, or the landscape in which it is set, be adapted in a passive way to resist or accept this transformation or erosion?

REACTIVE ELEMENTS
Second: invent a set of characteristic details as working drawings of building elements or components constituting enclosure, openings or thresholds that actively resist this force when required, but can transform when it is not present.

In both cases (above) we are looking for surrogate, simulated or realistic technical details (plagiarise specific exemplars or generic details) that recognize and exploit the questions we have raised about the responsiveness of the chosen building. These working drawings should be rendered so as to be at home in an art gallery.

---

03 MANUFACTURED COMMUNITIES/ THE COMMUTARIAN PRESENT

001 manufactured communities
002 the communitarian present

001 INDIVIDUAL PROJECT
What alternative models may be proposed for the concept of a 'manufactured community'? Does the term suggest that urban or architectural form is to be conceived of as an instrument with which to forge a social ideal? Or should the proposition be taken more literally to define a direct relationship between a particular industry and the housing of its workforce? Both connotations were present at Nowa Huta, but neither have their original force today.

The instrumental legacy of the Modern Movement (with its origins in C19th coercion and philanthropy) is now open to question, and 'jobs for life' are a thing of the past given the volatility of a post-industrial economy conditioned by global capitalism.

Is the concept of 'manufactured communities' redundant, or is there a direct parallel between functionalism and the priorities of a 'sustainable' architecture informed by a concurrent social idealism reminiscent of utopian socialism? Or should we, accustomed as we are to a 'networked' economic and social milieu, be wary of such affiliations and identify with a fragmentary autonomy framed by market forces?

Both the ideological 'city' of Nowa Huta and the medieval spaces of the traditional urban core in Krakow have become tourist destinations, associated with different forms of nostalgia. Should contemporary interventions in the city recognize this polarity or pursue a different tack associated with new industries, the 'knowledge' economy and hybrid conceptions of urban space?

KRAKOW: MEDIEVAL SPACE – IDEOLOGICAL CITY

Consider these two extremes:

1) Choose one and analyse the typical relationship between urban space and architectural form you find there. The 'historic' centre of Krakow developed incrementally over several centuries whereas Nowa Huta, initially proposed in ideal form, was modified within a relatively short time-span. Rescale and re- present (distort, fragment, emphasize or repeat) the characteristics of one place in relation to the other, bearing in mind the process of historical change.

2) Secondly what residential/industrial model or ideal might you envisage to replace Nowa Huta (or another district of Krakow or Katowice)? A new peripheral enclave, or island of development, at the edge of the city? Consider the relationship between residential and industrial uses, density (low, high, or hyper- dense) and scale (height, and extent of infrastructure).

Utopian socialism, C19th industrial philanthropy, the linear city, the siedlung or garden city Le Corbusier's conception of urbanism, new towns, corporate organizational complexes, Silicon Valley, the urban grid, gated communities and the logics of globalisation. Adopt any one of these models and revisit a specific example, altered or adapted to your own vision and chosen context. Present accurately to scale in relation to the overall extent of Krakow or Katowice in plan or abstract model form.

08_KW_S_016_001_203_P212_HP

08_KW_S_036_002_204_P212_IP

08_KW_S_022_003_205_P212_M

08_KW_S_053_004_206_P212_EP

08_KW_S_008_008_210_P212_DI 08_KW_S_019_009_211_P213_S

08_KW_S_018_005_207_P213_S

POLMOS 3

08_KW_S_054_006_208_P213_EP

08_KW_S_017_007_209_P213_HP

08_KW_S_055_010_212_P214_EP

08_KW_S_011_012_214_P214_E

08_KW_S_020_011_213_P214_S

08_KW_S_009_013_215_P214_DI

08_KW_S_012_014_216_P215_E

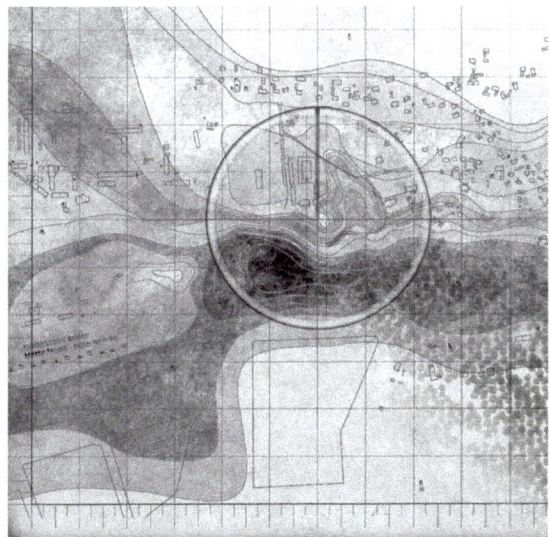

08_KW_S_010_015_217_P215_DI

08_KW_S_011_016_218_P215_SP

CATRIONA HUNTER

THE VALUE OF STUDIO CULTURE

My experience of studio culture was largely positive and I greatly enjoyed studying for my undergraduate degree at The University of Nottingham, followed by my Part II at The University of Westminster. Yet, as I will discuss in more detail, my professional route (post Part II) has been unusual in that as a consequence I have pursued a less traditional architectural role. My experience of an experimental and imaginative architectural education led me to reject a 'traditional' professional role, which I viewed as at odds with much of the design studio methodology that I had become accustomed to and found inspiring. Instead, I was drawn to a role which focuses more on design concepts, creative visualization and experimental design; which in hindsight reflects many of the habits and values which became instilled in my design work throughout an architectural education.

Architecture does not appear in a traditional school education, and consequently the design studio is a novel and important teaching opportunity for students faced with studying a subject of which they may have limited knowledge. The design studio allows the freedom to explore a myriad of subject matter that falls under the umbrella of 'architecture'. Students can interrogate, delve into, reject, and ultimately follow the topics that interest them. Yet although students are in theory able to research and follow their own inclinations, studio culture potentially offers an overall thematic framework; and a certain identity and a working brief; which, in my experience, was highly beneficial in provoking discussion and generating ideas. The University of Westminster's studio choices were extremely varied; ranging from mathematically based generative design, film and animation, to more historical or geographically based options. For a new student, anxious about doing well in their university degree, the design studio offers a degree of comfort, support and familiarity; as a base from which to branch out.

Architectural design is a non-linear process of learning. The architectural education offered in my own experience of design studio at the University of Westminster reflected this thinking in the style of work that was set. Weekly design tasks, often disparate from each other, encouraged students to think in a different ways and search for connections and threads of interest.

It was often surprising how seemingly unlinked threads of research could be connected to form the basis of a successful design proposal. Yet, on the other hand, short one-week projects also allowed students to discard a route they had explored, but found to be unproductive or unrewarding. Studio culture offered the discursive freedom to experiment and to 'get it wrong' without severe consequences. Personally, I found this opportunity hugely important and something that is often lacking in practice where, due to budget and time constraints, site practicalities and managing client expectations, there is often much more at stake. Design studio also encourages you to be self-critical, sometimes introspective, and to take risks. Risk-taking in turn generates discussion and some of the most interesting 'crits' were those in which the whole design studio pitched in with their thoughts. There was no right or wrong answer or solution—as is typical in design—but the methodology involved became the issue.

Having had the luxury of spending time researching and developing a concept over a number of weeks, if not months, one major change in professional practice is the speed of working and thinking that increases dramatically post-university. Working in an academic studio affords a certain level of procrastination; you can spend a whole day 'researching'. Obviously, however, when you are being paid by the hour a client expects substantive work to be delivered quickly. Nonetheless, studio culture and design research, I believe, builds the foundations for practice in allowing intuition to flourish.

After graduating from my Part II degree, and under financial, parental and self-inflicted pressure I, as previously, followed the traditional route of applying for a job as an architectural assistant at various architectural practices with whose work I identified (receiving an offer of employment shortly after my interviews). However, I had grown to love the more abstract and conceptual work generated in an academic design studio, and a traditional architectural role no longer had a great appeal. I had experienced a year in a London based architecture practice after completing my BA degree, and whilst I was offered a wide variety of typical Part I tasks, I found the work largely uninspiring and lacking in creativity. With this in mind, I decided to approach Banbury Walker Studio; a design agency which specialized in experiential design, exhibitions and events, and whose job description required creativity, experimental thinking and risk taking. My portfolio featured more explanation of experimental 'design research' processes; purposely generated by studio briefs; rather than overtly technical and traditional architectural drawings. I was offered the job I sought because the director admired my ideas, thought processes and ability to convey designs in an accessible and emotive manner.

In hindsight, Banbury Walker Studio appealed to me because it most reflected the studio culture to which I had become accustomed and enjoyed. Projects ranged from

the short one or two days to the longer, perhaps a month, but rarely spanned years as is common in building orientated architecture practice. Design processes and procedures at BWS were thoughtful, innovative and constantly evolving.

Perhaps paradoxically, studio culture or my experience of an architectural education at university, if I am honest, actually distanced me from pursuing a traditional architectural route into practice. I enjoyed an experimental architectural education to the point where I found the prospect of a 'traditional' role rather dull in comparison. I believe that there is a chasm between an architectural education (more obvious perhaps in the UK than elsewhere) and the 'real world' of an architectural practice. At university, imagination is the key; knowledge of budget constraints, client management and party walls, is unlikely to gain you a first-class degree. A result of this emphasis on 'creativity', is that a large proportion of graduates enter the profession with more theoretical than technical knowledge. Perhaps this is partly due to studio tutors' own desire for interesting and innovative projects, which informs or influences their students' work. It is often these tutors themselves who, tired of constraints of architectural practice, turn to education for something more interesting, fast-paced and ultimately fulfilling. However, this can leave aspiring architects feeling unfulfilled and bored once the explorative years of university study are over, a feeling that I succumbed to myself. I belong to a millennial generation predominantly defined by a habitually short attention span. In today's world of spectacle there is constant 'entertainment'—hundreds of TV channels, thousands of films, millions of YouTube videos; all available at the click of a mobile phone button. Perhaps I am symptomatic of my generation

in my attachment to one-week projects, where the transforming nature of the design studio was always in flux. The architectural profession often seemed devoid of the qualities I experienced in the studio and at odds with the transience of contemporary culture. The schism between architectural education and practice, seems fundamental. But can it be seen in a positive light in allowing the time and freedom to experiment (if only for a few years)? Or does it set students up for disappointment when they eventually join the 'world of work'? Perhaps this widening divide points to a future where architects dwindle numerically, as does the significance of their role? Or, on the contrary, does the pace of today's world suggest that studio culture's emphasis on the imagination is ever more relevant and important? Conventionally, a large part of design research involves precedent studies, but the exponential speed of development (technological, social and environmental) is already having a major influence on what can be achieved by architectural students as part of a university education. Many students are now inspired to invent new technologies, to create prototypes, and even build 'working structures' within the ambit of a year's work. Instead of looking to the past for inspiration, many now look to the future. And you cannot face the future without creativity, imagination and the ability to generate new ideas...

Catriona Hunter: BArch University of Nottingham, DipArch University of Westminster, Creative Director currently employed at Banbury Walker Studio (2013-2017)

ARCHIVE

STUDENT WORK AND PRACTICE
(pp.32-211)

The coded abbreviations for all illiustrations listed within this section follow a system that categorises each item as follows; Chapter Chronology_City_ Genre_Drawing Type Order_ Chapter Order_Book Order_ Page Number_Drawing Type.

* * * * *

The Abbreviations can be contextualised as follows:

CN -	Copenhagen
AP -	Antwerp
GA -	Genoa
TE -	Trieste
BT -	Budapest
WW -	Wroclaw
KW -	Krakow
S -	Student
SS -	Selected Student
P -	Practice
A -	Axonometric
C -	Collage
E -	Elevation
EP -	Exterior Perspective
HP -	Historic Photo
IP -	Interior Perspective
M -	Model
P -	Plan
PM -	Photo Montage
S -	Section
SK -	Sketch
SP -	Site Plan

P.44	01_CN_S_001_001_001_S
P.46	01_CN_S_001_002_002_EP
P.46	01_CN_S_001_003_003_HP
P.46	01_CN_S_002_004_004_EP
P.46	01_CN_S_001_005_005_SP
P.47	01_CN_S_003_006_006_EP
P.47	01_CN_S_002_007_007_HP
P.47	01_CN_S_001_008_008_P
P.47	01_CN_S_001_009_009_M
P.47	01_CN_S_004_010_010_EP
P.47	01_CN_S_001_011_011_IP
P.47	01_CN_S_001_012_012_C
P.47	01_CN_S_002_013_013_P
P.48	01_CN_S_002_014_014_IP
P.48	01_CN_S_002_015_015_M
P.48	01_CN_S_003_016_016_M
P.48	01_CN_S_004_017_017_M
P.48	01_CN_S_005_018_018_EP
P.48	01_CN_S_001_019_019_PM
P.49	01_CN_S_005_020_020_M
P.49	01_CN_S_003_021_021_IP
P.49	01_CN_S_006_022_022_M
P.49	01_CN_S_001_023_023_A
P.49	01_CN_S_001_024_024_SK
P.50	01_CN_S_001_025_025_D
P.51	01_CN_S_007_026_026_M
P.52	01_CN_S_006_027_027_EP
P.53	01_CN_P_008_028_028_M
P.54	01_CN_P_007_029_029_EP

P.69	02_AP_S_002_001_030_SK
P.70	02_AP_S_008_002_031_EP
P.70	02_AP_S_004_003_032_IP
P.71	02_AP_S_003_004_033_#HP
P.71	02_AP_S_009_005_034_M
P.71	02_AP_S_005_006_035_IP
P.71	02_AP_S_008_007_036_EP
P.71	02_AP_S_009_008_037_EP
P.71	02_AP_S_010_009_038_EP
P.71	02_AP_S_002_010_039_C
P.71	02_AP_S_003_011_040_C
P.72	02_AP_S_006_012_041_IP
P.72	02_AP_S_007_013_042_IP
P.72	02_AP_S_010_014_043_M
P.72	02_AP_S_004_015_044_HP
P.72	02_AP_S_008_016_045_IP
P.72	02_AP_S_005_017_046_HP
P.72	02_AP_S_011_018_047_EP
P.73	02_AP_S_009_019_048_IP
P.73	02_AP_S_011_020_049_M
P.72	02_AP_S_004_021_050_C
P.73	02_AP_S_003_022_051_P
P.74	02_AP_SS_012_023_052_EP
P.74	02_AP_SS_013_024_053_EP
P.75	02_AP_SS_010_025_054_IP
P.76	02_AP_SS_014_026_055_EP
P.77	02_AP_SS_011_027_056_IP
P.78	02_AP_SS_002_028_057_SP
P.80	02_AP_P_015_029_058_EP

224

Page	Code	Page	Code	Page	Code
P.92	03_GA_S_012_001_059_ _IP	P.114	04_TE_S_024_001_091_ _EP	P.134	05_TR_S_010_001_121_ _S
P.92	03_GA_S_013_002_060_ _IP	P.114	04_TE_S_013_002_092_ _M	P.134	05_TR_S_010_002_122_ _HP
P.92	03_GA_S_014_003_061_ _IP	P.114	04_TE_S_022_003_093_ _IP	P.134	05_TR_S_033_003_123_ _EP
P.92	03_GA_S_012_004_062_ _M	P.114	04_TE_S_004_004_094_ _S	P.134	05_TR_S_006_004_124_ _DI
P.92	03_GA_S_015_005_063_ _IP	P.115	04_TE_S_005_005_095_ _S	P.135	05_TR_S_026_005_125_ _IP
P.93	03_GA_S_017_006_064_ _EP	P.115	04_TE_S_004_006_096_ _SP	P.135	05_TR_S_014_006_126_ _M
P.93	03_GA_S_018_007_065_ _EP	P.115	04_TE_S_003_007_097_ _E	P.135	05_TR_S_027_007_127_ _IP
P.93	03_GA_S_019_008_066_ _EP	P.115	04_TE_S_025_008_098_ _EP	P.135	05_TR_S_005_008_128_ _E
P.93	03_GA_S_016_009_067_ _IP	P.115	04_TE_S_006_009_099_ _HP	P.135	05_TR_S_005_009_129_ _SP
P.93	03_GA_S_001_010_068_ _DI	P.115	04_TE_S_007_010_100_ _HP	P.135	05_TR_S_034_010_130_ _EP
P.93	03_GA_S_003_011_069_ _SP	P.114	04_TE_S_002_011_101_ _PM	P.134	05_TR_S_011_011_131_ _S
P.92	03_GA_S_005_012_070_ _P	P.116	04_TE_S_026_012_102_ _EP	P.136	05_TR_S_011_012_132_ _HP
P.93	03_GA_S_002_013_071_ _S	P.116	04_TE_S_023_013_103_ _IP	P.136	05_TR_S_015_013_133_ _M
P.94	03_GA_S_017_014_072_ _IP	P.116	04_TE_S_027_014_104_ _EP	P.136	05_TR_S_028_014_134_ _IP
P.94	03_GA_S_002_015_073_ _DI	P.116	04_TE_S_006_015_105_ _S	P.136	05_TR_S_006_015_135_ _P
P.94	03_GA_S_018_016_074_ _IP	P.116	04_TE_S_028_016_106_ _EP	P.136	05_TR_S_004_016_136_ _A
P.94	03_GA_S_001_017_075_ _E	P.116	04_TE_S_007_017_107_ _S	P.136	05_TR_S_035_017_137_ _EP
P.94	03_GA_S_003_018_076_ _DI	P.117	04_TE_S_029_018_108_ _EP	P.137	05_TR_S_012_018_138_ _S
P.94	03_GA_S_020_019_077_ _EP	P.117	04_TE_S_024_019_109_ _IP	P.137	05_TR_S_013_019_139_ _S
P.94	03_GA_S_005_020_078_ _C	P.117	04_TE_S_004_020_110_ _E	P.137	05_TR_S_029_020_140_ _IP
P.95	03_GA_S_019_021_079_ _IP	P.117	04_TE_S_008_021_111_ _S	P.137	05_TR_S_006_021_141_ _SP
P.95	03_GA_S_021_022_080_ _EP	P.117	04_TE_S_003_022_112_ _PM	P.137	05_TR_S_030_022_142_ _IP
P.95	03_GA_S_020_023_081_ _IP	P.117	04_TE_S_008_023_113_ _HP	P.137	05_TR_S_012_023_143_ _HP
P.95	03_GA_S_006_024_082_ _C	P.117	04_TE_S_009_024_114_ _S	P.136	05_TR_S_007_024_144_ _P
P.95	03_GA_S_004_025_083_ _DI	P.116	04_TE_S_003_025_115_ _A	P.136	05_TR_S_014_025_145_ _S
P.95	03_GA_S_002_026_084_ _E	P.118	04_TE_SS_030_026_116_ _EP	P.137	05_TR_S_006_026_146_ _E
P.95	03_GA_S_003_027_085_ _S	P.118	04_TE_SS_025_027_117_ _IP	P.137	05_TR_S_008_027_147_ _P
P.96	03_GA_SS_005_028_086_ _DI	P.120	04_TE_P_009_028_118_ _HP	P.138	05_TR_SS_036_028_148_ _EP
P.97	03_GA_SS_002_029_087_ _A	P.122	04_TE_P_031_029_119_ _EP	P.139	05_TR_SS_031_029_149_ _IP
P.98	03_GA_P_022_030_088_ _EP	P.122	04_TE_P_032_030_120_ _EP	P.140	05_TR_P_037_030_150_ _EP
P.99	03_GA_P_021_031_089_ _IP			P.142	05_TR_P_038_031_151_ _EP
P.100	03_GA_P_023_032_090_ _EP			P.144	05_TR_SS_007_032_152_ _E
				P.144	05_TR_SS_039_033_153_ _EP
				P.146	05_TR_SS_008_034_154_ _E
				P.146	05_TR_SS_040_035_155_ _EP
				P.148	05_TR_SS_007_036_156_ _DI

P.164	06_BT_SS_007_001_157_SP	P.189	07_WW_S_043_001_173_EP	P.212	08_KW_S_016_001_203_HP
P.164	06_BT_SS_041_002_158_EP	P.190	07_WW_S_013_002_174_HP	P.212	08_KW_S_036_002_204_IP
P.164	06_BT_SS_005_003_159_A	P.190	07_WW_S_032_003_175_IP	P.212	08_KW_S_022_003_205_M
P.164	06_BT_SS_009_004_160_E	P.190	07_WW_S_009_004_176_C	P.212	08_KW_S_053_004_206_EP
P.164	06_BT_SS_003_005_161_SK	P.190	07_WW_S_004_005_177_PM	P.213	08_KW_S_018_005_207_S
P.164	06_BT_SS_042_006_162_EP	P.190	07_WW_S_044_006_178_EP	P.213	08_KW_S_054_006_208_EP
P.164	06_BT_SS_006_007_163_A	P.190	07_WW_S_014_007_179_HP	P.213	08_KW_S_017_007_209_HP
P.164	06_BT_SS_015_008_164_S	P.191	07_WW_S_045_008_180_EP	P.212	08_KW_S_008_008_210_DI
P.165	06_BT_SS_010_009_165_E	P.191	07_WW_S_046_009_181_EP	P.213	08_KW_S_019_009_211_S
P.165	06_BT_SS_016_010_166_M	P.191	07_WW_S_017_010_182_M	P.214	08_KW_S_055_010_212_EP
P.165	06_BT_SS_004_011_167_SK	P.191	07_WW_S_047_011_183_EP	P.214	08_KW_S_020_011_213_S
P.165	06_BT_SS_007_012_168_A	P.191	07_WW_S_005_012_184_SK	P.214	08_KW_S_011_012_214_E
P.165	06_BT_SS_007_013_169_C	P.191	07_WW_S_008_013_185_SP	P.214	08_KW_S_009_013_215_DI
P.164	06_BT_SS_008_014_170_A	P.190	07_WW_S_033_015_187_IP	P.215	08_KW_S_012_014_216_E
P.166	06_BT_SS_008_015_171_C	P.192	07_WW_S_016_016_188_S	P.215	08_KW_S_010_015_217_DI
P.170	06_BT_SS_009_016_172_A	P.192	07_WW_S_048_017_189_EP	P.215	08_KW_S_011_016_218_SP
		P.192	07_WW_S_017_018_190_S	P.215	08_KW_S_006_017_219_SK
		P.192	07_WW_S_019_019_191_M	P.216	08_KW_S_011_018_220_DI
		P.192	07_WW_S_020_020_192_M	P.217	08_KW_S_012_019_221_SP
		P.192	07_WW_S_009_021_193_SP	P.218	08_KW_S_056_020_222_EP
		P.193	07_WW_S_021_022_194_M	P.219	08_KW_S_012_021_223_DI
		P.193	07_WW_S_034_023_195_IP	P.220	08_KW_S_037_022_224_EP
		P.193	07_WW_S_015_024_196_HP		
		P.192	07_WW_S_035_025_197_IP		
		P.194	07_WW_SS_049_026_198_EP		
		P.195	07_WW_SS_010_027_199_SP		
		P.196	07_WW_SS_050_028_200_EP		
		P.197	07_WW_P_051_029_201_EP		
		P.198	07_WW_P_052_030_202_EP		

STUDENT WORK AND PRACTICE
(pp.32-211)

The coded abbreviations for all illiustrations listed within this section follow a system that categorises each item as follows; Chapter Chronology_City_Genre_Drawing Type Order_Chapter Order_Book Order_Page Number_Drawing Type.

* * * * *

The Abbreviations can be contextualised as follows:

CN - Copenhagen
AP - Antwerp
GA - Genoa
TE - Trieste
BT - Budapest
WW - Wroclaw
KW - Krakow

S - Student
SS - Selected Student
P - Practice

A - Axonometric
C - Collage
DI - Digital Illustration
E - Elevation
EP - Exterior Perspective
HP - Historic Photo
IP - Interior Perspective
M - Model
P - Plan
PM - Photo Montage
S - Section
SK - Sketch
SP - Site Plan

001	01_CN_S_ _023_023_P49_ 03_GA_SS_	**A**	**001**	01_CN_S_ _012_012_P47_ 02_AP_S_	**C**
002	_029_087_P97_ 04_TE_S_	**A**	**002**	_010_039_P70_ 02_AP_S_	**C**
003	_025_115_P116_ 05_TR_S_	**A**	**003**	_011_040_P71_ 02_AP_S_	**C**
004	_016_136_P136_ 06_BT_SS_	**A**	**004**	_021_050_P72_ 03_GA_S_	**C**
005	_003_159_P164_ 06_BT_SS_	**A**	**005**	_020_078_P94_ 03_GA_S_	**C**
006	_007_163_P164_ 06_BT_SS_	**A**	**006**	_024_082_P95_ 06_BT_SS_	**C**
007	_012_168_P165_ 06_BT_SS_	**A**	**007**	_013_169_P165_ 06_BT_SS_	**C**
008	_014_170_P164_ 06_BT_SS_	**A**	**008**	_015_171_P166_ 07_WW_S_	**C**
009	_016_172_P170_	**A**	**009**	_004_176_P190_	**C**

001	03_GA_S_ _010_068_P93_	DI	001	03_GA_S_ _017_075_P94_	E	001	01_CN_S_ _002_002_P46_	EP
002	03_GA_S_ _015_073_P94_	DI	002	03_GA_S_ _026_084_P95_	E	002	01_CN_S_ _004_004_P46_	EP
003	03_GA_S_ _018_076_P94_	DI	003	04_TE_S_ _007_097_P115_	E	003	01_CN_S_ _006_006_P47_	EP
004	03_GA_S_ _025_083_P95_	DI	004	04_TE_S_ _020_110_P117_	E	004	01_CN_S_ _010_010_P47_	EP
005	03_GA_Ss_ _028_086_P96_	DI	005	05_TR_S_ _008_128_P135_	E	005	01_CN_S_ _018_018_P48_	EP
006	05_TR_S_ _004_124_P134_	DI	006	05_TR_S_ _026_146_P137_	E	006	01_CN_S_ _027_027_P52_	EP
007	05_TR_P_ _036_156_P148_	DI	007	05_TR_SS_ _032_152_P144_	E	007	01_CN_P_ _029_029_P54_	EP
008	08_KW_S_ _008_210_P212_	DI	008	05_TR_SS_ _034_154_P146_	E	008	02_AP_S_ _002_031_P70_	EP
009	08_KW_S_ _013_215_P214_	DI	009	06_BT_SS_ _004_160_P164_	E	009	02_AP_S_ _007_036_P71_	EP
010	08_KW_S_ _015_217_P215_	DI	010	06_BT_SS_ _009_165_P165_	E	010	02_AP_S_ _008_037_P71_	EP
011	08_KW_S_ _018_220_P216_	DI	011	08_KW_S_ _012_214_P214_	E	011	02_AP_S_ _009_038_P71_	EP
012	08_KW_S_ _021_223_P219_	DI	012	08_KW_S_ _014_216_P215_	E	012	02_AP_S_ _018_047_P72_	EP
						013	02_AP_SS_ _023_052_P74_	EP
						014	02_AP_SS_ _024_053_P74_	EP
						015	02_AP_SS_ _026_055_P76_	EP
						016	02_AP_P_ _029_058_P80_	EP
						017	03_GA_S_ _006_064_P93_	EP
						018	03_GA_S_ _007_065_P93_	EP
						019	03_GA_S_ _008_066_P93_	EP
						020	03_GA_S_ _019_077_P94_	EP
						021	03_GA_S_ _022_080_P95_	EP
						022	03_GA_P_ _030_088_P98_	EP
						023	03_GA_P_ _032_090_P100_	EP
						024	04_TE_S_ _001_091_P114_	EP
						025	04_TE_S_ _008_098_P115_	EP
						026	04_TE_S_ _012_102_P116_	EP
						027	04_TE_S_ _014_104_P116_	EP
						028	04_TE_S_ _016_106_P116_	EP
						029	04_TE_S_ _018_108_P117_	EP
						030	04_TE_SS_ _026_116_P118_	EP
						031	04_TE_P_ _029_119_P120_	EP
						032	04_TE_P_ _030_120_P122_	EP
						033	05_TR_S_ _003_123_P134_	EP

034	05_TR_S_ _010_130_P135_	EP	001	01_CN_S_ _003_003_P46_	HP	001	01_CN_S_ _011_011_P47_	IP
035	05_TR_S_ _017_137_P136_	EP	002	01_CN_S_ _007_007_P47_	HP	002	01_CN_S_ _014_014_P48_	IP
036	05_TR_SS_ _028_148_P138_	EP	003	02_AP_S_ _004_033_P71_	HP	003	01_CN_S_ _021_021_P49_	IP
037	05_TR_P_ _030_150_P140_	EP	004	02_AP_S_ _015_044_P72_	HP	004	02_AP_S_ _003_032_P70_	IP
038	05_TR_P_ _031_151_P142_	EP	005	02_AP_S_ _017_046_P72_	HP	005	02_AP_S_ _006_035_P71_	IP
039	05_TR_SS_ _033_153_P144_	EP	006	04_TE_S_ _009_099_P115_	HP	006	02_AP_S_ _012_041_P72_	IP
041	06_BT_SS_ _002_158_P164_	EP	007	04_TE_S_ _010_100_P115_	HP	007	02_AP_S_ _013_042_P72_	IP
042	06_BT_SS_ _006_162_P164_	EP	008	04_TE_S_ _023_113_P117_	HP	008	02_AP_S_ _016_045_P72_	IP
043	07_WW_S_ _001_173_P189_	EP	009	04_TE_P_ _028_118_P120_	HP	009	02_AP_S_ _019_048_P73_	IP
044	07_WW_S_ _006_178_P190_	EP	010	05_TR_S_ _002_122_P134_	HP	010	02_AP_SS_ _025_054_P75_	IP
045	07_WW_S_ _008_180_P191_	EP	011	05_TR_S_ _012_132_P136_	HP	011	02_AP_SS_ _027_056_P77_	IP
046	07_WW_S_ _009_181_P191_	EP	012	05_TR_S_ _023_143_P137_	HP	012	03_GA_S_ _001_059_P92_	IP
047	07_WW_S_ _011_183_P191_	EP	013	07_WW_S_ _002_174_P190_	HP	013	03_GA_S_ _002_060_P92_	IP
048	07_WW_S_ _017_189_P192_	EP	014	07_WW_S_ _007_179_P190_	HP	014	03_GA_S_ _003_061_P92_	IP
049	07_WW_SS_ _026_198_P194_	EP	015	07_WW_S_ _024_196_P193_	HP	015	03_GA_S_ _005_063_P92_	IP
050	07_WW_SS_ _028_200_P196_	EP	016	08_KW_S_ _001_203_P212_	HP	016	03_GA_S_ _009_067_P93_	IP
051	07_WW_P_ _029_201_P197_	EP	017	08_KW_S_ _007_209_P213_	HP	017	03_GA_S_ _014_072_P94_	IP
052	07_WW_P_ _030_202_P198_	EP				018	03_GA_S_ _016_074_P94_	IP
053	08_KW_S_ _004_206_P212_	EP				019	03_GA_S_ _021_079_P95_	IP
054	08_KW_S_ _006_208_P213_	EP				020	03_GA_S_ _023_081_P95_	IP
055	08_KW_S_ _010_212_P214_	EP				021	03_GA_P_ _031_089_P99_	IP
056	08_KW_S_ _020_222_P218_	EP				022	04_TE_S_ _003_093_P114_	IP
037	08_KW_S_ _022_224_P220_	EP				023	04_TE_S_ _013_103_P116_	IP
						024	04_TE_S_ _019_109_P117_	IP
						025	04_TE_SS_ _027_117_P118_	IP
						026	05_TR_S_ _005_125_P135_	IP
						027	05_TR_S_ _007_127_P135_	IP
						028	05_TR_S_ _014_134_P136_	IP
						029	05_TR_S_ _020_140_P137_	IP
						030	05_TR_S_ _022_142_P137_	IP
						031	05_TR_SS_ _029_149_P139_	IP
						032	07_WW_S_ _003_175_P180_	IP
						033	07_WW_S_ _015_187_P190_	IP

034	07_WW_S_ _023_195_P193_	IP	001	01_CN_S_ _009_009_P47_	M	001	01_CN_S_ _008_008_P47_	P
035	07_WW_S_ _025_197_P192_	IP	002	01_CN_S_ _015_015_P48_	M	002	01_CN_S_ _013_013_P47_	P
036	08_KW_S_ _002_204_P212_	IP	003	01_CN_S_ _016_016_P48_	M	003	02_AP_S_ _022_051_P73_	P
			004	01_CN_S_ _017_017_P48_	M	004	02_AP_SS_ _028_057_P78_	P
			005	01_CN_S_ _020_020_P49_	M	005	03_GA_S_ _012_070_P92_	P
			006	01_CN_S_ _022_022_P49_	M	006	05_TR_S_ _015_135_P136_	P
			007	01_CN_S_ _026_026_P51_	M	007	05_TR_S_ _024_144_P136_	P
			008	01_CN_P_ _028_028_P53_	M	008	05_TR_S_ _027_147_P137_	P
			009	02_AP_S_ _005_034_P71_	M			
			010	02_AP_S_ _014_043_P72_	M			
			011	02_AP_S_ _020_049_P73_	M			
			012	03_GA_S_ _004_062_P92_	M			
			013	04_TE_S_ _002_092_P114_	M			
			014	05_TR_S_ _006_126_P135_	M			
			015	05_TR_S_ _013_133_P136_	M			
			016	06_BT_SS_ _010_166_P165_	M			
			017	07_WW_S_ _010_182_P191_	M			
			018	07_WW_S_ _014_186_P191_	M			
			019	07_WW_S_ _019_191_P192_	M			
			020	07_WW_S_ _020_192_P192_	M			
			021	07_WW_S_ _022_194_P193_	M			
			022	08_KW_S_ _003_205_P212_	M			

001	01_CN_S_ _019_019_P48_ 04_TE_S_	**PM**	001	01_CN_S_ _001_001_P44_ 03_GA_S_	**S**	001	01_CN_S_ _024_024_P49_ 02_AP_S_	**SK**
002	_011_101_P114_ 04_TE_S_	**PM**	002	_013_071_P93_ 03_GA_S_	**S**	002	_001_030_P69_ 06_BT_SS_	**SK**
003	_022_112_P117_ 07_WW_S_	**PM**	003	_027_085_P95_ 04_TE_S_	**S**	003	_005_161_P164_ 06_BT_SS_	**SK**
004	_005_177_P190_	**PM**	004	_004_094_P114_ 04_TE_S_	**S**	004	_011_167_P165_ 07_WW_S_	**SK**
			005	_005_095_P115_ 04_TE_S_	**S**	005	_012_184_P191_ 08_KW_S_	**SK**
			006	_015_105_P116_ 04_TE_S_	**S**	006	_017_219_P215_	**SK**
			007	_017_107_P116_ 04_TE_S_	**S**			
			008	_021_111_P117_ 04_TE_S_	**S**			
			009	_024_114_P117_ 05_TR_S_	**S**			
			010	_001_121_P134_ 05_TR_S_	**S**			
			011	_011_131_P134_ 05_TR_S_	**S**			
			012	_018_138_P137_ 05_TR_S_	**S**			
			013	_019_139_P137_ 05_TR_S_	**S**			
			014	_025_145_P136_ 06_BT_SS_	**S**			
			015	_008_164_P164_ 07_WW_S_	**S**			
			016	_016_188_P192_ 07_WW_S_	**S**			
			017	_018_190_P192_ 08_KW_S_	**S**			
			018	_005_207_P213_ 08_KW_S_	**S**			
			019	_009_211_P213_ 08_KW_S_	**S**			
			020	_011_213_P214_	**S**			

001	01_CN_S_ _005_005_P46_	**SP**
002	02_AP_SS_ _028_057_P78_	**SP**
003	03_GA_S_ _011_069_P93_	**SP**
004	04_TE_S_ _006_096_P115_	**SP**
005	05_TR_S_ _009_129_P135_	**SP**
006	05_TR_S_ _021_141_P137_	**SP**
007	06_BT_SS_ _001_157_P164_	**SP**
008	07_WW_S_ _013_185_P191_	**SP**
009	07_WW_S_ _021_193_P192_	**SP**
010	07_WW_SS_ _027_199_P195_	**SP**
011	08_KW_S_ _016_218_P215_	**SP**
012	08_KW_S_ _019_221_P217_	**SP**

CREDITS

SB PROFESSIONAL ILLUSTRATION CREDITS
(pp.32-211)

A coded [_P_] in the previous archive chapter identifies work in practice. The full credits are listed here and numbered on the individual image or drawing.

* * * * *

001
1. **SIMHIKA RAO**
   ©Jack Hobhouse (Piercy&Company).
2. Digital imagery by INK (Piercy&Company).

002
3. **LOUISE SCANNELL**
   Rye Hill Park Housing, ©London Borough of Southwark (WestonWilliamson+Partners).

003
4. **TOBIAS PLUNKETT**
   Pattern Architects.
5. Ibid.
6. Ibid.

004
7. **JULIANNE CASSIDY**
   © Hunan TV Studios (HPP Architects, Shanghai).
8. Ibid.

005
9. **HANNAH GAZE**
   St Paul's School, General Teaching Building (Walters & Cohen Architects).
10. Lairdsland Primary School, ©Dennis Gilbert/VIEW (Walters & Cohen Architects).

006
11. **MATTHEW STEWART**
    Internet of Utopian Things (Yellow (smart) House or: Who will own data in Jarfalla?).

007
12. **HELEN MISSELBROOK**
    Circus Street Masterplan, Brighton, Helen Misselbrook Architects consultant at shedkm Architects.
13. Ibid.
14. ibid.

008
15. **CATRIONA HUNTER**
    Rugby Experience for M&C Saatchi (Banbury Walker Studio).
16. Porter Launch at London Fashion Week for My Beautiful City (Banbury Walker Studio).

009
17. **LUCY BROOKE**
    St. George's School, Azezo. Northern Ethiopia. (Northwood African Education Foundation [NAEF])
18. Ibid.

CITY CARTOGRAPHIC ILLUSTRATION CREDITS
(pp.32-211)

Every effort has been made to contact relevant copyright holders beyond the auspices of 'creative commons'. Where we have been unable to determine the exact source of the particular example of the map used, we have cited an archive where its equivalent may be accessed.

* * * * *

001 MAP OF COPENHAGEN 1779
Wikimedia US CC (PD-1923)
(Danish State Archives)

002 ANTWERP 1832
Courtesy, David Rumsey Map Collection, David Rumsey Map Center, Stanford
Libraries. https://purl.stanford.edu/ck406vy7856

003 GENOA 1872
Italy - Hand Book for Travellers. First Part.
(Northern Italy) Karl Baedeker
Wikimedia 'Old Maps of Genoa' 14783857853 CC (PD-1923)
(Emory University, Book Collection)

004 TOPOGRAPHICAL MAP OF TRIESTE 1850
Austro-Hungary 'Second Military Survey' (1806-1869)
© Österreichisches Staatsarchiv (Kriegsarchiv)

005 STREET PLAN OF TRIESTE 1911
From: Austria-Hungary, with excursions to Cetinje, Belgrade, and Bucharest: handbook for travellers
K. Baedeker, Leipzig, US CC
Internet Archive https://archive.org/
(Pennsylvania State University)

006 BUDAPEST 1918
Budapest 1:25000, 1918
Mario Kogutowicz (publisher Magyar foldrajzi intezet)
Budapest City Archives

007 WRATISLAVIA – BRESSLAW 1660
Matthäus Merian
Wikimedia US CC (PD-1923)
(University of Mannheim)

008 KRAKOW PLAN Z 1866
Wikimedia US CC (PD-1923)

**GOOGLE MAPS
ILLUSTRATION CREDITS**
(pp.32-211)

All map images presented within this publciation have been provided with the citation 'IMAGE © 2015 DIGITAL GLOBE' Corresponding numbers have also been provided to correspond with the adjacent list.

* * * * *

001 **AERIAL VIEW OF COPENHAGEN**
Google Maps. (2017). Google Maps. [online] Available at: https://www.google.co.uk/maps/place/Copenhagen,+Denmark/@55.6824996,12.5866127,5106m/data=!3m1!1e3!4m5!3m4!1s0x4652533c5c803d23:0x4dd7edde69467b8!8m2!3d55.6760968!4d12.5683372
[Accessed 12 Jul. 2017].

002 **AERIAL VIEW OF ANTWERP**
Google Maps. (2017). Google Maps. [online] Available at: https://www.google.co.uk/maps/place/Antwerp,+Belgium/@51.2128767,4.4104999,5674m/data=!3m1!1e3!4m5!3m4!1s0x47c3f68ebfc3887d:0x3eaf448482a88ab8!8m2!3d51.2194475!4d4.4024643
[Accessed 12 Jul. 2017].

003 **AERIAL VIEW OF GENOA**
Google Maps. (2017). Google Maps. [online] Available at: https://www.google.co.uk/maps/place/Genoa,+Metropolitan+City+of+Genoa,+Italy/@44.4136135,8.9076961,6470m/data=!3m1!1e3!4m5!3m4!1s0x12d34152dcd49aad:0x236a84f11881620a!8m2!3d44.4056499!4d8.946256
[Accessed 12 Jul. 2017].

004 **AERIAL VIEW OF TRIESTE**
Google Maps. (2017). Google Maps. [online] Available at: https://-www.google.co.uk/maps/place/Trieste,+Province+of+Trieste,+Italy/@45.6430746,13.766431,3166m/data=!3m1!1e3!4m5!3m4!1s0x477b6b06e4edf533:0x666a2484d4dd2b50!8m2!3d45.6495264!4d13.7768182
[Accessed 12 Jul. 2017].

005 **AERIAL VIEW OF BUDAPEST**
Google Maps. (2017). Google Maps. [online] Available at: https://www.google.co.uk/maps/place/Budapest,+Hungary/@47.4974836,19.0385864,6119m/data=!3m1!1e3!4m5!3m4!1s0x4741c334d1d4cfc9:0x400c4290c1e1160!8m2!3d47.497912!4d19.040235
[Accessed 12 Jul. 2017].

006 **AERIAL VIEW OF WROCŁAW**
Google Maps. (2017). Google Maps. [online] Available at: https://www.google.co.uk/maps/place/Wroc%C5%82aw,Poland/@51.1110197,17.0284003,2843m/data=!3m1!1e3!4m5!3m4!1s0x470fe9c2d4b58abf:0xb70956aec205e0f5!8m2!3d51.1078852!4d17.0385376
[Accessed 12 Jul. 2017].

007 **AERIAL VIEW OF KRAKÓW**
Google Maps. (2017). Google Maps. [online] Available at: https://www.google.co.uk/maps/place/Krak%C3%B3w,+Poland/@50.0559207,19.9323446,2908m/data=!3m1!1e3!4m5!3m4!1s0x471644c0354e18d1:0xb46bb6b576478abf!8m2!3d50.0646501!4d19.9449799
[Accessed 12 Jul. 2017].

BIBLIOGRAPHY

WROCLAW
2008–2009

Aman, A., Architecture and Ideology in Europe during the Stalin Era (Cambridge, Mass., MIT, 1992).

Beelitz, K., Förster, N., Breslau / Wroclaw: Die Architektur der Moderne (Berlin, Wasmuth, 2006).

Davies, N., Moorhouse, R., Microcosm: Portrait of a Central European City (London, Pimlico/Random House, 2003).

Gryglewska, A., Wroclawskie Hale Targowe 1908-2008 (Wroclaw, Muzeum Architektury we Wroclawiu, 2008).

Kapuscinski, R., Travels with Herodotus (London, Penguin, 2008).

Klimek, E., Wroclaw: Photographs from the Turn of the 20th Century (Wroclaw, Via Nova, 2002).

Muthesius, S., 'Hochhauser fur Breslau 1919-1932', JOSAH, 57, 4 (1998), pp. 476–477.

Muthsius, S., Art, Architecture and Design in Poland 966-1990: An Introduction (Konigstein, Langewiesche, 1994).

Sanford, G., Poland: the conquest of history (Amsterdam, Harwood Academic, 1999).

Welzbacher, C., 'Wroclaw: Europe's open end', Archis, 9 (2000), pp. 8-17

Wiblin, I., 'Recovered Territory: the spectral cities of Breslau and Wroclaw', The JoA, 11, 5 (2006), pp. 551–557.

TRIESTE
2009–2010 / 2013–2014

Ballinger, P., 'Imperial Nostalgia: Mythologizing Hapsburg Trieste', Journal of Italian Studies, 8, 1 (2003), pp. 84–101.

Bialasiewicz, L., 'Europe as/at the border: Trieste and the meaning of Europe', Social and Cultural Geography, 10, 3 (2009), pp. 319–336.

Cary, J., A Ghost in Trieste (Chicago/London, University of Chicago, 1993).

Drndic, D., Trieste (London, MacLehose, 2013)

Dubin, L., The Port Jews of Habsburg Trieste, (Stanford California, CUP, 1999).

Hametz, M., Making Trieste Italian (Woodbridge, Boydell, 2005).

Joyce, J., Ulysses (Dublin, Lilliput Press, 2000).

Magris, C., 'Who is on the Other Side: considerations about frontiers', various eds., Leopard III, Frontiers, (London, Harvill, 1994), pp. 8–25.

Magris, C., 'Caffè San Marco' and 'Public Garden', Microcosms (London, Harvill, 1999), pp. 3–30, 233–268.

McCourt, J., The Years of Bloom: James Joyce in Trieste 1904-1920 (Dublin, Lilliput, 2000).

Minca, C., 'Trieste Nazione' and its Geographies of Absence', Social and Cultural Geography, 10, 3 (2009), pp. 257–278.

Morris, J., Trieste and the Meaning of Nowhere (London, Faber, 2001).

Opara, C., Three Days in Trieste (Trieste, Beit, 2013).

Pizzi, K., A City in Search of an Author: the literary identity of Trieste (London, Sheffield Academic, 2001).

Svevo, I., Zeno's Conscience (London, Penguin, 2002).

Waley, P., 'Introducing Trieste: a cosmopolitan city?', Social and Cultural Geography, 10, 3 (2009), pp. 243–256.

ANTWERP / GHENT
2010–2011

Borret, et. al., eds., Homeward: contemporary architecture in Flanders (Antwerp, deSingel, 1998).

Borsi, F., Portoghesi, P., Horta (Braine-l'Alleud, Editions JM Collet, 1996).

Borsi, F., La Maison du Peuple (Bari, Dedalo Libri, 1978).

Brauman, A., Culot, M., et. al., eds., Maisons du Peuple (Bruxelles, AAM, 1984).

Caruso, A., 'Intimate Constructions', The Feeling of Things (Barcelona, Editions Polígrafa, 2008), pp. 61–71.

De Kooning, M., ed., Horta and After (Ghent, DAU Ghent University, 2001).

Dernie, D., Carew-Cox, A., Victor Horta (London, Academy Editions, 1995).

Honig, E., Painting and the Market in Early Modern Antwerp (New Haven/London, Yale UP, 1999).

O'Brien, P., Urban Achievement in Early Modern Europe (Cambridge, CUP, 2001).

Perez-Reverte, A., The Flanders Panel (London, Harvill, 1994).

Royle, N., Antwerp (London, Serpents Tail, 2004).

Wilssens, M., 365 Days Antwerp (Antwerpen, Lannoo/Stadsarchief, 2009).

KRAKOW / KATOWICE
2011-2012

Baldauf. A., 'Selling the Shtetl', in Ockman, J., Frausto, S., eds., Architourism (Munich/London/New York, Prestel, 2005), pp. 56–60.

Crowley, D., 'Architecture and the image of the future in the People's Republic of Poland', The JoA, 14, 1 (2009), pp. 67–84.

Davies, D., Heart of Europe: The Past in Poland's Present (Oxford, OUP, 2001).

Hoffmann, E., Lost in Translation (London, Minerva, 1991).

Millard, F., 'Environmental policy in Poland', Environmental Politics, 7, 1 (1998), pp. 145–161.

Stanek, L., 'Simulation or Hospitality - Beyond the Crisis of Representation in Nowa Huta', Frers, L., Meier, L., eds., Encountering Urban Places (Aldershot, Ashgate, 2007), pp. 135–154.

Stasiuk, A., Fado (Champaign/London, Dalkey, 2009).

Stenning, A., 'Placing (Post-) Socialism: The Making and Remaking of Nowa Huta, Poland', European Urban and Regional Studies, 7, 2 (2000), pp. 99–118.

Kudsen, B., T., 'The past as staged-real environment: communism revisited in The Crazy Guides Communism Tours, Krakow, Poland', Journal of Tourism and Cultural Change, 8, 3 (2010), pp. 139–153.

Whitehead, M., 'Between the Marvellous and the Mundane: Everyday Life in the Socialist City and the Politics of the Environment', Environment and Planning D: Society and Space, 23, 2 (2005), pp. 273–294.

COPENHAGEN / MALMO
2012–2013

Note: the histories of these two cities were less the focus than the narrative theme of Nordic Noir—hence these references.

Barthes, R., 'Introduction to the Structural Analysis of Narratives', Heath, S., ed., Image-Music-Text (Glasgow, Fontana/Collins, 1977), pp.79–124.

Calvino, I., If on a Winter's Night a Traveller (London, Minerva, 1992).

Ellis, T., 'The Discipline of the Route', AD (November 1960), pp. 481–482.

Evans, R., 'Figures, Doors and Passages', AD, 48, 4 (1978), pp. 267–278.

Heath, S., 'Narrative Space', Screen, 17, 3 (1976).

Lamster, M., Architecture and Film (New York, Princeton UP, 2000).

McQuillan, M., ed., The Narrative Reader (London/New York, Routledge, 2000).

Pai, H., The Portfolio and the Diagram (Cambridge Mass./London, MIT Press, 2002).

Psarra, S., Architecture and Narrative (London/New York, Routledge, 2009).

Tschumi, B., The Manhattan Transcripts (London, Academy, 1981).

Todorov, S., 'The Typology of Detective Fiction', The Poetics of Prose (Oxford, Blackwell, 1977).

GENOA
2015–2016

Bonfanti, F., Pallini, C., 'The Role of a Historic Townscape in City Reconstruction', Pendlebury, J., Erten, E., Larkham, P. J., Alternative Visions of Post-war Reconstruction: Creating the Modern Townscape (London, Routledge, 2015), pp. 142–160.

Cairns, S., Jacobs, J., M., Buildings Must Die: A Perverse View of Architecture (Cambridge, Mass., London, MIT Press, 2014).

Epstein, S., A., Genoa and the Genoese 958–1528 (Chapel Hill, University of North Carolina Press, 2001).

Leet, S., Franco Albini: Architecture and Design 1934-1977 (New York, Princeton Arch. Press, 1990).

Musso, S., F., 'Conservare il Moderno: Franco Albini e il Museo del Tesoro di San Lorenzo', Quaderni di'Ananke, 5 (2015).

Poleggi, E., 'The Strada Nuova in Genoa', Daidalos, 10 (1983), pp. 22–27.

Prina, V., Sant' Agostino a Genova, Stories of Buildings and Places, n.1 (Genova, SAGEP, 1992).

Rossi Prodi, F., Franco Albini (Roma, Officina Edizioni, 1996).

BUDAPEST
2016–2017

Alofsin, A., When Buildings Speak: Architecture as Language in the Habsburg Empire and its Aftermath, 1867-1933 (Chicago, the University of Chicago Press, 2006).

Anderson, W., et. al., The Grand Budapest Hotel: The Wes Anderson Collection (New York, Abrams, 2015).

Bodnár, J., Fin de Millenaire Budapest (Minneapolis/London, University of Minnesota, 2001).

Buarque, C., Budapest (London, Bloomsbury, 2005).

Csapó, T., Lenner., eds., Settlement Morphology of Budapest (Cham, Springer, 2016).

Clegg, E., Art, Design and Architecture in Central Europe 1890-1920 (New Haven, Yale UP, 2006).

Enzensberger, H., M., Europe, Europe: Forays into a Continent (London, Hutchinson Radius, 1989).

Esterházy, P., The Glance of Countess Hahn-Hahn (down the Danube) (Evanston, Northwestern UP, 1999).

Ferkai, A., 'Neues Bauen in Budapest', Blau, E., Platzer, M., eds., Shaping the Great City: Modern Architecture in Central Europe, 1890–1937 (Munich/London/New York, Prestel, 1999), pp. 178–180.

Firebrace, W., 'Location Gorlitz-Zgorzelec', AA Files, 69 (2014), pp. 65–76.

Gluck, G., The Invisible Jewish Budapest: Metropolitan Culture at the Fin de Siècle (Madison. University of Wisconsin Press, 2016).

Gyáni, G., Parlour and Kitchen: Housing and Domestic culture in Budapest,1870-1940 (Budapest/New York, CEUP, 2002).

Hanák, P., The Garden and the Workshop: Essays on the Cultural History of Vienna and Budapest (Princeton, Princeton UP, 1999).

Heathcote, E., Budapest: A Guide to Twentieth-Century Architecture (London, Ellipsis, 1997).

Judson, P., The Hapsburg Empire: A New History (Cambridge, Mass., The Belknap Press, 2016).

Konrad, G., The City Builder (Champaign/London, 2007).

Lesnikowski, ed., East European Modernism 1919-1939 (New York, Rizzoli, 1996).

Lukacs, J., Budapest 1900 (New York, Grove, 1988).

Magris, C., Danube (London, Collins Harvill, 1990).

Moravànszky, A., Competing Visions (Cambridge, Mass., London, MIT).

Sked, A., The Decline and fall of the Habsburg Empire 1815-1918 (Harlow, Longman, 2001).

QUOTES

1 -	p.48	Hilberseimer, L. *Größstadatarchiktur*, see A. Peckham, T. Schmiedknecht, eds., The Rationalist Reader (Abingdon, Routledge, 2014), p. 90.	COPENHAGEN NORDIC NOIR
2 -	p. 88	Epstein, S. A. *Genoa and the Genoese 958–1528* (Chapel Hill, University of North Carolina Press, 2001).	GENOA MODES OF EXCHANGE
3 -	p. 90	Barthes, R. *The Nautilus and the Drunken Boat*, Mythologies (St Albans, Paladin, 1973).	
4 -	p. 91	Saramago, J. *The Manual of Painting and Calligraphy: A Novel* (Manchester, Carcanet, 1995).	
5 -	p. 91	Leet, S. *Franco Albini: Architecture and Design 1934-1977* (New York, Princeton Arch. Press, 1990).	
6 -	p. 115	Morris, J. *Trieste the Meaning of Nowehere* (London, Faber, 2001), p. 4.	TRIESTE COSMOPOLITAN 'REGIONS'/ GLOBAL LOCALE
7 -	p. 130	Croset, P. *Microcosms of the Architect*, Rassegna, 9, 32 (1987), pp. 46–56.	TRIESTE/REVISITED CITY AS MEDIUM
8 -	p. 131	Puff, H. *Ruins as Models: Displaying Destruction in Postwar Germany*, J. Hell, A. Schönle, Ruins of Modernity (Durham/London, Duke UP, 2010), pp. 253–269.	
9 -	p. 134	Bialasiewicz, L. *Europe as/at the border: Trieste and the meaning of Europe*, Social and Cultural Geography, 10, 3 (2009), pp.319-336.	
10 -	p. 156	Esterházy, P. *The Glance of Countess Hahn-Hahn* (down the Danube) (Evanston, Northwestern UP, 1999). R. Kapuscinski, Travels with Herodotus (London, Penguin, 2008).	BUDAPEST ARCHITECTURE OF STASIS AND FLUX
11 - 12 - 14 -	p. 180 p. 180 p. 183	Welzbacher, C. *Wroclaw: Europe's open end*, Archis, 9 (2000), pp. 8–17.	WROCLAW RECOVERING WROCLAW/ CITY AS PALIMPSEST/ SILESIAN FIELDS

13 -	p.183	Kapuscinski, R. *Travels with Herodotus* (London, Penguin, 2008), p.71.	
15 -	p.192	Davies, N. & Moorhouse, R. *Microcosm: Portrait of a Central European City* (London, Pimlico/Random House, 2003), p. 457.	
16 -	p.193	Wiblin, I. *Recovered Territory: the spectral cities of Breslau and Wroclaw photographically revisited*, The JoA 11, 5 (2006), p.554.	
17 - 18 -	p. 206 p. 209	Whitehead, M. *Between the Marvellous and the Mundane: Everyday Life in the Socialist City and the Politics of the Environment*, Environment and Planning D: Society and Space, 23, 2 (2005), pp. 273–294.	KRAKOW DUAL IDENTITIES
19 -	p. 210	Koolhaas, R. Foster, H. *Junkspace with Running Room* (London, Notting Hill Editions, 2013), pp. 1-37.	
20 -	p. 210	Siza, A. *On Materials*, W.Wang ed., Alvaro Siza Figures and Configurations: Buildings and Projects 1986-1988 (New York, Rizzoli, 1988), p. 5.	

CATALOGUE

CATALOGUE AS CONSTRUCT/ARTEFACT

You are asked to draw up a catalogue that constitutes an inventory of the formal assets that you have acquired (individually and collectively) during the initial four weeks. It may incorporate additional material of your own and should register a conceptual intent, site and a theme or title for your design thesis. The idea is to ground your thesis project, in collecting, categorising and archiving visual material in order to establish a vocabulary and a thematic focus.

Inventoried Consciousness

Catalogues are typically lists or collections of products, commodities, artefacts, forms or elements. Your catalogue should be structured (or coded) systematically, whether alphabetically, numerically or under thematic headings, and completed as a publication (book or pamphlet) for the forthcoming X Reviews.

The architect's treatise (Serlio, Alberti, Di Georgio, Filarete, Palladio and Von Erlach) is also a form of catalogue where precedents from architectural history are juxtaposed with representative projects and explanatory text (or commentary). There are similar books elaborating the principles of the classical 'orders' – Vignola, Delorme and Scamozzi. In contrast C19th rationalist architects catalogued building types, typologies or construction elements (Durand), as did contemporary trade or craft manuals, or later empirical handbooks such as Neufert's Architects Data. Le Corbusier's books or in a more contemporary idiom Rem Koolhaas/OMA's publications (which have spawned a plethora of imitators – many influenced by Bruce Mau's Lifestyle) have similar characteristics.

Our conception of the Catalogue is located somewhere between a treatise and a manifest, the inference being that it is 'representative' but also useful. Consider spatial composition; constitutive form (typologies, elements, components or assemblies); referential images; sites or locations; programmes or building types and material precedents. How to formulate these as a foundation for your thesis project?

INITIAL PRESENTATION:
CATALOGUE AS ARTEFACT
At this early stage a draft format, structure and outline content should be presented in the form of an artefact:

01 Format
folded paper or individual pages
02 Structure
sections and headings
03 Content
a manifest or manifesto?
04 On The Wall

FINAL PRESENTATION:
EXHIBITED CATALOGUE
Pages of your catalogues are to be exhibited as a 'poster wall' of collective work in the studio (exhibiting their graphic currency in a form of seamless wallpaper). Display their visual narrative structure even if text may not read at a micro-scale.

Our final expectation is of a high quality publication, where the graphic design, paper quality, size, layout, binding and the cover, present an 'architectural' form to the publication as artefact.

TREATISE

H. F. Mallgrave, ed., Architectural Theory, vol. 1 (Oxford, Blackwell, 2006).
Useful extracts from the classical canon
T. Nebois, ed., Architectural Theory (London, Taschen, 2003).
Summaries and illustrations
Powers, 'The Architectural Book', K. Rattenbury, ed., This is Not Architecture (London/New York, Routledge, 2002).
R. Koolhaas, B. Mau, eds., S,M,L,XL (Rotterdam, 010 Publishers, 1995).
P. Ursprung, ed., Caruso St John: Almost Everything (Barcelona, Ediciones Poligrafa, 2008)
B. van Berkel, C. Bos, Move (Amsterdam, UNS/Goose, 1999) and UNSTUDIO.UNFOLD (Rotterdam, NAi, 2002)

LITTLE MAGAZINES

B. Colomina, C. Buckley eds., Clip/Stamp/Fold (Barcelona/Basel, Actar/Birkhäuser, 2010).

GRAPHIC DESIGN

S. De Bondt, F. Muggeridge, eds., The Form of the Book Book (London, Occasional Papers, 2009).
B. Mau, Life Style (London/New York, Phaidon, 2000)
A. Vinegar, I Am A Monument (Cambridge, Mass., MIT, 2008).
G. Mack, ed., Herzog & de Meuron: The Complete Works, vol. 2 and 4, (Basel, Birkhäuser, 1997 and 2008).
See book design by Mangold and Balland respectively
C. de Smet, Le Corbusier Architect of Books (Baden, Lars Müller, 2007).
G. Crespi, ed., ABC of 20th Century Graphics (Milano, Electa, 2002).
Accessible compendium

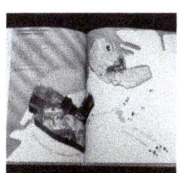

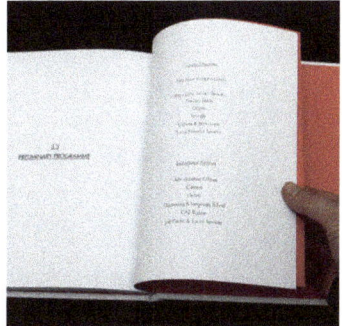

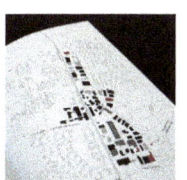

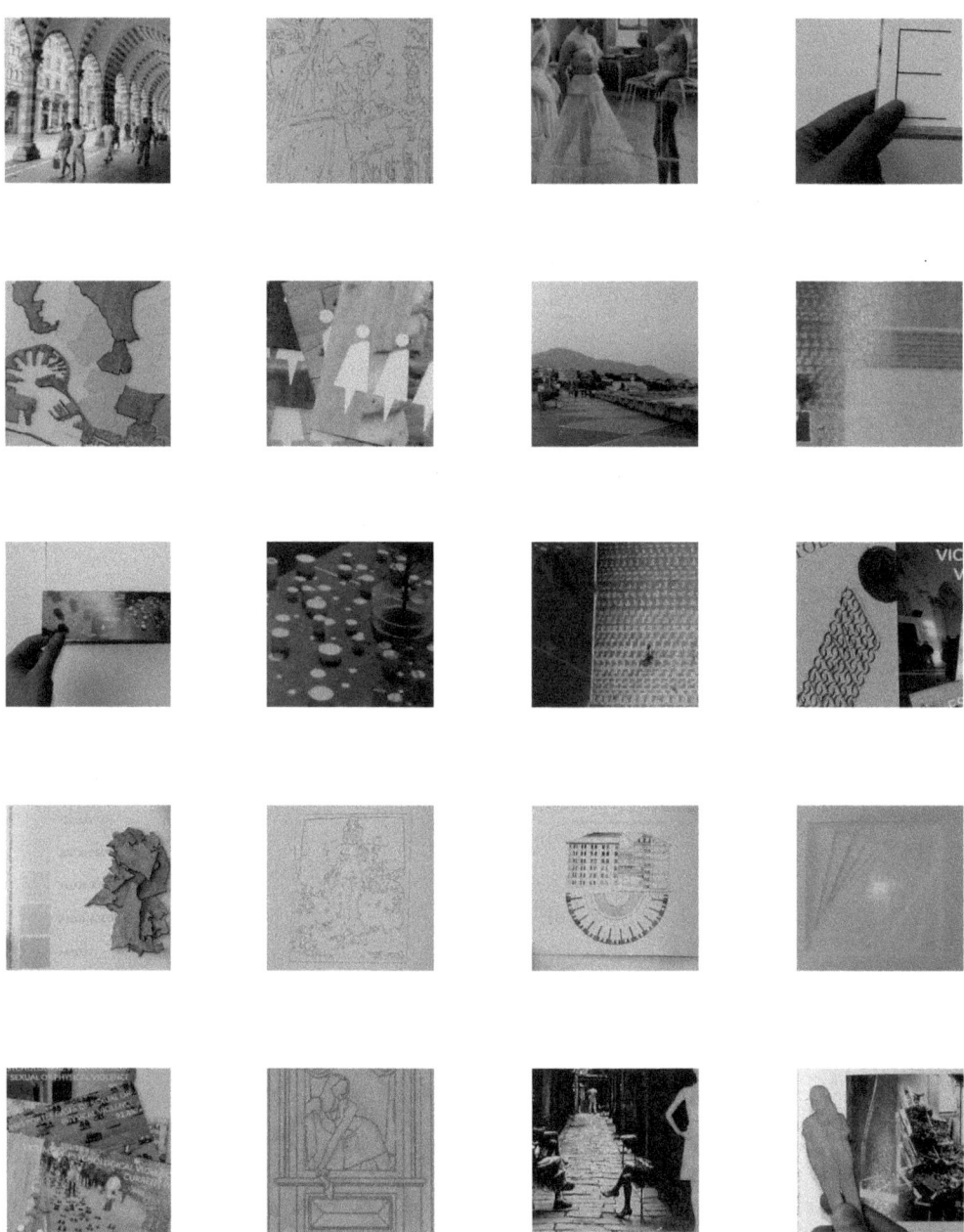

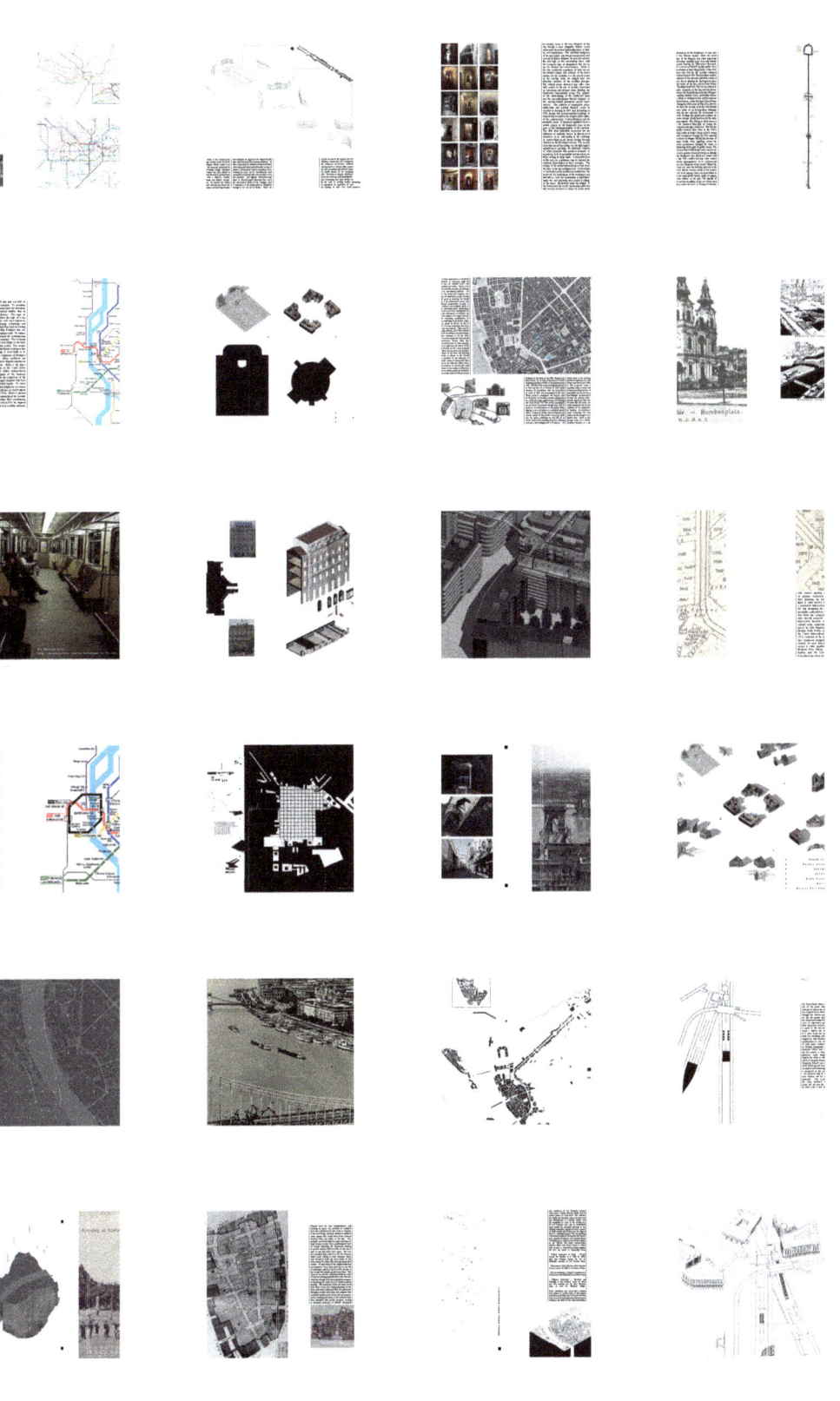

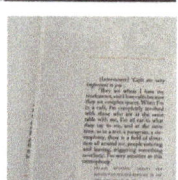

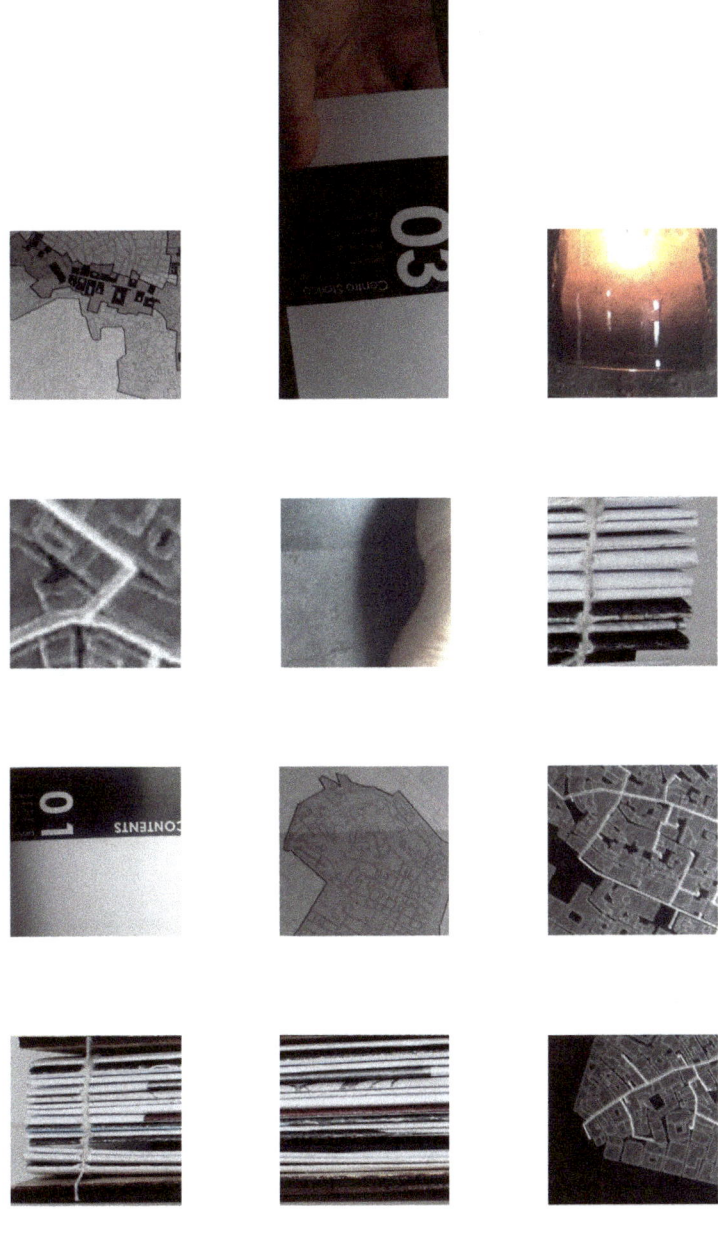

  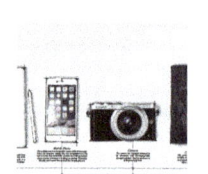 
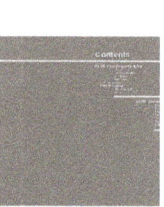   
  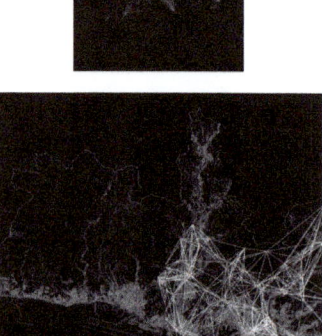 

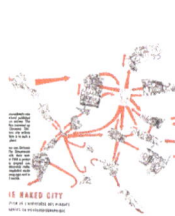   

AFTERWORD(S)

DIFFERENT REALMS OF PRACTICE

LUCY BROOKE

LUCY BROOKE

DIFFERENT REALMS OF PRACTICE

Since qualifying as an Architect I have worked across a range of sectors at varying scales. On leaving university, I was keen to establish a breadth of experience from which to apply the skills and further develop the applied knowledge of design I had acquired in the academic 'design studio'. To this end I see my career to date as a continuation of my education and my architectural experience in practice spans across infrastructure, culture, urban planning, education, and most recently the residential, sectors. My time in the design studio instilled in me the importance to come to each project with new eyes and to re-examine the set of principles within which I find myself working. Throughout the development of my final projects I was taught the importance the relationship between theory and design, and that you cannot place one before the other but rather, for the success of a project, they should be addressed in an active inter-relationship in order explore the working parameters set by the brief. Currently based in the UK I have also for the last three years been working freelance on the design and construction of a school in Ethiopia. The construction of the school is phased over ten years and will provide education for eight hundred pupils. Set in a rural area its aim is to provide education for under privileged children, funded from the UK. Working within a different cultural context required me to question and re-address habitual working assumptions.

Based in Ethiopia full-time for the first eight months, I initially struggled with how to progress the work required both in terms of the design, necessary team-work and construction expertise. I was working within the parameters of a master plan, but also largely working independently in constructing a local team for the project. Initially this was an isolating experience and during the first month I struggled to make headway and this led me to reflect on and revisit the practices I had been introduced to whilst at university. The transition to Africa and the contrast to working in the UK required an altered approach and so I started to tackle the project in the same way as I would have in a university design studio. This helped me to develop and ground my agency within a new framework and to form a new dialogue with the team involved. The language barrier meant that I became once again reliant on sketching and illustrative skills to convey ideas, much in the same manner as work was produced in the studio. My work took me from YouTube to check how to reinforce a slab, to handling the subtle cultural differences highlighted when I specified Vitreous china sanitary-ware to ensure it was suitable, only to discover that in Ethiopia 'china' is a term associated with inferior quality. An afternoon attempt to explain subsequently, was spent

handling crockery in the kitchen. Ethiopia is a country steeped in tradition, with a climate of extremes and an uncertain political landscape. With a limited palette of building materials and restricted access to water and electricity, I was presented with a unique set of challenges. Given a social responsibility to the wider community and the need to develop the means to finance the project, it is by a long chalk the most far reaching project I have worked on requiring the full breadth of everything I have learnt both in practice and architectural education. The projects I produced in the design studio instilled in me a broad set of disciplines and skills without which I would not be able to overcome many of the challenges I face in practice. Weekly 'crits' and tutorials taught me key presentation skills; how to engage with others and how to illustrate an 'idea'. This does prepare you in practical terms, whether presenting at regular meetings with thirty associated engineers, technicians, contractors and project managers, or having a gun waved in your face by a contractor out in Ethiopia (keep cool in the face of criticism). Both the courses at Edinburgh and Westminster taught me to constantly assess, reassess and examine the terms of a project. Wide-ranging exposure to the history and theory of architecture demonstrated how the process of design required aspiration but also an understanding of the status quo and technical exploration of available materials. My final project at Edinburgh addressed the polarisation between building regulations; critically viewed as 'external' to architecture; and creativity—the subjective freedom associated with design. I think in practice we commonly risk separating the two. Setting a precedent this approach has fed into my work, most notably whilst at Grimshaw Architects working on the London Bridge Station redevelopment. Based in a co-located office for over two years, working alongside the engineers and contractors, I quickly learnt that 'no' is flexible term in construction within the terms of cost, structure and compliance. The latter can be achieved without compromising design if you are willing to re-establish the terms with which you framed a design, and to engage in a renewed dialogue in order to achieve it. While one can argue that as a whole architectural education does not fully prepare the aspiring architect technically and practically for work beyond the academic studio, I would argue that many of these skills are best learnt on the job and at Part III. This is primarily due to the fact that architecture as a discipline is extremely diverse, and its practical terms vary hugely. However, all design projects require the discipline to formulate a concept, communicate an 'idea' and ground a project in its aesthetic, historical and sociological context. And these are the crucial skills developed in the design studio, where I would argue that it is through imaginative intuition that we begin to grasp the fundamental practices of architectural design. We cannot assume (or afford) that this can be learnt de novo in practice, and my continued involvement in the growth and development of the Ethiopia project is I think testament to this.

Lucy Brooke: MA University of Edinburgh, DipArch University of Westminster. Currently in practice (from July 2015) with Simon Smith and Michael Brooke Architects and also working Freelance since 2014. Previously with Aecom (2011), AND Architects (2012) and Grimshaw (2012-2014).

INTRINSIC AND EXTRINSIC CITY

INTRODUCTION

The Intrinsic and Extrinsic City sets out with the intention to explain the agenda behind the programmes DS11 pursued at Westminster during the period 2008-2017, when each year (bar one) there was a focus on a particular European city[1]. This served as the context for a range of short, weekly, thematic projects at the beginning of each academic year, and subsequently—via the production of catalogues and a city visit and survey—for the development of individual student projects pursued independently. The origins of this way of working stemmed from earlier endeavours (in Belgrade and Stockholm) and culminated during 2016-2017 in a final encounter with the city of Budapest. Preoccupied in urban terms to avoid, in the study of the past, a literal justification for design practice in the immediate present, we nonetheless ourselves sought to look back at what significance the work of our studio might have in retrospect, and that seemed more to do with the subsequent experience of our students in practice than with our own incipient nostalgia.

So, it was with some trepidation that we approached the production of this book, because we viewed attempts to theorise the 'teaching' of architectural design, and a 'performative' conception of design studio practice, with a degree of suspicion and ultimately disinterest. The former tended to propagate an institutional jargon endemic to a metalinguistic discourse about 'education', while the latter was identified with a rhetorical hype associated with the 'performance', the venues and the branding, of individual design studios marketed as a 'commodity' at the beginning of each academic year. Both were antithetical to our conception of teaching design. While we intended to distance ourselves from these predilections, it also became clear that our personal antipathy veiled a lack of theoretical substance to our own teaching practice, just as an expedient stance 'against the grain' was largely illusory given the pervasive nature of the marketing, high fee levels, and the 'consumption' of knowledge and skills, associated with the corporate values adopted in contemporary higher education. If we disliked the incestuous tone of 'research in education', and the superannuated pretension projected in competition between studios, equally we had to accept our own adoption of the habits and language of a certain educational practice, and our own tactics of persuasion in projecting our studio within a market culture. Not least, in this publication which within the 'Studio as Book' series considers the concept of 'design research' in relation to DS11's teaching practice.

With the benefit of hindsight looking back almost 10 years, we have collected together the first stage of a series of project programmes set annually, each identified with an overall theme: 'Recovering Wroclaw';

'Triestine Typologies'; 'Antwerp and Ghent: Recombinant Architecture', 'Kraków and Katowice: Mining and Manufacture'; 'Copenhagen and Malmo: Nordic Noir'; 'Triestinità: City as Medium'; 'Genoa: Modes of Exchange', and 'Budapest: Architectures of Stasis and Flux'. They are arranged retrospectively in a homogeneous outline format, but not in chronological order—to emphasise their independence (though each conformed to a similar logic).

This tended to identify (though not always) at first with a sculptural, and secondly with a thematic emphasis. The latter variously investigated: formal and spatial relationships; social or communal narratives; aesthetic and cultural issues, and on occasion environmental perspectives. In more specific terms these projects addressed a range of subjects: urban archaeology and artefacts; object types and building typologies; gallery sequences and co-operative space; force fields associated with pollution and weathering; noir narratives; strategies of demolition and imposition; building types associated with exchange and transaction, and contrasts between grid planning and aqueous fluidity in formal composition.

INTRINSIC AND EXTRINSIC

Our primary concern was to document and explain this chronological series of annual programmes. They all attempted to balance thematic, conceptual and material attention to the intrinsic (formal) nature of the city; urban fabric, infrastructure, institutions and architecture; with a parallel interest in the extrinsic (contingent) flux of the social, political and economic history engrained in its everyday life. Updated in contemporary experience, this could be vicariously sampled in the experience of the architectural visitor, but also studied in the available literature and documentation.

A duality between form and experience conditioned our interest in the literature associated with each city, placed somewhere between the historical monograph and the novel. That distinction stretches the boundaries between Norman Davies' and Roger Moorhouse's chronicle of the history of Wroclaw (where this series of annual city programmes started), *Microcosm: Portrait of a Central European City*[2], and two books on cities we never visited—Mark Mazower's lucid history of Thessalonika, *Salonica: City of Ghosts*[3], and Orhan's Pamuk's (auto) biographical *Istanbul: Memories of a City*[4]. Revisiting that city in his recent novel *A Strangeness in My Mind*[5], Pamuk's fictional protagonist experiences 'strangeness', located as he is between lived experience and historical transformation. We too experience this condition, but in an accelerated form, given the speed of change intrinsic to globalisation (prefaced in the growth of the imperial economies of C19th Europe—

assiduously compiled in Jürgen Osterhammel's *The Transformation of the World*[6]. It serves to define the territory of our conception of an urban architecture; one also projected in the relationship between Aldo Rossi's *The Architecture of the City* and the sentimental fragments of his *Scientific Autobiography*[7].

A condition, it should be said, that is fundamental to the terms of tourism and the studio-visit, an ambivalent aspect of studio culture (and our own choice of cities), participating—as a distant legacy of the 'Grand Tour'[8], and supported by budget airlines—in the contemporary 'experience economy' which permeates both the education and leisure 'industries'. For each studio, there is now the prospect of a 'destination'; reliant on the logistics and finance available, and its putative 'value' (over and beyond its carbon footprint). Typical, doubtless overlapping, tropes include: the 'didactic' study visit; the visit to an 'iconic' or archetypal city or place (monuments or capital cities); the corporate 'bonding' model; the 'global' variety aspiring to engage distance, speed of transformation or incipient 'conflict' (global cities), and the 'working' visit researching the context of ongoing project work ('on-site').

With these issues in mind we restricted our visits to cities peripheral, in some way, within contemporary Europe, generally avoiding capitals (with the exception of 'twin cities'). They tended to have a cosmopolitan identity, a fluctuating multi-cultural history, and to be the subject of contemporary trans-national or regional EU initiatives fundamental to our understanding of the 'European project'. A perspective latterly confounded by Brexit, since it was European professors who provided an intellectual engagement with urban history (not well understood on home ground)—just as the active municipal culture we experienced in town halls and city planners' offices exceeded the aspirations of many city authorities in the UK. Transformations associated with the Austro-Hungarian Empire, we discovered, were not so dissimilar to those effected by the neo-liberal economy of globalisation, if different in scale and temporality. Visiting the archives in Trieste we had the opportunity to view C19th maps projecting the entire northern coast of the Gulf of Trieste as port infrastructure, and a visit to the monumental Rozzol Melara housing complex (1968-1981) on the periphery of the city provided equally unlikely evidence of extremes of scale in an otherwise sedate urbanity. In the different context, of our visit to Wroclaw, Tomasz Ossowicz the city planner responsible, explained a wholly unsuspected and inspirational policy for urban development. These historical and contemporary insights referenced a landscape of urban transformation with its roots in the past, that grounded our students' projects whether in

---

the historic centre, its immediate periphery, or the suburbs and outlying districts of the expanded city. If the legacy neo-rationalism lurks in the background to one teaching partner's conceptual perspective (inherited from the architectural culture of the 1970's), only occasionally, or exceptionally, has this influence surfaced in the formal language of our students' architectural projects. We have therefore included, as a special case, a single project set in Budapest which, following in Vittorio Aureli's footsteps[9], proposes the polemical reconfiguration of the city's absent centre in neo-rationalist guise[10]. A knowing critique of the Hungarian government's current urban policies—evacuating existing cultural institutions in favour of token icons by celebrity architects—or a retrospective exercise in nostalgia, forty years after the publication of *Rational Architecture* (1978)[11], poised at a juncture between architecture and politics? Robin Evans noted of student projects at the AA in 1981, alluding to the work of Dalibor Veseley's studio: 'Rationalism has been overrun by existentialism' in a 'dominant species of urbanism' 'eminently reproducible as a style'.[12] A style which, much as its rationalist other (revived here), still gathers dust in the tutorial corridors of schools of architecture (beyond the bright lights of flexible studio space).

FRAMING DESIGN STUDIO

It should be emphasised that the design 'programmes' sampled here, represent only the initial body of six weeks of intense preliminary work each year, investigating the city concerned and constituting the ground-work for subsequent briefs (building design programmes in the first year, and final year students' design theses), prefaced by a 'catalogue', which was intended to edit and frame emergent design moves. A city visit and survey followed later in the year. The representations sampled, however, illustrate the character of work done over each year as a whole. There is, with only one exception, no attempt to describe individual projects in detail or to document their development. More importantly ex-student's 'reflections' on the academic design studio 'after the event' in practice, which were central to our enterprise, are inserted into their respective final year programme.

DS11 has always encouraged post-graduate students to acquire an agenda of their own, and resisted the kind of imitation that identifies too closely with tutors' formal interests which provide a recipe; a routine; or embed particular software, which generates a certain form, style, type or manner of architectural design. That is not intended to voice a value judgement about the production of a consistent vocabulary of form which conditions an individual student's interests, way of working and ownership of design-work. Rather it is the tautological implication of consensus between student and tutor which we were at pains to avoid in establishing a critical distance which put a premium on independent judgement. Architectural form is now typically produced either with reference to traditional 'convention' (typological, contextual or tectonic), or with recourse to digital techniques and methodologies (with their associated algorithms), where architectural form is delivered by default and justified by technical parameters, rhetorical jargon or arbitrary indexical procedures. Our students work may have occasionally touched on either extreme, but otherwise negotiated the middle ground of a historically aware urban architecture that recognises contemporary transformations of urban space and the valences of a digital visuality.

Wroclaw, Trieste, Antwerp, Ghent, Kraków, Katowice, Copenhagen, Malmo, Genoa and Budapest Set in the context of different European cities our programmes retained a pedagogic structure, which in general terms moved from working and researching at a distance, to visiting and surveying the reality of the city 'on-site'. This approach had its origins in the postgraduate Diploma studio culture of the 1990s, where an initial flurry of short projects; characteristically intemperate and often polemical; were set by selected studio tutors to provoke, disturb and dumbfound students who, it was contended, had become accustomed to the complacencies of a year out in practice. This allowed students from both years of the course a taste of what was on offer before selecting a studio, but what started as a year system then reverted to the familiar trope of a collection of semi-autonomous design studios (albeit conforming to a shared cross-studio programme for the first year). In the final year individually chosen design theses generally prevailed in each studio.[13] The system lapsed during the early 2000s in submitting to the unruly scenario of voting for an immediate studio choice at the beginning of each year, a choice spiced with the 'attraction' of a studio 'visit'. It was at this juncture that DS11 gradually reconstituted the logic of formative short projects, in order to introduce thematic avenues of urban research. This prioritised the availability of information on the web, subsequently tested in the direct experience of a city visit. The surplus of available digital information and data could be misleading, but working at a distance the initial choice of sites and programmes was not overburdened with details of physical context (habituated by contingencies at odds with a provisional conceptual rationale).

INTRODUCTORY SHORT PROJECTS

These short projects were informed by several key concerns. Firstly, they were intended to take issue with prior expectations; the work was to be intense and formulated at speed to be complete as 'exhibition' ready at the end of each project session (organised into two week-long slots). Oscillating between individual work for one week, and collective work (in a small group) for the other, they prioritised intuitive thinking, lack of prevarication and an ability to situate individual work in relation to group-work—the one leading into the other. Collective decision making involved selective use of individual work and co-ordination of a conclusive final piece of design. Always considered short 'design projects' with a definitive output; never as contextual or research orientated 'studies'; they all interfaced with the city we had chosen. Right from the start the 'designs' would in one way or another be directly incorporated into its formal context. In this manner, while research into specific aspects of each city was being promoted, each week required a design output that was conclusive and verifiable.

In this sense, they were not in themselves pieces of orthodox research, but required students to become acquainted with the city—always with the prospect of a design in mind. Their momentum and direct forms of engagement foregrounded a structured knowledge of the city; its history and current issues of the moment; which was being acquired in the background. Concurrently collective work, particularly, created a culture of expectation about complex pieces of architectural design, normally be deliberated over for weeks but which working in a small group could be delivered in a matter of days. While the briefs set discursive parameters designed to kick start deliberation and critical enquiry, they required careful reading and the confidence to follow set procedures (regardless of initial incomprehension). If high stakes were voiced in introduction, the exercises could be undertaken intuitively without too self-conscious a concern about what was right, wrong or appropriate.

OUTSIDE-IN

Investigation of sculptural concepts, whether in physical casting and moulding, or digital modelling, paid particular attention to the relation between the external form of the object and the spatiality of its interior subjected to 'sectioning', or interrogation of a threshold condition analogous to, or forming, an architectural façade. This tended to follow traditional sculptural conventions of moulding or carving, and casting or constructing; sometimes through digitally enhanced procedures. Subsequently, the architectural convention of the relationship between the room (or narrative sequence of rooms) and the city at large, would be introduced. In later projects this touched on the psycho-dynamics of the possession and occupation of 'space', whether conventionally understood in the character, form and configuration of a 'room', or understood as a tableau occupying a defined spatial field or enclosure (contesting the problematic concept of flexible space).

Conceived within an urban territory; viewing inwards into courts, slots, light-wells or atria; or conversely outwards to address the hierarchy of enclosure formed by the alley, street, square or arcade; the internal 'room' becomes associated with external public space read in its enclosure as an 'urban room'. Projects were preoccupied with digitally surveying facades to simulate, exemplify or transcend the experience of the city in the constitution of a touristic 'experience' or a museum environment that expressed the simulated hyper-reality enjoyed by the urban tourist. An alternative scenario identified with the conceptions of social life traditionally acted out in the street (within different national cultures), being displaced by changes in the relationship between concepts of public and private, where the culture of social media has challenged assumptions about public space in the generic 'European city'.

Whichever tack these initial projects took, their first (individual) stage involved sculptural modelling turned back into the formulation of an architectural interior in the (group) work that followed. Intended to encourage thinking beyond what, in some cases had become a 'comfort zone' associated with 'years out' in practice; the process of the 'making' (and unmaking) of a physical artefact sought conceptual insight beyond the finality of a crafted, or digitally made, artefact. This methodology was characterised by a certain 'porosity': in forms of lateral thinking; in the relation between the physical and the theoretical, and in the ownership of work which was shared or exchanged between individuals and groups. A psychological 'letting go' was encouraged, which could result in banality (or a reluctance to engage unknown territory), but also could manifest an unsuspected tactile sophistication or co-operative conceptual acumen.

THEMES: TOWARDS AN URBAN ARCHITECTURE

The second category of project covered a wide range of themes or subjects associated with the individual city interrogated for the qualities of its urban architecture, institutions, and local material detail. These exercises variously touched on the qualities of form and space, social occupation and narrative, through a thematic approach, which set out a basis for subsequent design projects. Themes were chosen for their discursive engagement with the history and urban characteristics of the cities selected. The concept of social and financial 'exchange', for example, embedded in the history of Genoa, or the notion of architectures of 'stasis and flux' epitomised in Budapest by the grid planning (of Pest) and the flow of the Danube.

That said, our conception of the thematization of architecture was not predicated purely on formal autonomy or architectural doctrine[14], but oscillated between issues fundamental to architecture and those which one could alternately characterize as belonging equally to aesthetic, historical, sociological or technical disciplines. The art of these exercises was to negotiate specific architectural terms while stretching an ability to conceptualize an urban architecture.

These themes might be considered overarching or grandiose abstract ideas, incidental in strictly architectural terms and of only a general applicability, unlike the direct engagement with built architecture conventionally pursued in exemplary 'case studies' (of urban morphologies, individual urban buildings, building typologies or tectonic elements). Most degree courses in architecture include this approach which, in the context of studio teaching, through copying and imitation aspires to high quality work produced in a particular formal vocabulary. But the art of the DS11 short projects lay elsewhere, first in acting as an imaginative prompt which compelled us to question and think through each year what their applicability and implications might be; whether in terms of the individual city and its history; the characteristics of its urban fabric, or the qualities of its individual buildings. The themes and cities changed each year, and although the permutations of the short projects varied their structural logic remained fairly consistent and subject to gradual refinement.

Given the demise of the claims made for the 'European City' disseminated by Leon Krier in 1978 (almost forty years ago)[15], following Aldo Rossi's publication of *The Architecture of the City* (1966)[16]; and the subsequent practice of contextualism concurrent with the rise of 'urban design'; a generalised anti-modernist and apparently traditional model of urban space had by the turn millennium become largely generic. In an increasingly globalised digital culture, these urban conventions retained plausibility primarily as spaces of tourism, while in the transformative areas of development and 'reconstruction', the canons of 'urbanism' (or urbanity) had largely dissolved, given the scale of infrastructural transformations (bigness) and the indeterminate spatiality theorised by Rem Koolhaas[17]. Meanwhile there were also attempts to reclaim a topographical aspect to 'urban landscape', the natural metaphor veiling the singularity of isolated complexes, or the over-scaled and reductive configuration of standard residential and commercial typologies.

Bearing this oversimplified but not entirely misguided perspective in mind, we sought an urban architecture that could respond to traditional parameters were appropriate, but which on the other hand was engaged (we hoped) with contemporary realities of densification, simulation and transformations in scale, set within the regional context pertinent to the more peripheral cities within the EU. Many were ironically identified with planning policies announcing their centrality, or prime logistical location, both for tourism and for the service industries they sought to attract, bolstering what often seemed fictional 'hubs' of development. In short, we offered students opportunities for developing an oblique approach to conventional architectural subjects—typified in Genoa, where the concept of 'exchange' could be conceived as a building type or a social, financial or legal transaction, informing different building typologies: the market, the maritime courthouse; the activity of an auction house, or the independent social relationship between districts formed by the city's topography (identified with student projects for a 'social condenser', a leisure centre or spa). All these possibilities were raised in the investigations prompted by the early projects, to be developed later as consolidated design theses. In more ambitious projects the initial parameters would be exceeded: for example, when 'exchange' was identified with the control of the perennial flooding caused by the discharge of water from the adjacent alps, or an unlikely and surreal relationship was explored between a maritime breakers yard and a performance space for music. Aside from our cultural themes, the environmental problems of a high water-table and the impact of the polluted river Oder in Wroclaw, stimulated a later interest in the contrasting geology and underground spaces of Trieste's limestone landscape 'with its cavities, caves and rivers—something akin to the terrain of the Buda hills. As the series of city programmes developed, a concept of environmental 'interfaces' emerged prominently in projects related to Kraków and its adjoining region, with its legacy of mining and heavy industries—focused on the deterioration of the fabric of the inner city and the renewal of Nowa Huta with its adjacent, largely redundant, steelworks. Overall this pattern of diverse speculative projects was typically reformulated in two subsequent pieces of work, the production of a catalogue and the conduct of a city survey: the first as a decisive step towards an individual design thesis and the second exploring the intrinsic and extrinsic qualities urban form and everyday life.

A CONCEPTUAL CHALLENGE

The catalogue which we expected each final year student to produce was proposed as an artefact that emerged from the initial four weeks' work, in a first move towards a design thesis. A selection of material from the initial individual, group or collective work of the studio, it could also incorporate pertinent external sources. This was interpreted as a conceptual challenge given the opportunity to explore a graphic formal repertoire, or thematic, which informed the

move towards a specific programme and a site in the city chosen as the focus of the year's work.

The catalogue was not intended to be a description of a potential thesis, or an outline version of the initial work done, but in visual terms sought the formulation of a coded, indexical and structured visual narrative that provided the groundwork for the later consolidation of a design thesis. Exemplified in the choice and presentation of the material, a conceptual agenda was to be presented in graphic form, rather than an 'illustrated' introduction to a design report. A premium was placed on typographical literacy, and an ability to 'construct' a publication conceived as an artefact in constituting a visual narrative[18]. While this raised the stakes in terms of graphic representation, it also tested an ability to conceptualise a visual proposition (with a mind to importance of reports, publications and other graphic media in contemporary architectural practice).

CITY SURVEY: TYPOLOGIES, FABRIC, FABLES AND SOCIAL LIFE

The nature of the city survey served to complement each student's choice of site and programme for their main-stream design project. Working in their previous project groups, students were asked to complete a formal survey and, individually, a systematic collection of photographs.

The survey process developed out of examining the different neighbourhoods and districts of Wroclaw, conceived as city 'islands' on the flood plain of the river Oder[19]. This was confounded as a technique in confrontation with the complex topography of Trieste, caught between the escarpment of the adjoining karst and the sea, where the studio developed a strategy for 'sectioning' its profile, adapting orthographic projections to determine different scales, durations, moments, and depths of city fabric. A similar pattern followed later in Genoa, which was modified for application to the contrasting Buda hills and flatland grid of Pest.

The strategy varied in its application to different cities, in the first instance by walking (or travelling), and recording at fixed intervals a linear section through the city's topology. In principle, this engaged urban enclosure, characteristic detail, facades and their institutions, and the contingencies of itinerant street life. This procedure, not uninfluenced by the routines of psycho-geographers[20], was modified to incorporate a temporal dimension and relative perception of distance or proximity (one group in Trieste, alternately expanding and compressing the literal profile of their journey up to the karsk from the porto antico).

The other technique related to the formulation of the themes put forward each year from which to approach each city. This involved the selection of 10 paradigmatic photographs, a simple enough proposition. But intended to be taken, selected, edited and formatted, with (absolute) precision to address a focus on detail or the selection of viewpoints, they served to examine pertinent issues: from recording social interaction; cultural or material detail; environmental conditions or visual panoramas. Their primary role, however, was to highlight the difference between unmediated documentation and seeking to constitute an informed focus on a characteristic theme. They also served to emphasise the ambivalence of the architectural tourist whose cursory visit could only obtain a selective insight into the everyday life of the city and its characteristic architecture, yet who aspired to a status beyond that of a 'partial' observer.

THE DIDACTIC TURN: RESEARCH IN DESIGN

Design research: a figment of the imagination or a procedure fundamental to the practice of architectural design? Both these responses have a certain plausibility, which detracts from a doctrinaire approach to the subject. Historically Beaux-arts ateliers, whether 'official' or 'open' remained tied to principles of composition and formal continuity, while Neo-rationalism sought a theory of architecture where research functioned as a methodology of design (best expressed rhetorically by Georgio Grassi). This elision contributed to the movement's downfall, since it conceived an inflexible design methodology viewed as a form of research, one engrained in the culture of Italian schools of architecture until well past its sell-by date. It is with that in mind that we have approached the didactic role of the design studio.

The days are long gone when teaching architectural design was simply focused on the pragmatics of programme and physical context. Contemporary complexities (digital, technical, managerial, contractual and environmental), as well as superannuated academic pretension, have tended to subsume the formal virtues of studying precedent, adhering to typological rigour, or following the norms of urban design.

Our contention was that the practice of studio teaching is best visualized as an open framework of investigation, setting out the terms within which students operate and within which local research is done: examining design mores, the social life and urban history of the cities, in which our design programmes have been set (as prescriptive, yet open to selective engagement). Typically, the city's volatility and historical complexity confounded the notion of a predetermined or single research agenda, which in any case goes against the grain of our conception of studio practice. It would be disingenuous, however, not to qualify this position. Rather than argue for a consistent content, or focus, to applied research in the studio, our interest was in its structure and how non-linear patterns emerge to inform design procedures.

The art of the short projects collected here, which constitute a form of research, is to negotiate an oblique approach to strictly architectural issues, while confronting themes that stretch the conceptualization of an urban architecture. Christopher Frayling's categorization of different types of design research in his entertaining paper 'Research in Art and Design' (1993)[21], set out three definitions for the relationship between the two disciplines, a starting point for many writers on the subject. Substituting 'architecture' for 'design' these definitions become: research 'into' architecture, research 'for' architecture, and research 'through' architecture. This compartmentation has a certain plausibility, with which Jeremy Till later broadly concurs. In his 'Three Myths and One Model' (2007) he shifts the emphasis towards research 'into' architecture—that is architecture itself as subject (as in education), and research 'through' architecture—directed towards methodology (or self-referential practice) which is identified with the 'architectural institute'—or is it the broader agenda of 'the institution of architecture'? Regardless, research 'for' architecture is seen to constitute a grey area between the two extremes, applicable to future developments (as his main area of interest). Frayling's initial trinity is returned by Till to an essential duality in architecture between professional 'practice' and the 'academy', and the focus predictably enough is on the relationship, and the communication, between the two cultures. He argues for academia to recognize the virtue of 'tacit research' in practice, and to offer an 'archaeology of production' as research with professional mores or praxis in mind (which for example would be epitomized by ProBE[22] here at Westminster).[23] That proposition significantly aligns with the development, in the last ten years or so, of contrasting 'practice' and 'project' based PhD's, whether identified with a decline in academic rigour or viewed more positively in terms of the 'communication' Till had in mind. Murray Fraser's introduction to Design Research in Architecture (2013)[24] provides a more recent update in a comprehensive summary of the state of play in this area. Intriguingly he quotes Aldo Rossi on 'analysis and design' where 'For the archaeologist and the artist alike, the ruins of a city constitute[s] a starting point for invention [...]'.[25] While we do not claim for DS11 the 'precision' and 'systematic' approach advocated by Rossi, his sentiments incline with our own. Without wishing to be unduly pedantic, 'Research as Prospect' best describes the nature of the short projects outlined here where structured investigation or research activity was initiated, but is conceived with two aims in mind. The literal 'output' of the design proposal (which requires an imaginative leap at some point), and, as in the nature of prospecting, whether or not the object sought may be found, the process and the procedures carried out refine the skill and knowledge required to obtain it in future.[26]

CONCLUSION: STUDIO CULTURE

We don't make any great claims for the originality of our approach to an urban or extra-urban architecture, and many of our themes and interests are quite conventional; the expectations of DS11 are doubtless not untypical of work to be found in the design studios of most schools of architecture, constituting a loose amalgam of research and design practice.

What we would assert though, is a didactic logic to our approach to setting architectural projects. This does not exemplify or verify the academic, technological or professional confines of a 'research agenda' (architect as researcher); or the artistic shibboleth of a 'creative romanticism' (the architect as fine-artist or contemporary purveyor of structures). Both perspectives are grafted onto, inherent in, or claimed for, much contemporary design studio practice, where tautological procedures often disguise the limitations of what used to be categorized as 'intuitive' judgement. All the more imperative then to restore the 'critical project' of dialectical reason, whether or not that is recognized in a form of architecture or architectural critique. There is a 'built' architecture procured and realized, and an architecture 'represented', described, modelled or simulated—in graphic, mediated or project form alone. Then there is the occupation, alteration, and everyday use and inhabitation ascribed to a 'social' or lived conception of architecture, and finally a surrounding architectural culture and research produced in different forms of media (sometimes critical but often complacent) with its entrées into other areas and the disciplines of journalism, historical discourse, technological development and culture criticism. While it is often contended that all these different aspects are bound together in an inclusive comprehension of 'architecture'; that seems to treat elasticity and appropriation with an undeserved abandon. Only the first two categories are intrinsically architectural in a formal sense, and doubtless this explains 'local' revivals of neo-rationalism (to be scorned or celebrated) where, rather than being seen as a straightjacket, a paradigm, a mirage, or an autonomous discipline; rationalism has resurfaced as a positive value[27]. It would be foolish however to ignore contemporary sensibilities in architectural academia, indebted as they may, or may not be, to their 'other' the realm of normative architectural practice, which in its commercial form represents the ideological face of neo-liberalism (more insidious in its everyday, rather than its iconic,[28] guise). In the recent past the post-graduate course at Westminster sought to educate 'thinking architects' (who could design, write and think 'critically')—wishful thinking perhaps, since who would entertain the thoughtless variety? It was, though, with that concept in mind that we sought to examine the afterlife of DS11. For whatever we as tutors thought we were doing, that was alternately confounded, misunderstood, celebrated or heroically exceeded by our students who always, kept us in our place.

1 - With the intent to reform the well-worn phrase 'the architecture of the city' in the contemporary context of the C21st.

2 - N. Davies, R. Moorehouse, *Microcosm: Portrait of a Central European City* (Pimlico/Random House, London, 2003).

3 M. Mazower, *Salonica City of Ghosts: Christians, Muslims and Jews 1450-1950* (London, Harper Perennial, 2004).

4 O. Pamuk, *Istanbul: Memories of a City* (London, Faber and Faber, 2005).

5 O. Pamuk, A *Strangeness in My Mind* (London, Faber and Faber, 2016).

6 J. Osterhammel, *The Transformation of the World: A Global History of the Nineteenth Century* (Princeton and Oxford, Princeton UP, 2014).

7 A. Rossi, *The Architecture of the City* (Cambridge, Mass., London, MIT Press, 1982) and A. Rossi, A Scientific Autobiography (Cambridge, Mass., London, MIT Press, 1981).

8 See Perspecta, *41* (2008), and J. Ockman, S. Frausto, eds., Architourism (Munich/London/New York, Prestel Publishing, 2005)

9 Initiated in P. V. Aureli, *The Project of Autonomy: Politics and Architecture Within and Against Capitalism* (New York, Princeton Arch. Press, 2008).

10 Redolent of mega-structural schemes for the city in the late 1960s. For general accounts of Neo-rationalism see A. Peckham, T. Schmiedeknecht, eds., *The Rationalist Reader: Architecture and Rationalism in Western Europe 1920-1940 / 1960-1990* (Abingdon, Routledge, 2014) and H. Engel, *Autonomous Architecture and the Project of the City*, OASE, 62 (2003), pp. 20-69.

11 Rational Architecture Rationelle (Bruxelles, AAM Editions, 1978).

12 R. Evans, *From Axes to Violins*, AA Files, 1, 1 (1981), pp. 116-120.

13 Or 'interest group' as they had been termed previously.

14 See Peckham and Schmiedeknecht, eds., op. cit., n. 10, pp. 283-315.

15 *Rational Architecture*, op. cit., n. 11.

16 A Rossi, *The Architecture of the City*, op. cit., n. 7.

17 R. Koolhaas, *Bigness, or the problem of Large* in OMA, R. Koolhaas, B. Mau, eds., S,M,L,XL (Rotterdam, 010 Publishers, 1995), pp. 494-516, and 'Junkspace' most accessibly published in R. Koolhaas, H.Foster, Junkspace with Running Room (London, Notting Hill Editions, 2013), pp. 1-37.

18 See S. De Bondt, F. Muggeridge, eds., *The Form of the Book Book*, (London, Occasional Papers, 2009), and R. Kinross, 'Judging a book by its material embodiment: a German-English example', in his Unjustified Texts: perspectives on typography (London, Hyphen Press, 2011), pp. 186-199.

19 Influenced by O. M. Ungers. See F. Hertweck, S. Marot, eds., *The City in the City / Berlin: A Green Archipelago* (Zurich, Lars Müller, 2013).

20 See M. Coverley, *Psychogeography* (Harpenden, Pocket Essentials, 2006).

21 C. Frayling, *Research in Art and Design*, Royal College of Art Research Papers, 1, 1 (1993).

22 Christine Wall's *An Architecture of Parts: Architects, Building Workers and Industrialisation in Britain 1940-1970* (Abingdon, Routledge, 2013) is a case in point.

23 J. Till, *Three Myths and One Model*, Building Material, v. 17 (2008).

24 M. Fraser, ed., *Design Research in Architecture: An Overview* (Farnham/Burlington, Ashgate, 2013), pp. 1-14.

25 A. Rossi, *The Architecture of the City*, op. cit., n. 16, p. 166 (Preface to the Second Italian Edition).

26 Both aspects reside in Till's grey area of *Research for Architecture*.

27 M. Jay, *Reason After its Eclipse: On Late Critical Theory* (Madison/London, University of Winconsin Press, 2016).

28 Critiqued in D. Spencer, *The Architecture of Neoliberalism* (London, Bloomsbury, 2016).

NOTES FROM THE HEART

DUSAN DECERMIC

Balkan born. Beograd. Bad boy. After many returns home from island exile, this visit seems different. It's three am, the balcony of a tenement block, typical remnant of the socialist paradise of Tito's fairytale Yugoslavia, overlooks the rooftops of an older city, Ottoman in its script, Slavic in its demographics. All quiet below. Time to descend and thread oneself back through to the other part of town. The route is instinctive, navigable by a myriad of fragments, laying, waiting to be encountered once again, sediments of memory, layers built over years of roaming, loving, hating, waiting. On previous visits, each fragment was connected by a living thread, leading back to the self. Roots. Not this time. A strange and disturbing levitation occurs, full of dread, but also of relief. It's as if shards of temporal reality are now part of a distant cinematic screen drifting past in front of one's eyes, the viewpoint slowly receding to the back of the hall. A painting of Marc Chagall's comes flickering to mind, 'Over the Town'... The fear of severance now erupts into a sense of freedom, a final acceptance of existing nowhere in particular, rootless, weightless. This town does not belong to me anymore, now unhomely and virtual despite its physical presence. A feeling of estrangement. The whole nation has been displaced, flooded by recurrent nightmare, erased, replaced by a new Balkan archipelago, non-navigable, treacherous. Now there truly is nothing for a Balkan born in 1962, in Tito's Utopia.

This experience of exile and loss, a European story like many others, lends a certain grit of legitimacy to the teaching partnership in the studio, with its keen interest in the contested territories embedded in the palimpsest of the continental history, past and present. Other legacies, much less poetic or fashionably psychic, lie in years of experience fashioned by the tried and tested instruments of practice; a procured and built architecture of a high level of quality and detail. Anxiety had no place, drove the obsessive re-working of a tangible, haptic architecture, sanctuaries in the drift. No longer concrete works in practice, a loss perhaps but also the virtue of conjectural practice in the studio.

In spite of the emergence of 'virtual' applications and current rather sensational technological inventions which permeate our manic culture, a certain deep-seated orthodoxy paradoxically still operates in the body of studio practice, unchanged, persisting; in the form of its relevance to the humanities; in the teaching of architecture. Beyond the modish concern with producing form relevant to current cultural and economic dynamics, there is something fundamentally critical to the relevance of this practice, and its survival in architectural thinking. This sounds as if inherently present or already taken for granted, but just when access to this fundamental process is required one is surprised to find that there is a disturbing void opening up, where substance is meant to be. Architectural thinking is a form of practice, one that is strangely slippery in its nature; not a monolithic body but one structured and coaxed into a particular form. Its nature is manifold, elusive, and as such resistant to being taught through a singularly effective, efficient process available to many. It must be nurtured and propagated over time, and offered as fundamental to each individual subjective mind. The method of propagation is one embedded in a carefully calibrated discourse, prone to multitude of minor 'failures' that are inherent and necessary part of design practice, often an anathema to profit driven institutional educational processes, eager to embrace the technological fix.

Ten years of teaching is compacted into this book, containing as a rough calculation seven thousand and two hundred individual conversations. Each one, precariously negotiated between public and private discourse, each fraught with a mild dose of danger, anxiety and inevitable emotion. This is an ancient construct, alive today, and at the core of what we do. Exhausting, a wearing river of erosion; but exuberant and dangerous, part of what makes us architects of the mind as well as of materials; from territories nowhere, to the expectant places of belonging. This piece is short, as the future holds many more conversations that are urgently needed, right now. They will not be 'written', but will remain shimmering in the ether. We hope that this modest book will serve as a brief history of our meetings and travels together.

ACKNOWLEDGEMENTS

First and foremost, we should like to thank: Julianne, Hannah, Louise, Matthew, Helen, Simhika, Catriona, Sam, Lucy and Toby, for taking 'time out' to write their reflections on studio and practice.

Double thanks then are also due to Sam Giles without whose sterling work on formatting, graphic design and typography, this book would never have reached publication; and similarly, to Toby Plunkett for his knowledge of technical aspects of printing and the cover design.

Almost ten years was a long way back, and we are grateful to all our ex-students who searched their files and provided the drawings and images that we never thought to keep. Special mention goes to Sophie Determann for following up work and people we had given up for lost.

Our contacts in Trieste were fundamental to our enterprise. Elena Carlini beyond any call of duty, went out of her way during two study visits to offer welcome advice, information and connections, and who in the first instance put us in touch with Luciano Lazzari. Meeting with Luciano we discovered several mutual coincidences, and his generosity made our visits memorable; not least in the good use we made of his extensive professional and academic contacts, but also now in his foreword for our book.

We were indebted to city planning and development offices on all our visits, but it was Thomasz Ossowicz in Wroclaw who raised our expectations. Foregoing lunch, his presentation provided the inspiration for us to repeat the experience of that successful visit elsewhere in Europe (in Ghent they were to run him a close second).

Finally, and in an academic context, we were fortunate to enjoy lectures on urban history from university colleagues who unfailingly offered their services, and others', at short notice. With enlightened thanks to professors Stefano Musso in Genoa and András Ferkai in Budapest.

Which brings us closer to home, where Elantha Evans and Ana Serrano covered our absences while providing incisive and generous criticism, as did our design critics over the years (too many to mention).

Looking back, course leaders Murray Fraser and William Firebrace provided a stalwart independence, a light touch, and a high culture of expectation. Well appreciated, as was the sense of humour experienced here in William's 'short cuts'.

Finally, thanks are in order to Lindsay Bremner, Harry Charrington and the editorial panel, for supporting our proposal in the first place. We hope we have done it justice.

We have refrained from crediting individual student work done under the collective auspices of DS11. However subsequent work has been credited to the architectural practices concerned to whom we are particularly grateful. For external sources, we have endeavoured to follow Creative Commons and Fair Dealing criteria, for which thanks to Flickr and Google Earth. Historic maps are variously indebted to Wikimedia and individual map collections

**ANDREW PECKHAM
& DUSAN DECERMIC**

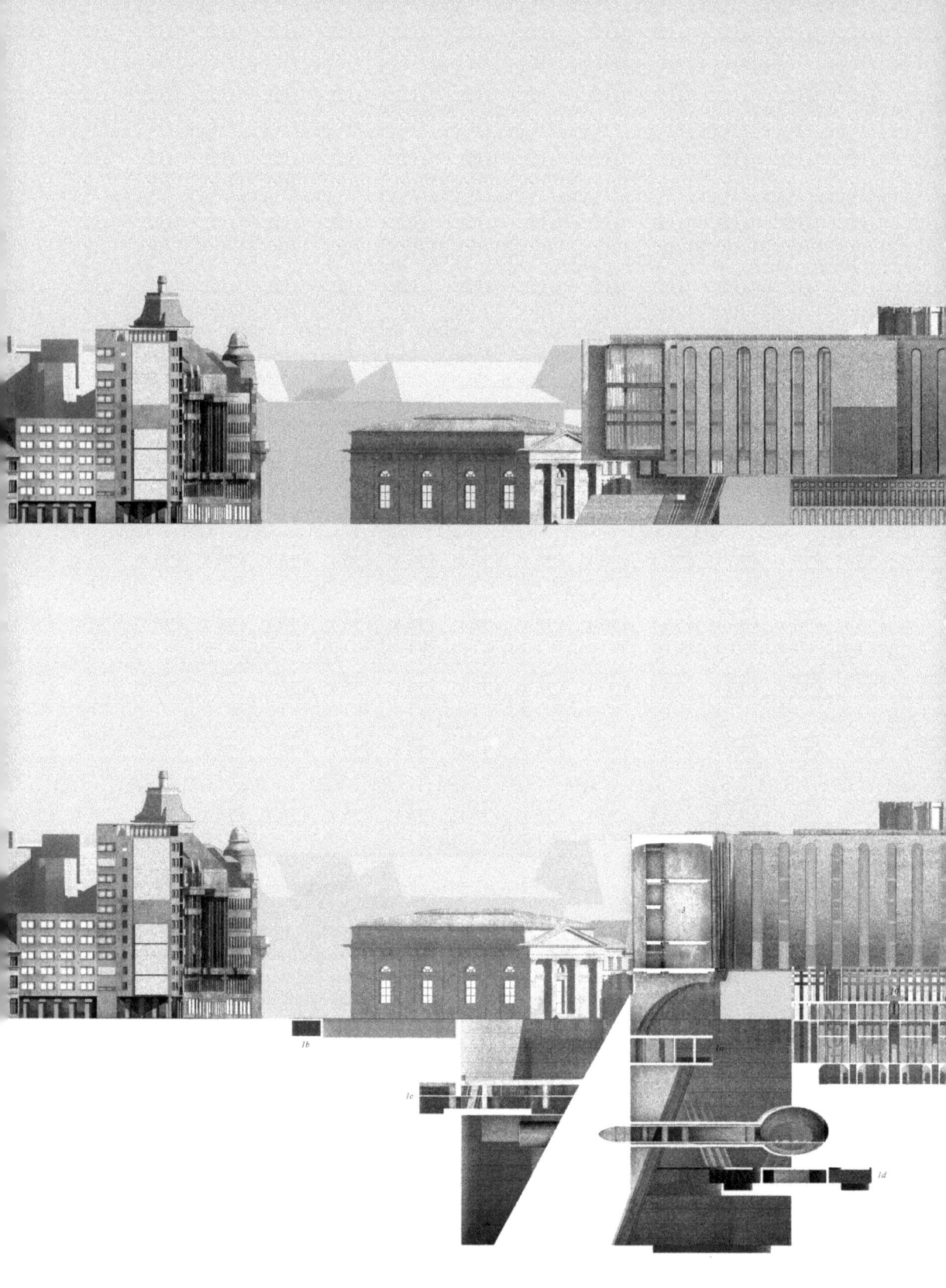

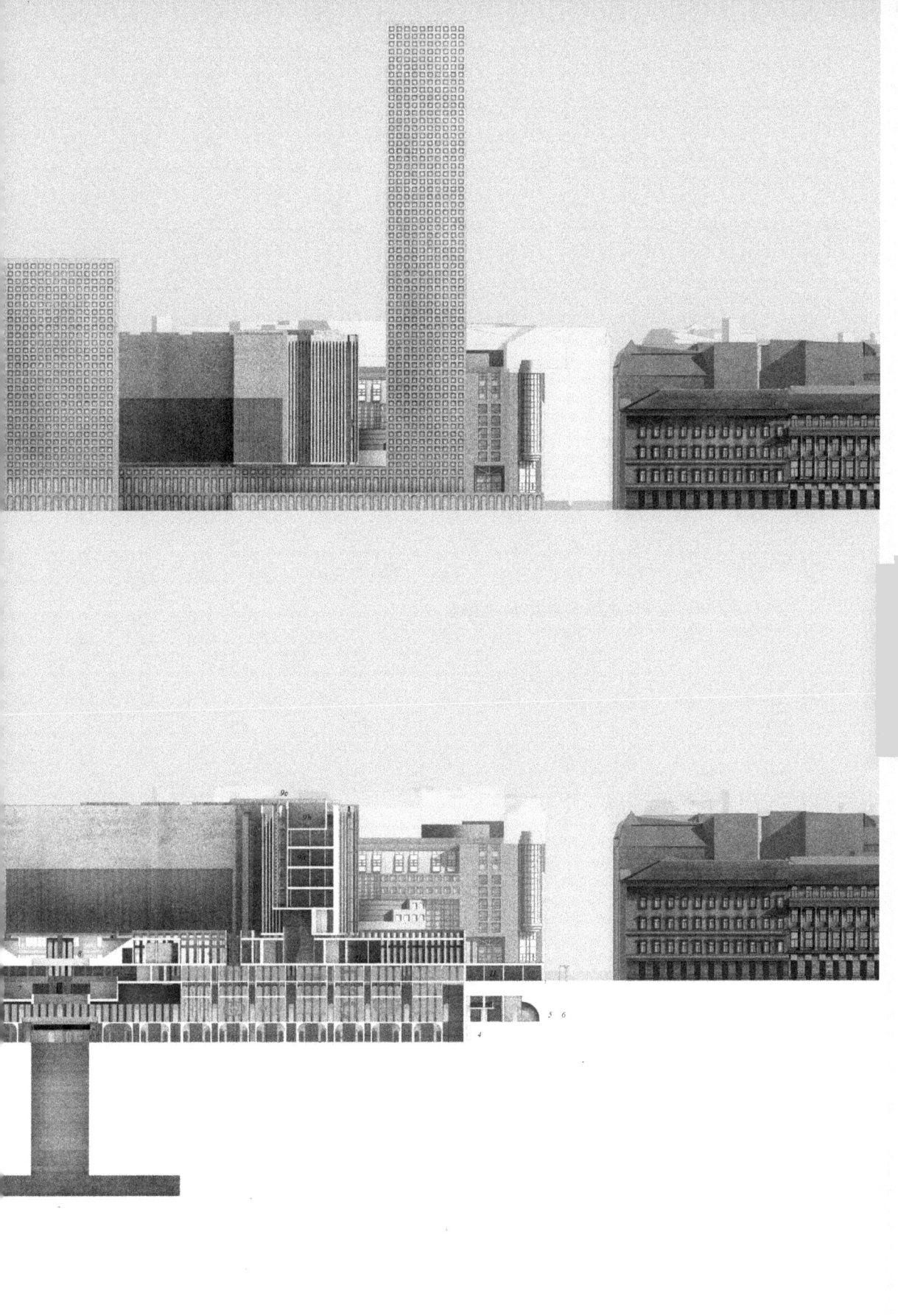

The Intrinsic and Extrinsic City

DS11-2008-2017

Edited By Andrew Peckham & Dusan Decermic
With Sam Giles & Tobias Plunkett

A University of Westminster
Department of Architecture Publications
Template Design by Mark Boyce
Printed by Lightening Source

All texts ©2018 the authors

This work is subject to copyright. All rights are reserved, whether the whole or part of the material is concerned, specifically the rights of translation, reprinting, re-use of illustrations, recitation, broadcasting, reproduction on micro films or in other ways, and storage in database. For any kind of use, permission of the copyright owner must be obtained.

ISBN 978-0-9955893-0-8

The Studio as Book series are available to purchase through www.studioasbook.com and other online stores.

The editors have endeavoured to acknowledge all sources of images and quotations used and apologise in advance for any errors and omissions

Department of Architecture
University of Westminster
35 Marylebone Road
London
NW1 5LS

www.ingramcontent.com/pod-product-compliance
Lightning Source LLC
Chambersburg PA
CBHW041246240426
43669CB00026B/2993